THE LIFE AND TIMES
OF A
LOCOMOTIVE
ENGINEER

Charles F. Steffes

Old World Publishers
California

ISBN Number 1-880365-13-8

Illustrations   Loren Knowles

Published by Old World Publishers,
Darlene Steffes, Publisher

Old World Publishers
P.O. Box 81686
Bakersfield, CA 93380

Printed in the United States of America
96 95 94 93 92   10 9 8 7 6 5 4 3 2 1

*This book is dedicated to the men
and women, past and present, of
the American railroads*

THE LIFE AND TIMES
OF A
LOCOMOTIVE
ENGINEER

Acknowledgements

In writing this account of my life working on the Southern Pacific railroad, I wish to thank those people who helped me so much, including J. W. Sulliven, Bill Coffelt, Elmer Fowler, Bruce Sprayberry, Fred Enloe, Mrs. J. S. Simpson, and many, many others, whose names would fill another book. I would also like to thank my wife and publisher, Darlene Steffes, who was the inspiration behind the book, and Bryan Aubrey, who edited the manuscript.

In writing, I did not give the exact time or day of many of the events, because they happened so many years ago. But the sequence of events down through the years is correct, and also the events are true.

The time I have written about is like a fluttering candle burning out and soon there will be nothing left but a wisp of smoke. And that too will disappear in the dusty, empty pages of history. So I hope this book will be somewhat of an epitaph for our times.

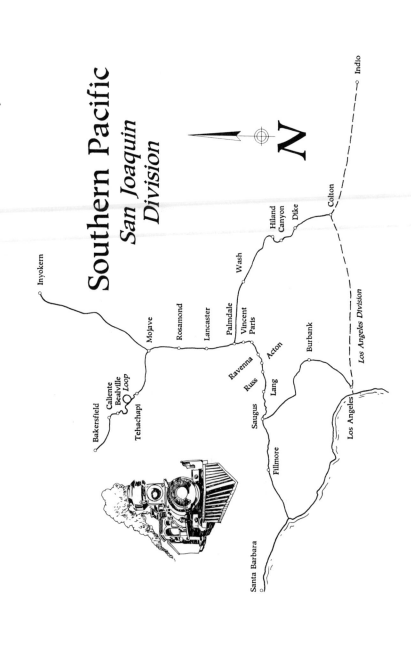

Southern Pacific
San Joaquin Division

N

Inyokern

Bakersfield
Caliente
Bealville
Loop
Tehachapi

Mojave

Rosamond

Lancaster

Palmdale

Vincent
Paris

Ravenna

Russ

Lang

Acton

Saugus

Burbank

Wash

Hiland
Canyon

Dike

Colton

Indio

Los Angeles Division

Los Angeles

Fillmore

Santa Barbara

"The Malley"

1. The Early Years

Going to work that morning, my heart was vibrant and joyful. This was the beginning! At twenty-three years of age, I was an engineer! Prior to this time, it had taken years to become an engineer. During the Great Depression, the railroad in the United States lay dormant as far as hiring was concerned. From about 1928 to 1937 scarcely anyone was hired. But coming out of the Depression, and being faced with the war in Europe, every thing had to be geared up, and I was caught in the rising tide.

This was the beginning of the grand and glorious years in railroading! The next thirty years would produce the most fabulous scientific inventions the world would ever know. It would be the most fantastic era in all modern history.

Six-thirty that morning the phone rang loud and clear on the wall in the kitchen. I woke up, and with one eye open, looked around, then covered my head with a pillow. I was not due out on my assignment, firing for Curly Farrow on train #51, the San Joaquin Daylight to Bakersfield, until the next day. Probably a wrong number anyway, I thought to myself. I had worn myself out wrestling for sex half the night (and not succeeding), and I wanted a little more sleep. But Margie finally went to the kitchen and answered the phone.

1

"The railroad is calling you," she shouted.

She came back and shook me. It turned out that I was being called for the one and only switch engine the San Joaquin had in the yard. A demoter trip meant that I was being called to fill a vacancy for an engineer, even though I was still a fireman, on account of the shortage of employees. Many times in this situation I was paid double—as engineer and fireman.

I took a promotion in late 1942 but did not officially become an engineer until early 1944. Since I worked as an engineer and a fireman during this time, making the double pay was certainly nice.

After my very first trip as an engineer, the next morning I left with Curley Farrow, firing my regular assignment on #51 and returning on the Portland train #60 the next morning to Los Angeles. It was raining quite heavily all the way to Bakersfield and back, so we received a train order to watch out for floods and wash-outs.

Everything seemed to be in good shape, except that when we left the station of Vincent on the way back from Bakersfield down through the Soledad Canyon where the Santa Clara River began, the water exceeded its banks in places. The rain continued through that day and night. The sky had cleared in the morning, when the persistently ringing phone almost shook itself off the wall, calling me to be an engineer on a work train, destination Soledad Canyon. My first main line work! Boy, was I excited. I started to shake, then danced around; even Margie got caught up in my jubilant attitude. Settling down, I began to wonder what could have happened up the canyon. The water was high, but fortunately, there was no wash-out as we came by.

After getting our engine, the 4102, ready, Frank Pucket, my fireman, and I took it to the "A" yard where our train waited

2

with twenty-one flat cars of rick-raft, great heavy granite stones used for damming-up purposes. I was wondering if this old cab ahead 4102 malley could pull this tonnage up the mountain. But the instruction in the timetable informed me that the engine was rated for tonnage. Frank and I had worked together on steel frame houses before we went railroading. Frank was a welder and I did what little woodwork was needed.

Receiving an airbrake test, then leaving town for Burbank Junction (the end of double track where the San Joaquin Valley and the Coast Lines separated), we received a train order giving us right of track over all trains to Saugus, where we were to meet two trains.

Killing a little time in the side track waiting for the trains we were meeting at Saugus to arrive, I and the rest of the crew crossed the street to the cafe for a cup of coffee. Sitting at the counter having coffee was the crane operator.

"What are you going to use for unloading that rock with?" the conductor asked.

"I'm going to use the flat-bed truck with the crane on it," he replied.

"How bad is it up there?" the conductor asked again.

"Enough," he replied. "Some banks on the fill are washed out, but the track isn't disturbed yet."

The first train we were to meet blasted through Saugus making a run for Newhall hill, the last grade before reaching Los Angeles.

"The other guy is supposed to be on his block," the conductor informed us, so we all scrambled back across the street. Sure enough, the semaphore arm on the signal was up in red position. Searchlight-type signals were just beginning to replace the semaphore arm signals, but it would be some time before the replacement would be completed. The conductor delivered our train orders from the operator's office, giving us the right over all trains to Vincent, at the top of the hill twenty-nine miles away. We put the flat cars in the house track at Ravenna and then went to Vincent to turn the engine and caboose on the Wye. Our orders were to work between Vincent and Russ until seven-fifty in the evening. Train number 52 was running two hours and forty-five minutes late. The Owl's time at Russ was 7.37 p.m.

Working to unload rock at different locations between Ravenna and Russ, we only had half of it unloaded by 7.20 p.m., when the conductor and one brakeman climbed on the engine.

"We have seven flat cars of rock and three empties, the rest are at Ravenna with the rear breakeman in the house track," the conductor said. "Let's go to Russ for the Owl and unload one car in the sidetrack and then back up the hill, following the Owl out of Russ," he continued.

"OK, let's go," I replied. Russ was about five miles from where we quit working. I released the engine brakes and let the train roll down the grade, which at some places was about two percent, and had a speed limit of twenty-five miles per hour. Letting the speed climb to that level, I reduced the air pressure by ten pounds, not letting the engine brakes apply. Nothing happened. We kept going and the speed climbed to thirty miles per hour. The conductor and brakeman were talking to Frank and I was glad they had not noticed. I was applying the engine brakes fully, but the speed still did not diminish. I had to do something and do it quick. In my mind I was seeing a head-on collison with the Owl. How many passengers would be killed or hurt, not counting the engine crew? With two miles left, I did things automatically. I believe that in a crisis, a sixth sense

4

comes into play and you do things without knowing why. I was keeping the engine brakes applied and recharging the train line, then I went to emergency. The sweat poured from my body. Going through the same procedure again, the speed started to diminish. Slowing down to about fifteen miles per hour, I then thought of reversing the engine, because this speed was much too fast for anyone leaving the engine and running to line the switch for the sidetrack.

Wet with sweat, a calm came over me; it no longer mattered, I had done all that I could. Frank and the trainmen were laughing and joking and I was on the other side of the cab with my toes dug into the floor boards of the locomotive and with a little water trickling down my legs inside my pants. The others never sensed the gravity of what I was experiencing. The switch for the siding was about a thousand feet around a curve and a loaf of a mountain hid it from view. It was quite dark by now and I could see a slither of the Owl's headlights as we approached the siding.

By now the rest of the crew was aware that I was on the engine also and were waiting for me to slow down more, so the brakeman could run for the switch. They didn't know I could do nothing more to slow the train down. The time was 7.45 p.m. The Owl was a little ahead of time and as we got closer, I was about ready to yell jump, when at the switch, a man waved us into the siding with his flashlight. The fireman on the Owl walked up and lined the switch for the siding. My body felt like an oversized balloon, inflated as tight as it could be, which had suddenly had the air let out of it. Every part of my body ached as we rolled into the siding. "Thank you, God," I murmured, and I meant it.

The grade at Russ leveled to about nothing and I was able to stop. I sat still for a full minute because my arms and body would not move. My mind was searching, trying to figure out the whys and wherefores of all this. I did know one thing, however; I was much smarter and wiser than I had been a few minutes before. I had gained insights into what an engineer had to be. He was by himself. Even though the conductor and engineer were equally responsible for the safety and operation of the train, the conductor was most always many cars back in the caboose. It was the engineer who had to have the skill to make the right decisions and to act on any emergency with no mistakes. He must know what to do and then be able to do it. I became a man that day. I learned a lesson that I never forgot. Safety must be remembered at all times, which is a very hard thing for a young person to learn. The company also had to learn it. Years later, when tons per operative brake were in effect, that train would have been restricted to slower speed and more empty cars would have been added for extra braking power.

I was moving the train to where the crane operator wanted to unload a flat car of rock. All the signals would be given on Puckets side of the train, so I leaned back to rest. All I could do was reminisce, going back to the first time I ever thought about the railroad, when a friend of my family, Charlie Allen, asked me if I would like a job on the railroad. Being between jobs at the time I said "yes," so he coached me what to say and how to find the railroad headquarters.

"Now remember," he cautioned me, "be sure to say that I am your uncle; I'll call tomorrow to let you know what day to go down there."

Parking my '29 model "A" Ford in the dirt parking lot at Taylor yard by the river in Los Angeles, I had to walk a long way to the master mechanic's office to apply for a job with the Southren Pacific railroad. On my way I passed by a building

6

that housed the steam boilers for the mechanics of the operation in the round-house. Glancing up at the tall smoke stacks, with the blue sky beyond, made me feel small and insignificant. Thinking of going to work for this big outfit was invigorating to my soul. Quickening my steps I walked by many other buildings before reaching the round-house, which was a large brick building shaped like a horse-shoe, with the inner side left open, creating stalls for about twenty-five to thirty-five locomotives. In front of the U-shaped or half-circle round-house was a large round cemented hole, about one hundred and twenty feet in diameter and six feet deep. Across this hole was a bridge-like contraption with rails for locomotives to run on. The bridge pivote in the middle, making it possible for the turntable to move in a full circle with a motor operating two iron wheels that ran on a rail going around the bottom of the hole near the outer edge. Each stall had a track leading to the turntable.

It was a magnificent sight, seeing the workers going about their business and the sounds that filled the air, iron clanking on iron, plus all the other unusual sounds not heard elsewhere. I had to remind myself it was a job that I had come for, so I moved on to find the master mechanic's office, which was not far from the round-house. I walked up the steps to an old wooden building with a railed-in porch, and opened a door into a plain but well-used office. The clerk behind the counter stood up behind his desk to greet me, as if he had been expecting me.

"Howdy," he greeted me casually. "Can I help you?"

"Well, I was told to come here to apply for a job."

"Who told you to come here?"

"Charlie Allen, my uncle," I stammered, knowing that the clerk was testing me, and hoping that my memory of Charlie's coaching would serve me well.

"Charlie Allen! Does he work here?" the clerk prodded.

"He sure does. He is supervisor of the rip track."

"Rip track, what's that?" He kept prodding, which irritated me.

"You should know,' I said, putting him on the defensive. "Where box cars are repaired."

The clerk grinned. "I guess he's your uncle all right. You know we have to make sure of these things or every brother, sister, aunt or uncle would be in here for a job. Charlie did tell me you would be in this morning. I was only making sure," the clerk said, shoving me some papers to fill out.

That was how I started out working for Southern Pacific railroad.

I was to have a physical Monday morning, and after that I would report for work. I did not ask what kind of work, only what I should wear. The clerk told me how to dress, how much the starting pay would be, and that I should report to foreman Pablow for instructions.

Margie

I met her at the high school prom. She was a cute, nice-looking girl with blonde hair, hazel eyes, and clear, milky white complexion. Margie really caught my fancy. She had firm bosoms that made my mouth twitch and a small firm butt packed the way it should be. We had been keeping company for over a year and I really enjoyed the relationship. But sometimes she would get serious. That being a warning sign, I always tried to change the subject. Other than that, she was delightful to be around.

"What will your wages be like? Any more money than your last job?" Margie asked, about my new position.

"It will be a little more than I have been making," I assured her. "Thirty-three cents an hour, but that's only for starting. I shall make more as I progress and there are lots of chances for advancement." Thirty-three cents an hour was slightly higher than the average at that time. It went quite a long way—a loaf of bread cost only five cents, a quart of milk was sometimes as low as four cents, and three dollars could buy the best Florsheims on the market.

"Why all the concern about my making more money?" I grinned, thinking maybe she wanted me to spend more money on her. She was probably getting tired of going to the Pasadena Civic Auditorium for a dance on Friday or Saturday night, which only cost fifty cents for each of us. I would buy one coke, and we would share it, using two straws, during each intermission. Margie knew how hard money was to come by in those times; she would not let me spend any more. We always had quite an enjoyable evening, dancing to the big bands like Arty Shaw, Glen Miller, Guy Lombardo, Les Brown, Tommy Dorsey, and many others.

"Don't you think a girl would like to marry some day?" she said, looking out of the corner of her eye. Not expecting a remark anything like this, I was speechless. Not only that, I was confused; she had caught me off my guard. True, I had had the urge to have sex with her for a long time, and the urge became greater as time continued, but in those times—it was January, 1937—things were very unlike what they are today. The fear of God was put into you about sex; the rule was, marriage before sex. Hell, we didn't know what the word sex meant. No pill at that time, only warm bottles of coke and the hope that the girl did not become pregnant.

With a warm goodnight kiss and a hug, with my hands groping for something without success, I bid her good night.

Driving home, I thought about how many times I had walked these three miles in the cold of the night before I bought my first automobile, aching in my stomach and groin because I was not permitted the natural act of lovemaking. The cool of the night was like a cold shower. But now, with the warm heater, there was no cold air to stop the plangent beating of my heart. I had received the ultimatum tonight: "Get on the pot or get off." The only thing left to do was marry the woman, and that I finally did.

The Beginner

Four months of steam-cleaning locomotive cabs, then wiping down the brass handles and valves. Cleaning the windows with water and alcohol, making sure they were spotless. After cleaning was complete came the supplying. All the tools had to be in place: hammer, coal chisel wrenches, long oilers torches, lubricating oil for automatic lubricators. Time went by. Eventually I was promoted to boiler-maker helper. This advancement, or demotion (I did not know which) paid five cents an hour more. But for that I had to work at midnight and either wash out boilers or clean out carbon from the fire-boxes, or do any miserable job the boiler-maker didn't like.

Receiving the wet job of washing out boilers, another employee and myself were issued a large wrench with a bar to unscrew all the wash-out plugs from the boiler end of the locomotive, located around the outside lower edge of the boiler. If the water and steam were not completely emptied in the boiler, and sometimes they weren't, the first plug that we removed would give one of us a hot bath. But we learned very quickly to be careful. Another employee and I worked from midnight to eight in the morning, six days a week, pulling heavy black rubber hoses from one locomotive to another, hooking one end to a faucet and the nozzle end to the locomotive. Completing that task, I would let out a "whoop" to the other employee, which told him to turn the water on at the faucet. I would watch the water gushing from the other wash-out plugs until it came out clear, without shale or sludge. Then I would yell "hip" and he would turn the water off. Both sides of the locomotive had to be treated in this way.

Five weeks passed and I was still doing this miserable job. The only thing that changed was that my companion who worked with me left and went out on the road as a student fireman. Another person was assigned to help me, but within a week, he began to talk about going out on the road also. I started to think there must be something better than this onerous work of yelling whoop and hip all night. Winter was about to set in, and my bones would soon be rattling in the cold wet night.

But just about the time when this job had completely exasperated me, I was notified of a changed assignment. From the quagmire of sludge and water, I went to the heat of hell, working in the fire-boxes, cleaning out carbon and laying and replacing fire bricks. Oh, yes, the pay was forty-two cents an hour, but it was hard work, particularly for a skinny-ass kid like me.

I never forgot the night I reported for my new assignment. Waiting for me was a four-by-four man in a suit of ill-fitting overalls with a denim jacket reaching down to his knees and a red handkerchief hanging out of one pocket. He was looking at me as if I was some kind of a nincompoop.

"You'll do, follow me," he said, as tobacco juice streamed down each corner of his mouth. And I followed him. Securing a bar and a shovel we climbed the ladder into the cab of a newer

11

locomotive. The steam had been removed from the boiler and the round-house steam was connected at the smokestack portion of the locomotive. This created a strong draft of cold air through the fire door, making it more comfortable for a person working in the fire-boxes. Inside of the open iron door to the fire-box a light burned from an extension cord and I noticed a build-up of glowing red carbon on the fire-box floor.

"Well! What are you waiting for?" the little fat man blurted out.

"You want me to get in there?" I asked.

"Who do you expect, Santa Claus?" was his sarcastic reply. Maybe he was referring to himself as Santa, he being about the same size. But his remarks and his attitude were perturbing me, all because I didn't know exactly what to do. Me, a skinny lanky kid, not quite dry behind the ears, with no experience of what I was about to do. I could see why he wanted me to go into the fire-box—because his belly and posterior would not fit through the fire-door. After uttering some quiet expletives to myself, I wiggled through the fire-door into the fire-box. The blower brought in cool fresh air and cooled me from my waist up, but the bottom half was roasting and boy, were my feet starting to catch fire!

"Get that carbon cleaned out," he yelled, throwing me a bar and a shovel through the fire-door. "Work fast or you'll burn up," he added.

That was my introduction to Herman. He wasn't so bad after working with him for a few days. If things were done Herman's way, he saw to it that a little rest was forthcoming on his shift. So I tried to do what he expected. Sometimes it turned out to be a hard job but it paid off.

I recall one incident in particular. We had worked through our regular lunch period to get a particular locomotive ready because it was wanted for a special assignment. Finishing the job, we went on our lunch period. After eating my sandwich, I found I had fifteen minutes left, and I climbed up into the cab on the next engine that we were scheduled to work. I settled down on the fireman's seat box and waited for Herman. I closed my eyes and must have dozed off for a few seconds, when all of a sudden there was a tumult of noise and a shower of stars and my head was being rolled around like a bowling ball. I was being shook.

"No one sleeps on this shift. You're fired!" said the earthquake that had me by the collar. And that earthquake was the round-house foreman, George Orsiline. I got that sick feeling in my stomach; it was like being stepped on by an elephant. I was flabbergasted!

"But, but . . ." I tried to find the right words. "I'm on my lunch hour," I finally stammered.

"Why, hell, lunch-time was over an hour and a half ago. Who you trying to kid?" he growled at me. "Where is Herman?"

"I'm right here, George," Herman said as he climbed up the ladder and entered the cab. He could see the difficult spot I was in.

"What in the hell you doing?" he asked George.

"What the hell you think I'm doing? This man was asleep and I just fired him," George bellowed.

"So what?" Herman came back. "A man can do what he wishes on his lunch time and we were at lunch. Besides it wasn't ten minutes ago that I saw you sitting in your office nodding at everyone that passed by, and furthermore, if you don't get away from here, I'll call the shop steward."

By this time Herman was shouting loud enough for everyone in the round-house to hear. The two men looked each other over with provocative eyes. Neither said anything more until finally George shrugged his shoulders and left. He knew he was licked.

After a couple of months working in the fire-boxes and doing as well as anyone in my category, I became, like any young person, careless. I would go into the boilers without my jumper coat, do my work and come out into the cold night air dripping wet with sweat. Not surprisingly, I caught pneumonia.

Two weeks in the hospital gave me time to think. One thing was certain, going back into the fire-boxes was over! Perhaps I could go on the road as a student fireman and work in engine service? The idea intrigued me very much. Lying in bed and daydreaming about locomotives, I thought of their smell and sounds, especially the sound of the air pumps spitting when they were actuated by steam. I thought of the sight of a lonely engine standing on a turn-out track patiently waiting for her crew, with a small throbbing fire in the fire-box, just enough to maintain the steam pressure up until her crew came and took her out to a train waiting somewhere out in the yard. Thinking of the places it would travel, winding its way over the mountains and then down through the desert. What a great place the desert is! Such pure air, nothing like the city, all gassed up and stinking with fumes. The early morning desert breeze blows against your face and vibrantly bathes the lungs. The desert is a quiet place until the wind starts marauding about; without that, the air would be as it is in the cities, stagnant. Men go out on the desert like a bunch of scrounging ants upsetting the balance of nature. Man has the right of survival, but he must respect nature too.

Mr. Macdonald, the master mechanic, was glad to see me after my discharge from the hospital. I told him that I would like to go firing, and he said that would be fine because of the shortage of firemen. I was to start immediately on my student trips. Student firemen at that time were required to go out on the road for thirty days, receiving no compensation. The requirements were to make one trip a day and go over the entire division. Los Angeles division consists of all the city and clear to Yuma Arizona, including all the branch lines.

Driving home I felt jubilant about my new adventure, but what about Margie? Why, hell, we are not married yet, I am still my own boss, I mused almost aloud to myself. Then I started wondering how I could finance the trips. I had only twenty-one dollars saved up, not enough to last thirty days, during which I would have to pay for meals and room rent.

I arrived home still thinking how to raise the money for my trips.

"Here," my mom said to me, "you'll need this for your trips." She handed me fifty dollars. I was preoccupied with my problem and not paying attention, but then suddenly it struck me! How did she know that I needed money for trips? Nobody in the world was that psychic.

"Charlie Allen called and told me that you were going out on the road as a student fireman," Mom said, "so I though you might need a little money." Mom smiled; she was always coming to my rescue. That explained everything; nothing psychic, just the swift way news traveled.

The Neophyte

I took a written test of the book of rules published by the Southern Pacific Railroad, which I studied over the weekend. Then I received a pad of thirty different individual papers, one for each engineer to sign at the end of every trip, stating that I had been instructed by the regular fireman in the art of firing a locomotive and that he would or would not recommend me to continue. At first I was anxious, afraid, and lonely, starting

15

my student trips scarcely knowing where to go or what to say. But after a few starts of introducing myself to the engineer and fireman that I was to work with, it became easier.

I learned about the different types of water injectors, also water pumps, how to use the atomizer with the blower, epsecially on switch engines, and the damper keeping a bright red fire in the fire-box so no smoke would come out of the stack. Smoke out of the stack was unburnt oil and a waste. All our locomotives in the west burned oil. On road trips I learned to keep the water at the right level in the water glass at all times, uphill or down, and to look for signals ahead or behind at all times. Many other things a fireman must know but I picked those up as I gained experience. The most important was to know the engine you were in charge of.

Thirty long days finally ended. Then I returned to Los Angeles to be put on the fireman's extra board, once again being on the payroll. With my wallet empty, I was eager to earn some money. Not too many years later the Brotherhoods (the unions) negotiated with the railroads to partially pay the student firemen for their time and expense. The company, knowing that the young firemen were low on money at the end of their trips, issued meal ticket books, worth five dollars, which were accepted by the cafes and hotels along the routes of the railroads. Each fireman could acquire as many books as he needed and then the money would be taken from his wages at payday. The books became popular with all the train and engine crews. Unfortunately, some began using them for gambling, and when that started, the wives complained to officials and the books were discontinued.

My first pay trip, starting at midnight, was a switch engine down in the center of town, a place called Ferguson Alley. The nice old engineer that night said to me, "Don't you worry, lad;

we all had to learn." His remark eased my anxiety and fear a little. Firing that old twelve hundred slide valve teakettle with an antique monitor water injector that spilled more water on the ground than it put into the boiler, wasn't easy, but I made it! Boy, I was making four dollars and nineteen cents for eight hours work, and that was good wages in those days. An engineer's pay for a switch engine amounted to five dollars and twenty-five cents for eight hours work. Today, an engineer on a clean diesel makes about one hundred and thirty-one dollars for eight hours work.

I struggled through a week of switch engines and then drew a "dead head" to Indio in the hot Imperial Valley way below Palm Springs, to augment the fireman's extra board. "Dead heading" was to ride the passenger train or bus to the destination being called for.

Air conditioning was in its infancy back in 1937 and 1938. Before that time, we only had fans for cooling, but I saw one of the first squirrel cage water coolers made, sitting in Woods garages in Indio. I did not know who had made it, but I did know that whoever had contrived this innovation was a genius. Keeping cool in this hot climate was a challenge. Some of the older engineers working out of Indio had "subs," a quonset-hut with burlap stretched over the top and sides and along the full length of the top ran a water pipe with sprinklers keeping the burlap wet. This made the insides very cool but the air became stagnant because only a few had windows. These huts were built under the palm trees along the railroad property right-of-way.

Arriving at Indio, I did not have much choice for sleeping quarters, using the dormitory above the depot for the employees' convenience. Each divided room had a clean bed with a top and bottom sheet, a bucket of water and a fan. When retiring you soaked the top sheet in the water, then wrung it out and lay down with it over your body. It acted as an air conditioner until the sheet dried out; then the heat of the day or night woke you up and you started the procedure over again. This way of sleeping was not very healthy, but at least you did receive some sleep.

The next morning I was on a freight train to Yuma, Arizona, with engineer Van Leiur. It was my first mainline pay trip, and boy, was I excited. I was also apprehensive, although I did not know that no one liked to work with Van Leiur, which was probabaly why I had caught the trip with him.

The temperature at seven-thirty that morning registered one hundred and eight on the thermometer at the depot, but it would be much, much hotter on a steam engine. The train was located on the ice-house track while the reefers (refrigerator cars) were re-iced. Reefers were made of steel supports sided with tongue-and-groove 1" x 4" Douglas Fir outside and thick insulated walls having plywood inside walls, as well as insulated floors and ceilings. A compartment at each end of the car held an enormous amount of block ice, which was fed through doors in the roof.

Designated yards along the railroad system had ice-house tracks for re-icing purposes. Along the track, there was an elevated walkway high as the top of the refers, having a roller ramp from a large concrete ice plant feeding large blocks of ice to workmen stationed on the walkway icing the refers. Ice-house tracks varied in length according to the demand of the locality.

Checking the engine over, I was trying to recall my student training, but in my excitement I forgot some things. Engineer Van Leiur was quick to notice.

"I'm always getting these green firemen," he mumbled,

walking away. He would not show me anything; all he did was complain.

I thought, 'Oh, my, what an experience this is going to be.' I guess he had never been a student fireman; maybe he was just born with the knowledge. As we moved out of Indio yard and before the train was completely on the high rail (main line) Van shouted his instructions.

"Come on, boy, more atomizer, get the steam up, cut the blower down, more oil, more oil." Being commanded to do so many things at once, and qucikly forgetting what had been said at the beginning, did not bother me as much as the arrogant and acidic way this guy talked.

We ascended the Niland grade for about ten or more miles. Most trains received a helper to boost them up the hill but our tonnage did not require any help.

"Sand her out. Come on, what's the hell the matter with you? Damn dumb firemen, that's all I ever get is bastards like you."

As the hair on a wolf bristles when he is angry, so the hair on the back of my neck was bristling up after that remark. With slow and easy movements, I stepped over to the sand box, took out sand scoop and turned to Van, shaking it in his face.

"I ought to throw you into the fire-box for that last remark. Now if you want this engine sanded out, do it yourself," I said. Hooking the business end of the sand scoop over his reverse lever, I returned to do my work. bewildered and astonished, he sanded the engine. The procedure consists of scooping sand from the sand-box through the peep hole in the fire door so the sand went through the flues and out the smoke stack, cleaning all the carbon build-up on the metal in the flues.

With the front window of the cab open for air, a grain of sand out of the stack came through the window, lodging in my left eye, making the situation worse during the completion of the trip. I welcomed being told the right way of doing things, but not in the sarcastic and abusive way Van Leiur related to me.

The returning trip from Yuma the next morning was no better. Taking the same punishment and abuse, and with the pain in my eye nearly killing me, I made up my mind to quit upon arriving at Indio. Having a doctor's order for my eye and after showering at the round-house washroom, I walked up to the club-house at the depot, looking for someone to direct me to the doctor's office.

"Where in the dickens did you get that?" one of my friends asked me after directing me to the doctor's office.

"A piece of sand got to me when Van Leiur sanded the engine."

"Van sanded the engine out? How did you get him to do that?" one of the other firemen asked with great excitement. "Why in the hell do you want to quit?"

I related all that had happened on my ill-fated trip.

"You want to quit account of that?" one of the older engineers, who had been listening along with two others, asked.

"Didn't I deliver the *Herold Express* to your house while I was going to school?" I inquired of one of the other two.

"You sure did and don't quit," came the encouragement from my subscriber; years have long erased his name from my mind.

"We'll straighten Van up; he won't bother anyone else when we've finished with him."

In those days of railroading, train and engine men were proud of their positions, and discipline came from the men themselves rather than an official of the company.

20

"OK, I'll give it another try," I responded after some thought, and then I left to have my eye taken care of.

I made many helper trips from Indio to Beaumont, and also some trips to Yuma, without any trouble. The engineers that I worked with were kind enough to teach me things that helped improve my job performance. On the last trip I was called to fire again with Van Leiur, but this time I was ready for him. When I arrived at the round-house, I found that he had laid off on the call because he had been paired with me. I figured one of two things could have changed his mind. Either he was afraid I might throw him in the fire-box, or the chastising by his associates had taken effect. Probably the latter.

Returning from Yuma I found a note pinned on the register book, informing me that I was to dead head to Niland for helper service because the regular fireman on the job wanted some time off. I felt very fortunate to be asked to fill this assignment because of the good pay involved. Sometimes we covered three hundred miles per day. Train and engine men worked by the miles; one hundred miles equalled one eight-hour day; the time we went on duty, or whether we actually took the full eight hours, made no difference. The average time taken on a helper trip between Niland and Amos was about two to three hours, and if three hours elapsed between trips, it constituted one hundred miles each, so making it possible to make three trips or more in twenty-four hours.

Niland was a busy railroad junction where a branch line to the rich Imperial Valley connected to the Southern Pacific main artery to the east or west. Local freight trains brought train loads of produce in each day to be picked up by trains going east or west. The town seemed small when I first saw it, but it had potential and the possibility for growth. At the time of year when I arrived, the crickets were at their height; they

21

were *all over*, six inches deep, piled against the store fronts, on the sidewalks, walking across the ceilings in the hotel rooms, just about every place possible. After about five or six weeks the crickets would leave as fast as they had appeared. My biggest worry was when eating—perhaps if I bit into one of these critters, it would be the end. But the natives said they were delicious. I said, "horse hockey."

Weathering four good money days on the helper, with crickets as constant companions, I was called in the early morning with engineer Banta, one of the nicest and most congenial people I had ever met. The night had been fairly cool and it was just about sunrise when we arrived at Amos. Amos siding was removed many years ago, and I do not know if that was the correct name. But I believe it was, because the name stuck with me because of what happened that fifth day, so long ago.

After the train had stopped, engineer Banta seemed to be having difficulty moving; it seemed as if he was in pain. I asked him if he was able to run the engine for us to be cut out from the train. He replied that he could.

One of the brakemen walked up from the caboose to cut us off the train. He continued on walking, inspecting the train. Backing up with the engine and caboose another brakeman dropped off at the siding switch while the conductor rode the caboose's step between the engine to lift the draw-bar lever pin, cutting us away from the caboose as we made a drop of it to the train and entered the siding. Everything went well until entering the siding, when Banta passed out. He had the engine speed revved up very fast and I was frightened. Beads of sweat popped out everywhere on my body. Noticing Banta was on the verge of tumbling out of his seat, I ran and propped him up; then I closed down the throttle and put on the "jam" (slang for engine brakes), finally stopping the engine, which was half-way through the siding by that time. The train that we helped had already left for Yuma, so I could not have any help from them. Throwing some water on Banta's face revived him a little, and with my help he was able to lie down on the sand-box. I released the air on the engine and let it roll back to the beginning of the siding, where a telephone was located for talking to the dispatcher. It was the only way I would be able to summon help.

Naturally the phone was busy, but my patience ended and I cut in.

"Dispatcher, I have an emergency."

"Who is this? Don't you hear, this line is busy?"

"Damn it," I replied, "we need help, medical help." He then listened to my plight.

"There isn't any road up there for an ambulance to travel by, so you better run the engine to Niland and we will have help waiting. You have my permission to use the main line between the Amos and Niland. I will hold all trains at Niland for you. Be calm and good luck."

And that was it. For the first time in my life, I felt like a boy called upon to do a man's job. Beads of perspiration started forming on Banta's forehead as the day started to warm up. Knowing time was of the essence, I worked quickly. I ran to the mainline switch and lined it for the side track for bringing out the engine. I released the brakes and let the engine roll out on the high rail, stopped, ran back and lined the switch for normal operation. Then everything was ready to depart for Niland. I looked at Banta. His eyes were closed and he was moaning. At least I knew he was still alive.

Now came the test! Could I do what must be done? I had no experience of running an engine. My knowledge came from observing the engineers at work. I nudged the engine with the throttle to get it rolling down the hill. Not knowing how to use my watch with the mile posts for checking speed, all I could do was guess how fast we were traveling and hope it was correct.

Backing up to Niland, running, firing and making sure that Banta did not fall off the sand-box, proved to be a busy job for a greenhorn like me. Very shortly Niland loomed up. Standing by the depot was an ambulance and a group of people. Stopping by the depot, and taking in a big breath of air, I thought, 'thank God for letting me bring Banta down the hill for help.' Somebody shook my hand after the ambulance attendants removed Banta, but my trembling inside made it feel like a dream. I was in shock. Someone put the engine on the relief track for me, then going into the depot, I sat for a long time.

The regular fireman reported for his assignment, relieving me to go back for the Indio extra board. Staying at Indio for another week, I was released to my home terminal, Los Angeles. And Banta? After a few days, he was fine.

2. Blind Ordainment

Having several hundred dollars in a newly acquired bank account I made the mistake of telling Margie about it. The making of good money and the bank account prevailed upon her; she wanted to get married as soon as possible, and with a big wedding. I argued against it, telling her that my seniority as of then might not keep us afloat because it was an unknown quantity. I might be able to work permanently from now on or I might get laid off. After talking for hours and not making any headway, I gave in. There are some women who just can't be reasoned with. I gave her the money I had in the bank so she could arrange whatever she wanted. Two months later we were married.

For several months, it was fine. Margie kept me worn out— at home, always in bed, sometimes on the floor, on the couch or table, it made no difference where. I would go to work dragging my butt, glad to get away. It wasn't long before Margie took sick, mostly in the morning. Boy, was I scared! Nobody had told me that anything like this would happen. All the advice given me was: Go to bed, boy, have sex and enjoy it, which I sure did!

It did not take long for us to confirm that Margie was pregnant. At the same time the company cut me off the extra board. Being laid off at that time meant that the pay check stopped. What a hell of a fix we would have been in, if I had not had a little money saved. Social Security, and unemployment benefits, were being formulated in Washington in those days, but had not yet been put into effect.

The Southern Pacific tried to keep their cut-off employees working by putting them in the shops or coachyards and any other place they could use them. But if there wasn't a place for you, that was it. I happened to be in the crew dispatcher's office when Frank Miller, the assistant chief dispatcher, received a wire from the Coast Division, stating they needed a fireman at San Francisco.

"Would you care to borrow out to Frisco, Charlie? Frank asked. "They need firemen up there."

"Absolutely. I'll leave tonight if you have pass on #69. You know with a baby coming, I have to work."

The San Francisco jaunt lasted two months. Then it was back to Los Angeles. Still not being able to find work there, I visited Frank again.

"We're sending three firemen to the San Joaquin Division at Bakersfield tonight on the Owl #25," he informed me. The Owl was #25 then and later changed to #57.

"Who else is going besides me? I asked. Frank looked a the crew sheet.

"Let's see—Hector, Powell, Mays, and then you."

"What happened to Cecil Miller?" I asked.

"Oh, he went up two weeks ago and there were a lot of others but most of them came back. Got homesick, I guess."

"Don't worry about me until they cut me off or I am called back here," I assured Frank.

Arriving at Bakersfield around midnight, the weather was hot. None of us knew the location of the round-house. We

26

started walking towards the rear end of the train, which was now leaving, thinking that maybe this was the right direction. Bordering the broad asphalt walk was a row of well-kept company houses, with manicured lawns. The green, lush lawns looked inviting in the heat of the night and as the houses were in darkness I allowed myself to stretch out for a few minutes on one of the cool lawns. My three companions followed. Not knowing where to go or what to do, this was a relief. Lying there in the black of the night, looking up at the galaxy, I was almost falling asleep. But suddenly, night was flooded out with light.

"What are you fellows doing and who are you?" shouted a voice from the lighted porch as the floodlights on the tall pole beamed down on us. The voice had a sound of authority but was not without compassion.

"We're firemen from the Los Angeles Division. We're here to work the extra board." Hector did the talking.

"That is fine, we need you boys. I judge you dead headed on the Owl? the man asked.

"We did," Bob Powell replied.

"Good, now make yourself comfortable, I'll have someone here very soon and get all of you on the extra board and help you find a room." With that the man retreated into the house; the lights remained on.

Little did we know that the man was Mr. Brennan, Superintendent of the San Joaquin Division. But we soon found out he wasn't the only nice person in Bakersfield. It seemed like everyone was a caring person in this small town. Here I would put down roots and stay; as a matter of fact, all of us stayed.

After transferring to the San Joaquin Division my seniority climbed up fast, on account of the war in Europe. Hitler's

27

threat to the world geared up production in the United States tremendously. I bid for the extra board firing in Los Angeles belonging to Bakersfield. I worked to Santa Barbara, Bakersfield, and many local places, and with a lot of helpers.

By the time the second baby, Charoline, was born, my seniority allowed me to have a regular pool freight assignment between Los Angeles and Bakersfield. Seniority acted like the stock market—it just kept climbing. Soon it came about that I was firing a regular passenger train to Bakersfield. Those were the glory years, but not for long. Time moved on, and my turn for promotion to engineer was growing close. I used every available minute for studying. Concluding that the older engineers were the library of resources, all the young upstarts like myself bombarded them with questions. It must have been a grueling and trying time for them, but not one refused to help. I remember one tough old engineer called Blacky Young. He had a swarthy complexion and never smiled much, but I liked to fire for him because he would take time to explain the actions of various trains and why they differed. It was against the rules of the company to let a fireman, unless he was promoted, run the engine, and I often wondered how a young person could expect to gain experience. But Blacky was one of the few who let me handle a train, and he would instruct me on different procedures of the work.

Three days of continuous writing about the rules left blisters on my fingers. My last day of writing looked like some chicken had walked over my papers. But my work was accepted. Then there were two days of visual and oral examinations, and one day in which all the different areas of knowledge were brought together.

Everyone in our group passed the test, and returning home on the train relief and jubilation prevailed amongst us all. I enjoyed the family for a day and then reported for work.

The Demoters

A demoter was a fireman who had been promoted to engineer, but who was not yet on the engineers' roster, or who had been reduced down to a fireman on account of a reduction in business. A demoter was the envy of working engineers, because he usually made double pay. Here's how it happened. When the engineers' extra board was exhausted and no one was on the list of engineers, the first senior promoted fireman would be used to fill the vacancy. He would be paid for his assignment as a fireman as well as for his position as an engineer. I was in the demote bracket for almost fifteen months after being promoted to an engineer and the money came rolling in!

I made many trips as a demoter before being called on my regular passenger assignment firing, and it felt good having someone else at the helm for a while, but having a locomotive at your command exceeded any excitement there could ever be. The romance of railroading in those times was stupendous and inconceivable. As engineer Lee Nelms once said to me, "a good engine is like a good woman, you pet 'em, you pamper 'em and treat 'em nice and they'll do anything for you." Lee could make a steam whistle moan like no other person could. People laid awake nights to hear Lee's moaning whistle coming down the San Joaquin Valley. When the diesels replaced the steam locomotives, Lee faded out; diesels held no romance for him and it was not long before he took his pension.

The Quincy Hotel was a resting place for most engineers and firemen, as well as some train crews out of Los Angeles. Never was there a closer bunch of men, knitted together, always ready to help one another. Engineer John Simpson once told me, "Damn, I spend more time out here with you guys than I spend with my wife," and he was correct. The Quincy was probably the first hotel to have air coolers piped to each room. The hotel was immaculately clean and very quiet, and the lodging only seventy-five cents per day.

The Frolics

One day I was on my regular passenger assignment which arrived at Bakersfield in the early afternoon on train #51. I would be on duty the following morning at two-forty for train #60.

At Bakersfield, there was time to kill. Curly Farrow, my engineer, and I walked to the Quincy Hotel and secured a room, then left for a bite of lunch. After eating, I dropped into the Eight Ball, instead of taking my usual walk up and down Baker Street. I sat down to watch and wait for a chance of a game of pool with the four young enginemen who were finishing their game.

"Hey, fellows, what say we visit the girls in the houses?" Glenn Porter, one of the firemen, blurted out. It was one of those afternoons; pool was a bore. None of us took him seriously at first, but when young minds get together, something is bound to happen. None of us drank, because then the use of alcohol was strictly forbidden by the railroads, on or off the job. This was "Rule G" in the rule book and was rigorously enforced by the company.

No one answered Glenn. Maybe, like me, they had never been inside one of the girlie houses.

"Come on," he continued. "Let's go see what it's like inside one of them." Back in the forties, Bakersfield had about as many whore-houses as churches; perhaps that had something to do with the fact that there were not very many rapes or attempted rapes at that time. I remember one time, when making a demoter trip, sitting on my engine, parked directly across the Edison highway from the Tacoma, a well-known whore-house at that time. It was nine-thirty in the evening and I counted forty-two patrons entering the premises in a period of thirty minutes.

On this occasion we doggedly put all our cue sticks away and reluctantly followed Glenn, not wanting to be called chicken.

We visited four bordellos that afternoon. Each one had expensive thick carpets with heavy drapes darkening the heavily perfumed parlor on entry. We were greeted by a Madam, usually an older woman who had outgrown her whoring days.

"What will it be, boys?" The question was always the same.

"Can we see the girls, please?" Porter would ask, as we all sat with strained grins on our faces. I wished that I was not there. The women that were not busy presented themselves in flimsy see-through attire. The heavy make-up on their faces was ugly and their presence intolerable. They had no femininity; they were neither old nor young, just used and tired. What a repulsive thought to even contemplate an intimate relationship with any of them. But some men did. Well, each to his own.

After making a complete inspection, Glenn would inform the Madam that they weren't exactly what we wanted. The Madam would be dumbfounded and watch with open mouth as we walked out.

"You bastards don't ever come in here again," she would scream.

After thinking about it later I realized what a cruel thing we did. These people were in business like anyone else, regardless of what the business was. We had no right using it for our own amusement. Back at the Quincy for rest, I had a rueful and gamy feeling about the incident.

My next trip was on a coast train to Santa Susana as an engineer. Margie made me a lunch and also gave me hot jello in a thermos to drink. I never drank much coffee because it bloated me and also added to the amber stream. That was sometimes hard to take care of because there were no toilets provided on the locomotives, only a sand-box.

Arriving for work at two o'clock in the morning, I discovered my fireman D. J. Barr was going on his first trip firing oil, although he had fired coal in the East some place. He was nicknamed Billy for some reason which I never found out.

"The blind is leading the blind tonight," Frank Miller, the crew dispatcher, kidded me.

"Well, maybe so," I joshed back, "but he won't be treated like I was on my first train mainline trip." Frank nodded his head, knowing what I meant.

Our powerful Consolidated 2700 type locomotive had small drivers (wheels) but we still called her a teakettle. The Southern Pacific had many new locomotives on order but mostly newer cab ahead articulated malley engines of the 4200 class.

With the teakettle cut in the train we were about to help, I proceeded to show Billy a few things about oil burners. He was a quick learner. It was about four-fifteen in the morning when we started on our way up the coast, receiving orders at Burbank Junction to meet extra east 4201 at Hewitt. If the opposing train were in the side track at Hewitt, then we would go to Chatsworth for the fleet, the fleet being all the morning passengers and express trains.

Billy did a wonderful job of keeping the teakettle happy

with steam, and luckily the extra 4201 was in the siding at Hewitt. So we pushed on to Chatsworth, which was located on a long right-hand curve slightly uphill. The east end of the mainline and siding where we stood was located on a built-up fill, making the natural grade lower than the railroad track. On the inner side of the long curve of the track, there were vast farm lands and some farmer had planted the most luscious-looking cantaloupes. On a cold dark early morning like this, just before dawn, I betted they would taste good. A story was told that this farmer would shoot anyone with rock salt if he caught them exploiting his field, but most of us figured it was a trainmaster's story for keeping us out of the field.

"Billy, how about a good cold melon this morning?"

"No, I think I'll just sit here and rest," Billy Barr, who was older than me, replied. I remembered how, several years ago, when firing for old Tom Graham on the helper to Vincent, Tom would have me put the lights and the fire out of the engine and at the lower end of siding Humphreys, where the grade leveled off a bit, Tom would stop and we would do a little raiding of a melon patch which had been planted close to the track. But old Tom was a hog; he filled a burlap bag with melons. I am sure the farmer did not mind one or two melons, but a hundred pound bag? After grabbing the loot and climbing back on the engine, Tom would release the engine brakes and coast down the hill for a mile. Then he would instruct me to put a fire in the engine and turn the lights on.

I decide to go it alone, leaving Billy asleep. Seeing by the engine's firelight, I tapped each melon to find a ripe one. But when I looked up, there he stood! Seen against the flickering firelight, holding a gun, was the farmer. What in the hell was I to do? This wasn't any trainmaster's story; this was very real. I was relieved that I did not have any melon in my hands, and was also thankful Billy wasn't with me. The idea popped into my confused mind: make like you're going to the toilet. Not knowing what other course of action to follow in a fast situation like this, I unhooked my overalls and began shaking like an Aspen leaf in the breeze—not from the cold but from the fear of buck-shot in my butt!

After a minute or so in a squatting position the cold began to take over and I got cramp in my legs. Sweat beaded on my forehead and the lower part of me felt like icicles were forming on my rear end. I was afraid to move and afraid that if I didn't, I would freeze to death. Talk about a rock and a hard spot! I could see the newspaper headlines: 'Man frozen in melon patch'. What would my family and friends say? In fact, it was not cold enough to freeze anything, but it sure seemed so to me.

To exacerbate the situation, two long sounds of the whistle moaned in the dark from the head end of the train, telling me they wanted to move. The train order office was located near the head end of the train and they must have gotten orders to meet the fleet farther up the line at Santa Susana.

The train backed up against my engine trying to start, and I supposed the conductor would be walking up from the caboose, wondering what the trouble might be. The first streak of dawn was brightening the eastern sky, and looking up at the farmer, I could see him much clearer now. Hell, it was not a person but only a scarecrow holding a stick over its shoulder! I hastily pulled up my overalls and took out for the engine, never telling anyone until years later what happened in that melon patch.

3. The War Years

On December 7, 1941, as a result of Pearl Harbor, the United States was faced with the reality of war. We were not prepared but we had something more than preparedness. We had determination and anger, and when the American people are angered, nothing can stop them. The men were drafted and the women went out to work and worked like men. Anyone who could walk or not, had something to do.

On the railroad we worked sixteen hours a day, seven days a week. Old men came out of retirement and were firing for young engineers who could very easily have been their grandsons. Sometimes the sixteen hour law (a law passed by Congress limiting the working hours of a railroad employee to sixteen hours before receiving eight hours rest) would trap us outside of Los Angeles, no farther than San Fernando or Saugus, a distance of twenty-one or thirty-two miles. The reason for this detainment of train movements was far beyond my comprehension. We had so many long grueling trips that seemed to get us nowhere. To keep our nerves from snapping, we were informed that the security of getting our train from point A to point B depended on the FBI and other government secret services. We were told that saboteurs and enemy agents would try to delay the supplies and troop movements, so everything had to be checked out before any movement was made. Soldiers guarded all the bridges and tunnels and other important facilities. If air raid sirens sounded, the engineer would put out his headlight, and if the train was in a siding, the fire was to be extinguished.

Throughout the history of the United States there has never been a more well-oiled organization of work force and military operation in such a quick time. Everyone was required to stay on their jobs unless it was not in the interests of defense. If this was the case he could change to defense work or join the military.

Wages increased substantially from 1937 to 1942, but during the war years they were kept stable. The long hard-working hours made the pay check look enormous. Many times after working sixteen hours, we stayed on the engine and rested for eight hours then went back to work again. It was hell.

Old Turkey Neck

I was called one night for a demote to help a passenger train going to Portland. Helping to Eric, six miles east of Tehachapi. In the steam locomotive days, Eric was the station where Mojave helpers were cut off to return. All that was there was a spur with a Y for turning engines, a water plug to water engines, and of course a dispatcher's phone.

The train engine, a brand new cab ahead malley 4297, was a smooth rider, not like my pile of old iron, the 3614, that didn't even have a speedometer. But that did not bother me, because, not being qualified for passenger service, I would have to trade with the regular engineer until getting to Eric. Sometimes a disqualified engineer would be called for passenger if there wasn't a passenger man available. So many train trips were required before an engineer was approved for passenger, and I hadn't at that time made the standard amount.

Old Turkey Neck—I do not recall his real name but his nickname has stuck—sensed the situation and decided he was not going to run that hard-riding antique without a speedometer.

"You're qualified to ride the point tonight," he told me in a rough voice. Not wanting an argument, I accepted the assignment, although I knew it was wrong.

After leaving Los Angeles Union Passenger Terminal, everything went fine until going down Newhall Hill. I looked back at my train, as required by the rules. Old Turkey Neck was having a fit, with his cab light on, his long neck and head sticking out the window and a flashlight in his hands, gesticulating with his arms. He looked somewhat like a turkey with its wings flapping for take off. It then dawned on me the reason for his nickname.

"What do you think is wrong with old Turkey Neck?" I asked my fireman, Ivan McKibbon. "He is having a fit back there."

About that time the 110 pounds of air pressure on the air gauge went; he had stopped me with an emergency application of the brakes. As soon as the train came to a rest, I slid down the handrails of the ladder to the ground and went back to his engine. Turkey was on the ground by this time.

"What's wrong?" I shouted.

"What in the hell are you trying to do, get me fired?" he yelled back at me. "You were doing forty and the speed is thirty and you better make damn sure you live up to it. I don't give a damn if you get fired but you're not taking me with you!" He kept raving on, frothing at the mouth and gesticulating.

I felt the crimson flow of blood in my neck and up to my head; my ears twitched with the rise in temperature.

37

"Listen and listen good," I yelled, standing close to him so he would understand. "You are supposed to be on the point of this train, not me. Now with this short hill, it's less than two miles before the speed limit increases to forty. I didn't have time to check my watch against the mile boards. But you can sit on your ass back there and look at your speedometer which I haven't got. Now either you get on my engine or I'll get on yours, but if you get on yours, don't look at the speedometer and don't ever pull the air on me again, understand?" We stared at each other, then he turned without a word and climbed the ladder of the malley. I went back to my engine, and experienced no more trouble. We arrived at Eric on time.

After cutting off from the train and going around the Y with our engine, Ivan filled the water tender as I phoned the dispatcher for permission to cross over the double tracks on our returning from our helper trip. The dispatcher informed me that we were stuck because of a Santa Fe passenger train. After he had gone by, we were to give the dispatcher another call. Five hours passed and nothing happened. I called the dispatcher.

"Can't get you out yet," he replied.

"We could have walked to Mojave by this time, and besides, we're hungry."

"Sorry, the chief says to hold you there," he said. Nothing arrived or left for several more hours. Finally, we were told to cross over and upon arriving at Mojave, to tie up for rest and we would be called to help when they needed us.

The Southern Pacific had a nice bunk house at Mojave with partitioned-off rooms with clean beds, a shower room, and toilets. Ivan McKibbon and I remained there, on call and on overtime pay, for seven long days. Our clothes were standing by themselves. Taking two showers a day and washing our underwear out manually did not help the awful stink. We assumed the only ones who could stand us were each other, since we both smelled the same. I wanted to go home in the worst way. Not only was I a stinking mess but I was running out of cash. But how were we going to get there? We were too smelly to ride the passenger train or bus. We were called the next morning to dead head on train #60. McKibbon came up with a solution—we rode the baggage car. One thing for sure, from now on, there would be no leaving home without an extra change of clothes.

In and Out

The war effort was escalating. The military was drafting men with families, and I knew that my number could come up soon. I thought about what course to follow. If I waited to be drafted, it would be the regular army for me, but my family could have a larger allotment if I enlisted in the Sea-Bee's, a new branch of the Navy. I knew construction quite well, maybe well enough to receive a rating. I talked about it with Margie and although like millions of other women, she did not want to lose her husband, we decided it was the smart thing to do under the circumstances. It was a Tuesday when I left to enlist. The recruiting office location was on Hill Street in downtown Los Angeles, upstairs in a huge loft.

When filling out my papers, I omitted to mention that I was working on the railroad, figuring they would not find out about it and in that way I was a cinch for enlistment. With the paperwork finished, the next step was to strip off our clothes in the far corner of the loft. I have never witnessed such an array of gangling bodies, all arms and legs, with white butts and washboard ribs in my life. After the doctor finished listening to the hearts and taking blood pressure, came the short-arm inspection, and finally one for flat feet. In passing, all of us stood at attention.

"You are now in the United States Sea-Bee's, a branch of the Navy. All of you are starting with a third class rating," an officer yelled as loud as he could. "You are to report back here two weeks from today!" he continued, "and be ready to leave for boot camp."

Driving home I wasn't very happy. Actually I had mixed emotions; all kinds of thoughts rolled around in my head, as I tried to ferret out what was right. I had two weeks in which to cram a lifetime of living and to get my affairs in order. I decided the best thing was for me to lay off sick from work, and, when leaving for the service, I would notify the company. In that way if or when I returned, my job would be waiting for me.

Two weeks elapsed; like the wind it came and was gone. With a heavy heart and a light satchel I bid my family goodbye. Even Margie cried. As I boarded a streetcar for the city I realized I was no different, in the way I thought and felt going off to war, from thousands of other men who had gone before me. Honor and duty and pride are part of man's roots. A call to arms means, stand up and be counted. The welfare of our country is just as important as anything we personally possess. To me it is a great privilege to be an American.

I realized I was on the other side of the fence now; I was going to serve and not be the server. I would be fighting, not supplying. As I considered this I experienced an altogether different kind of emotion than I was accustomed to. In the service, one is told what to do; there would no more doing what you think should be done.

Leaving the streetcar at Fifth and Broadway, I walked up to Hill Street in the morning sun. It was a beautiful day, a day for

40

having a light train to Bakersfield with power to spare. Not being an engineer anymore hit me in the solar plexus as I climbed up the steps to the loft. A few recruits were ahead of me at the recruiting officer's desk. Looking about me I saw many bleak, anxious faces, but I knew they were filled with a resolution to do what they must do.

"Your name, please?" the officer said, bringing me out of the trance I was in.

"My name is . . . is . . . " I stammered, "Charles Steffes."

"Oh, yes, I have something on you. Let me see." He mused and fumbled through some papers. "Now, here it is." He hesitated, then frowned and said, "your job is a railroad engineer. Mister, you are wasting my time." He was now bellowing at me. "And your time, also the railroad's time. The railroad went to Washington D.C. to get you a deferment. Now get your ass out of here and don't come back. You are far more essential where you are then anywhere else."

How did they find out that I tried to join the service? Must have been through my Social Security number somehow. The officer handed me a reassignment of my draft card and I left.

Well, I was on the other side of the fence again and it was good.

The Laughter and the Grief

I was at Los Angeles station, observing the large crowd of people on the depot platform while waiting for the train inspection and departure of a troop train, destination, San Francisco, for the western theater of the war. Regular passenger trains took a far second to troop trains, which always had priority. Girlfriends, wives, moms and dads, or sisters, and more, were saying goodbye to their loved ones. There was hugging, kissing and lots of laughter. The servicemen would

41

jokingly say, "We'll be right back; a few weeks and the war will be over! Wait till we get over there—we'll show them." This buoyant hubbub would soon give way to last moment tears as the parting approached.

The conductor shouted the all-board and the servicemen scrambled to get on the train. The conductor then turned and gave me a "high ball" (an arm signal) to proceed. After receiving the light signal on the ground by the tower man we slowly moved out.

With the train on the roll, the rules required a running air test, which I complied with. We heading up the westbound Southern Pacific main track to Burbank Junction, thence to Santa Barbara, where the Coast Division engine crews boarded. After taking on water in the tender, they left.

After making out the work report and time slip for the fireman and myself, I decided to eat a snack before retiring. But after being told that we were scheduled for a funeral train back to Los Angeles, eating was impossible. It was a troop train of the dead in coffins coming home. Not too long ago they had been laughing just like the ones we had just taken out. In addition to these trains there were the hospital trains with the wounded and maimed. The dead were not actually coming home; they had gone home already, the day they were killed, home to their God. Grief and sorrow lies deep in the hearts of the living. The bodies came home to pacify the living, not the dead.

It took only a run of three hours to arrive at Santa Barbara, but returning to Los Angeles with the coffins took over seven hours. On arriving at the passenger station we came to rest on a back track as far from the public eye as possible, and I was thankful when that day was over.

The Grind and the Loneliness

The day of my demotes were over; the glory year was done. Seniority moved me onto the engineer's roster, and this meant the end of double pay. I would be making the "dead heads" like all the other engineers who had to relieve men working on outside points, if they wanted off. The outside stations on the San Joaquin Division at Los Angeles were Santa Barbara, Oxnard, one job at Mojave, Filmore, and some helper jobs at Lancaster.

To complicate things, Margie was almost due for her third baby, making it imperative that I work harder without any loss of time. That was very easy to accomplish because the war effort was escalating rapidly, resulting in heavy movements of trains. So working harder created no problem, but I encountered many "dead heads."

Working on the railroad in either engine or train service required a great amount of night work and daylight sleeping. Resting during the day was almost impossible with a young family coming up. I had the idea of building a room out from the house, heavily insulated with sawdust to keep the noise out. I put in a heater and cooler with a circulating fan, a toilet and a washstand, making the room very comfortable. A phone was installed with an off and on switch for the bell if I so desired. With this kind of arrangement things were easier for my family, and I would have my much-needed rest, only sometimes it would be two or three days before I would see the family. Looking back, I realize this was not good for my kids, but I had to work.

As time elapsed, like any male I would get horny, so I would go into the house on a night that I didn't work, and crawl into bed with Margie. But since the last baby she wasn't herself. Her reception of me was cool, almost foreign.

"Come on, get it over with," she complained, "I don't know why you have to do this anyway." I dismissed this remark at first, thinking that she was just not herself. But it continued for several years. One night I went to bed with her, still hoping things would be different. We had had a beautiful evening taking the kids to a restaurant and having a delicious dinner. After coming home I had romped with the girls for a while and then put them to bed. Things seemed like old times again, and in bed Margie talked of what a nice time we had had. Then like some stranger in bed with me, she displayed a different personality entirely.

"Well! I see you got your tent up," she said. (That was her expression when I was sexy.) "Come on get this over with. And another thing, the next time you're in this shape, I want you to take the money and get yourself a whore, because I don't want you to touch me again, understand?"

Never was a tent hauled down so rapidly, and my feelings were drained. It was like the time when I handled the runaway train to Russ and the fireman on the passenger had us lined into the siding averting a collision. My body was limp. It felt as if someone had a paddle and was stirring around and around in my stomach until I was ready to puke.

I slipped out of bed for the last time with Margie, and went to my outside room, feeling rejected and lonely. I never touched her again. I thought of packing and leaving, but then what about the children? They needed me too, so I stayed.

I lived like a hermit and kept smiling for the kids. Making them think that everything was fine was difficult, but I would try. Then lying down I hoped that I might sleep it all away.

Unbelievable Truths

On a nice afternoon day in the early Spring of 1945 I

received a call for a trip to Bakersfield. With me was a crew of the finest bunch of men there ever was. Having a train load of ammunition, we were given right of track over all trains, including train #52, the San Joaquin Daylight to Bakersfield, but they made it to Junction for us. Our tonnage being light without any helper, I would manage to run the speed limit. Having a train order, "Handle the train with the greatest of care on account of high explosives," made all of us feel edgy. My fireman, Jess Pound, and I went along with conductor Earl Owens and his crew to run the beans (eating) at Mojave. After taking water at Mojave, we chugged up the hill to Tehachapi. We stopped to let the trainmen turn up the retainers on the box cars so that the air leaving the brake cylinders of each car was restricted. In that way the trainline could be recharged with air. The rules stated that an engineer must use the standard set and release method in braking a train from Tehachapi down to Caliente, but ninety percent of us used our own technique, either bridging or reducing the feed valve pressure. I used the feed valve method. All trains were required to stop at Woodford, half way down the hill, to cool wheels, equalizing the heat so as not to crack and break a wheel. After arriving at Caliente the retainers would be tuned down.

A warm zephyr breeze fanned my face on leaving Tehachapi at one o'clock that morning. Jess had worked hard, firing that cab ahead Malley, so he would rest going down the hill. The head brakeman rode the box cars down the hill, watching for any defects of the running gear.

Centralized Traffic Control, (C.T.C.), had been installed almost a year earlier and was operated by the dispatcher in Bakersfield. He had the use of power switches and signal control for dispatching the trains up and down the mountain.

Having the speed set at twenty miles per hour between

45

Tehachapi and the next siding Cable, my eyelids started to get heavy; I was battling sleep. I did not remember anything from Cable until we had almost arrived at Woodford six miles farther down the mountain. I woke up with a jolt, wide-awake, trembling like an earthquake and scared, not knowing how many red signals we had passed or how many trains we had met. My speed was still twenty miles per hour, with the approaching signal showing yellow over green, a siding indication for Woodford, to cool wheels. Sweat poured from me and a change of underwear would be due when arriving at Bakersfield. The Lord had his arms around me; this I know because this is one of many experiences I have had while working on the railroad. I believe in the Supreme Being because of the evidence in my everyday adventures, especially on the railroad. I also believe what Kahil Gibran wrote, "Your blessed Spirits are all about you." I saw so much evidence of it in my work. In remembering this incident, I only have to think of what might of happened if I had passed a red signal and ran head on into a train coming up the hill. Having all those explosives we were transporting, I think of the many lives that would have been lost and the huge damage caused.

For the remainder of the trip to Bakersfield I never closed or even blinked my eyes. Registering in at the round-house, no one remarked how good or bad the trip was, but I made up my mind that never again would I go through a situation like that. So when John's pipe shop opened that same morning, I became a new owner of a pipe and some tobacco. In that way, if sleepiness overtook me, the pipe would fall from my mouth and awaken me. Of course my shirt would sometimes have several little burn holes, but every hole might signify someone's life.

The call came around eleven o'clock that night for an extra

express train to Los Angeles. All the crew ate at Doll-Ray Cafe before going to work. When I lit up my pipe after eating I at once became the center of attraction. They knew that I never smoked and wanted to know what was going on. I told them nothing; only that I wanted to smoke. I did not say why.

After leaving Tehachapi the most awesome thing happened at Summit Switch. At three o'clock in the morning the night disappeared. For almost ten seconds it came as light as the noon day. There was no noise, just brightness. The head brakeman yelled at me, "that's the atomic bomb they're testing at Nevada; it was supposed to be released this morning."

What a bomb! It must be, lighting up the country several hundred miles away. Something big must be going to take place, although we never realized that it was going to be used on Japan. This experience reduced us all to silence, and an unobtrusive quietness remained with all three of us as we rode in the cab of the locomotive for the rest of the trip home.

One evening later that week, the phone rang and crew dispatcher Frank Dwyer called me for a light engine to Bakersfield. The thirty-six-ten was the engine, a 2-10-2 class. "But," Frank said, "you'll be firing the engine for Fritz Iverson, because we are out of firemen."

"Well that is fine," I replied. "It will still give me engineer's pay."

Fritz Iverson was a young engineer with an even temper and a perpetual smile. He did good work, like the average San Joaquin engineers. It looked like a good trip ahead for us. The night was balmy, not too hot or cold, with just a little breeze. Everything went just fine; the first train to meet would be at Ravenna. Having the green light clear to the east end of siding Humphreys, there we encountered a yellow signal. Fritz

47

slowed the engine down and then looked at me, trying to figure out why there was a yellow signal.

"We must be catching up with one of the 807s, because #801 wasn't called when we left," Fritz yelled at me. Traveling up the main to the other end of the siding where the signal was in red position, the stench of the hog farm nearby grew almost intolerable, and we were down wind from it. Being a very large operation, much of the garbage came in gondolas from Los Angeles. One train load, twice a week was set out on a spur track for the purpose of feeding the hogs. The terrain thereabouts was very primitive and wild and accessible only by dirt roads. Today it is suburban, with paved roads.

We stopped at the red signal. It was my job to protect the rear end of our light engine by flagging, which required me to walk back a sufficient distance leaving two torpedoes on the rail, return halfway and remain, until recalled by the engineer's whistle to return to the engine, leaving a lighted fuse. I had forgotten my flashlight when coming to work so I used the white, "hay burner," kerosene lantern along with the red one, with the torpedoes and fusees in my pocket. I started walking back, complying with rule #99, the flagging rule in the book. Walking slowly back about one fourth of a mile, I glanced back at the engine and wished Fritz had taken it very slowly up to the signal, then I would not have had to be so long out there smelling this foul air full of hog stink. Besides, my white lantern was acting up.

At that same moment, in a drainage ditch on my right, an awful loud scream, sounding like a woman pierced the night air. It made my hair stiff on top of my head (even though there was not much left to stand up—I was bald at an early age.) I looked quickly to my right and there, not too far away, were two large green fiery eyes, staring at me. I knew instantly that

48

they belonged to a cougar that had come down from the mountains for a pig dinner. Not wanting to be included in a pig dinner, I ran faster then I have ever done in my life. Dropping a lighted fusee and running back to the engine, I did not realize that the cougar was running in the opposite direction. It seemed like only two steps and I was going up the back end of the tender, over the top and down into the cab, panting like I'd just run the marathon race.

"I did not call you in." Fritz looked puzzled.

"No," I replied after catching my breath, "and I ain't going back. Any more flagging tonight, you're going to do it." Then I related my experience to him. Fritz chuckled a little, then he said, "I believe it. Just the other day coming down from Vincent with a train, that second tunnel from Lang, I chased a brown bear out of it, just missing him with the engine. I believe the food is getting scarce in the high country and all the animals are coming down for pig dinners or garbage spilled out of the gondolas."

"Yea," I laughed, "it stinks so bad it must reach the high country; they wouldn't have any trouble finding it."

By that time the signal cleared to a yellow and we continued slowly up the hill following the train ahead of us.

4. Post War Boom

In 1945, the United States ended the war by using the atomic bomb on Japan. Business still escalated on the railroad but for several months I and many others had to travel the 217 miles from Los Angeles to Fresno to find work. This was all because I was an engineer. Men younger than me in seniority remained at home doing well-paying firing jobs while I and the other engineers worked a low-paying switch engine or a local freight job at Fresno. This happened every spring for the next five years. There was one passenger job working the local mail train between Fresno and Bakersfield, but it was held by a regular engineer so none of us outer-towners would get that run. This was because of a local agreement: when the regular man wanted off he would let his intentions be known to some of the home guards and they could take a "hold-down" on the job until he returned to work.

On one very foggy night someone did not want to work the mail and passenger train and I was called for it. To make things worse the fireman who went with me was a new man; I have forgotten his name. We did not know the location of the stops, and the dense fog made things particularly difficult. Well, it was back up, go ahead all night, and we came into Bakersfield an hour and a half late, even though we had left on time.

"Boy, you better go back up on the mountain where you belong," the conductor said to me, shaking his head.

"And you know," I replied, "I would like that."

I never took a call for that train again after returning to Fresno, but it seemed like midnight switch engines were my speciality. I did not mind the night work because the hotel Saint Francis, where I stayed, was cool and dark in the day time. The proprietor, Lillian Owen, was the sister of engineer Bob Fowler and conductor Elmer Fowler, so she knew that train and engine crews had to sleep in the daytime.

It was not all railroad people who stayed at the Saint Francis, however. I remember one very good-looking young girl; she was especially nice, with black, wavy hair and a Marilyn Monroe shape of which she was very aware. I could tell this by the way she switched her butt as she walked, making all the men drool and slobber at the mouth. Lillian told me her name was Alice and she was off limits to the railroad men. Alice must have known that all these birds around the hotel would have liked to have gotten into her pants. Ray Trusty, an engineer friend of mine, tried very hard to make acquaintance with her but he failed, like a great many others who made similar attempts.

Working the same midnight switch engine three nights in a row was getting boring, but that was all there seemed to be for me in Fresno. Other men like Trusty seemed to get by these midnight jobs by tying up for eight hours when finishing a daylight tour, that way by-passing the midnight work. But I was afraid of losing some time that way.

Completing my midnight tour and climbing the stairs to the hotel, which was on the second floor of the building over shops and business, I felt very lonesome and a little rejected because I was not having a good home life. I was living in a false marriage, although it was always a joy to see the kids. On reaching the top of the stairs I encountered Alice, who was about to come down.

"Good morning," I greeted her.

Alice nodded her head, smiled, and said: "Do you happen to know where I might purchase some thread for my sewing machine?" Her voice had a very soft, beautiful tone that reminded me of something like angels talking.

"Yes, I imagine the ten cent store a few blocks over and down several blocks would have some." For some reason I was being excessively courteous.

"Would you mind going with me?" she said. "I do have an awful time following directions. Please go with me?"

"Well," I replied, looking around the foyer and down the hallway, where many heads came popping out from the doors of each room, including that of Ray Trusty. And I think I also saw Hector's gleaming eyes. "I'm just getting off of work but if you don't mind my working clothes, and walking."

"Oh, I have a car we can use," she replied. With that, Alice grabbed my arm and we proceeded down the stairs, looking back at all the comical looks on many faces.

After obtaining the thread at the store, I suggested a little breakfast. While eating she told me that she worked as a cocktail waitress somewhere in the East but she wanted to find work in Fresno. So far she had had no luck. But seeing how attractive she was, I knew she would be able to find the work she wanted.

"Look," I said to her, "you been looking at wrong places. Go out to the Fig Gardens or the better places. With your looks they will be more than glad to put you on the payroll."

"You think so?" Alice asked, her big beautiful eyes searching.

"Of course. But why don't you go to school and learn some kind of office work?"

"I was thinking of that," she replied. "But that takes money and I only have $1,800 left."

"Hell, that should see you through, and if it doesn't, get a part-time waitress job," I suggested.

"You know, I'm going to do that," she declared. We sat, eating and enjoying each other's company. Going back to the Saint Francis we were greeted by raised eyebrows and inquisitive looks from everyone in the lobby. But we walked by them with an air of superiority. Boy, did I rub it into those guys!

After making sure that Alice got to her room, I went for a shower and a clean up and a much-needed rest. The doors of the rooms were always left open. Across the opening of the door a heavy drape hung on a rod about six inches from the top and about a foot up from the floor. This enabled the cool air to circulate through the room from the hallways, where there was an air conditioner. As I lay sprawled on the double bed I thought how nice it was to enjoy the company of a female. But not for long—the arms of Morpheus soon wrapped around me and scooted me off to dreamland.

I must have slept a good six hours without moving. But when I did roll over something warm and soft was beside me. Not quite awake, I thought it was a dream, but no, there was someone in bed beside me! Sitting straight up in bed in the still dark room, I could barely make out a nude body lying on my bed. Was somebody playing a joke on me? No, it was real. Alice had her arms stretched out for me to lay back down. What a magnificent, beautiful body she had, soft like a kitten but resilient like a lion. Electrifying shocks dashed through my mind. What is happening here, I thought to myself? I am

53

a married man and have no business doing this, but God! It had been almost two years since I had been with a woman. I finally gave way to the beating desire within me. I sank into her arms. Her wet red lips started a roaring fire inside of me, as hot as any furnace on earth. We indulged in the kind of lovemaking I never before had thought possible. It was like a hot sirocco wind blowing across the waters and the undulating breakers beating their music on the sands. It was all this and more, again and again, until, exhausted, we closed our eyes. Once again Morpheus took over and I slept the night through.

I awoke and looked at my watch. Seven o'clock. But was it a.m. or p.m? Looking around the window shade, I saw that the sun had risen and people were stirring in the streets below. Morning! I was having trouble reconstructing in my mind the events of the past eighteen or twenty hours. The night before, oh yes, the night before! Things started to take shape in my waking mind as I remembered the most beautiful dream of my life. But it wasn't a dream; the events were very real, and she had laid beside me, so soft and smelling so fragrant, just like a woman. should. But where was Alice? She must have gone back to her room during the night. Feelings of shame began to form within my mind. What in the world were you doing? You are a married man; what would Margie say? Well, she told you to get someone else! But that is not the way it is supposed to be. A mass of confusing thoughts flooded into my mind, until finally I put my hands to my head and almost yelled out loud, "no more, no more."

After taking a shower and shaving, I felt much better, and I left my room to see how the rest of the world was faring. Passing by Alice's room I noticed the maid was cleaning.

"Where is Alice this morning?" I asked.

"Why, she checked out early this morning. I don't know

where she went to because she didn't tell me. Are you Charlie?"

I felt as if a cold bucket of water had just been thrown on me. "Yes," I answered weakly.

"She told me to give you this." The maid handed me an envelope. I took it and returned to my room. Trembling, I opened the envelope and found a picture of Alice. There was an inscription on the back: "Thanks for the most precious moments of my life and if anything should come of this, it shall follow our names, Alice or Charles. Love you so much. Please don't try to find me, Alice."

I sat for a long while trying to put the puzzle together. It had been so beautiful and yet all Alice had wanted was a baby, my baby. And I'll never know.

* * *

I put in a bid for a job on the extra board at Los Angeles and received it. I was going home and glad to be leaving Fresno, but the episode with Alice lingered in my mind. Going home might banish some of it. A few mainline trips to Santa Barbara and Bakersfield helped considerably, and soon it was my turn for a "dead head"; I was called to work a sugar beet job at Oxnard, working twelve to sixteen hours a day. That would pay good money, more than twice what a switch engine paid in Fresno, and I needed the money. I could drive to Oxnard because it was only fifty miles from Los Angeles, and that way, if I wanted to get home fast, it was possible.

There were not many places to stay at Oxnard because Navy personnel and their dependents took most of the lodging. To ease the shortage, the Southern Pacific parked a Pullman car on a spur for train and engine employees to sleep in. They also provided a porter to clean and make beds with clean linen, etc.

But by the fifth day, we realized that something was wrong. I and the rest of the twenty-odd men began to itch, especially on the hairy parts of our bodies. After comparing notes we decided someone had brought in a case of crabs (or walking dandruff) and now we all were infested. This was a serious situation. How were we going to explain our affliction to our wives? The trainmaster saved the day by giving out typewritten memos to each man, saying the operation would be shut down for thirty-six hours to fumigate the car for crabs.

We all knew who the guilty person was. He had brought a woman with a considerably shady reputation into the Pullman car, and evidently she was the source of the crabs. I went to the druggist and purchased some medicine to kill the varmints. That day also, the regular man reported, leaving me to go home.

Driving down Ventura boulevard on the way home, the Highway Patrol stopped me for going thirty-five miles per hour. This was not my day!

Arriving back home, the family wanted to visit grandma and grandpa on Margie's side of the family. Figuring a few days off wouldn't hurt, we all went to Littlerock, a small farming community ten miles east of Palmdale. Peaches and pear orchids were the main crop, along with melons. Margie's father was on the water board and they had some undeveloped land for sale that he wanted me to look at. I bought about four acres with water and electric available, and the contract payable in four years. Margie didn't make much comment about the land, but she never did voice her opinion until later. Then it was, "why," or "if you didn't . . . ," which made it very hard for me to know what she wanted.

After staying a few days and catching up on some work at home, it was time to report.

The Movie Trains

The old diamond stack was our engine and its location was at station and siding Lang in the Soledad Canyon. Clark Anson, my fireman, and I were to dead head in a carry-all to Lang. When we arrived there, number nine was deader than a doornail—not one pound of steam. The crew the night before had put the fire out and left.

"Is there any water in the boiler?" I asked Clark.

"Yeah, there's a half a glass of water, but nothing else," Clark reported. Although that much water in the boiler was plenty, with no steam pressure to work the atomizer or blower, not counting heating the oil in the tender so it could flow to the fire-box, things were in a hell of a fix. The old #9 burned oil as a fuel but had a facade of cord wood piled around the top of her tender to create the appearance of a wood burner.

"I'll go to the office and see what the dispatcher wants us to do with the damn mess," I informed Clark, starting for the train order office. Inside the office the operator handed me the phone.

"What are we to do?" I asked Pop Galyan, the dispatcher. "The engine is stone dead. Why didn't they have a watchman here last night, or better still take it to Saugus."

"Well, I guess they just forgot," Pop replied in his quiet, unexcited voice. "But Charlie, I would appreciate it if you can do anything to make a fire in her and get it going, because actor Roy Rogers is going to be there with all the cast. Say if you can use wood, take that stuff from the tank and I'll order a load out from Saugus, or use any wood you can lay your hands on." Pop Galyan was the best in his line of work and he had his boys and some of his relatives working as dispatchers. He taught them all he knew and they could not be beat for dispatching trains.

"OK," I replied, "order the wood." Then I went back to help Clark build a fire. Clark started the fire with waste soaked in kerosene. Using dried tumble weeds, paper or any burnable trash we collected from around the vicinity, we had the wood burning. But it wasn't enough. After using all the wood on the tank the steam pressure was nil.

"When this burns down in there, that's it," Clark remarked. "I tried to get the oil running but it's still too cold."

"Yeah," I replied gloomily, sitting on the engineer's seat box staring out the window in a gaze, void of thought. But with a quick return to reality, I saw the solution! On the ground below me was a nice large stack of new railroad ties—just the thing. It did not take long to handle the ties onto the fire-box. We burned over half of the stack until there was enough steam pressure for normal steam operation.

"What in the hell are you doing with my ties?" Someone was bellowing up at us from the ground. We looked down into the face of the roadmaster.

"They made a beautiful hot fire," I said. "And besides we had permission to use anything we needed to fire up this engine."

"Not my ties you weren't." He was angry.

"Oh, they're your ties?" I fired back at him. "Damn, I thought all this time, they belonged to the Southern Pacific Company, didn't you, Clark? I'll tell you what, give me a bill for how much they are and then I'll pay you."

The roadmaster was boiling over and he shouted, "I'll have both of you fired for this." He walked away still shouting threats.

"He fired me a hundred times when I worked on the bridge gang before going firing," Clark chuckled.

On the dirt road coming into Lang, the motion picture

equipment came in trucks and trailers, then the limousine filled with actors.

"Not enough steam yet to move her." Clark called me back from gazing at the activity.

"Yeah, I know, but keep patting her on the butt while I oil around," I instructed him, grabbing the long oiler.

Soon everything was buzzing with prop men, setting up the decor. Down at the dirt crossing workers were driving long steel stakes into the ground then attaching large pulley wheels onto them. The stakes were placed near the rails. Not being able to figure what they might be used for, I asked Clark, but he had no idea either.

"Well, we have fifty pounds of steam but not enough to move her yet," I said.

"It should come up faster now that the oil is getting warmer," Clark replied.

"I hope so because here comes the rest of the crew with the trainmaster."

"Is everything ready?" the trainmaster inquired.

"Not yet, but soon, we have a little over fifty pounds of steam and here comes our load of wood which you guys can help load on the engine."

"What the hell you been doing all of this time?" conductor Red Griffin asked jokingly.

"Clark and I have been discussing where we're going when we get fired." Then I related our experience of the morning. The trainmaster laughed and said, "I'll take care of the roadmaster but when you're ready, back up to the cars and bring them out on the pass track." With that he left and disappeared for the day.

About the time we were ready to move, someone climbed the ladder to the cab, dressed in a neat cowboy outfit.

"Howdy," he greeted us with a genuine smile, as perky as the morning sun. "I wanted to see how these thing looked inside, do you mind?" Clark about dropped his eyeballs. It was Roy Rogers. He was the nicest actor I have met in all my time working on movie locations.

"You are surely welcome," I finally managed to say, and showed him the simple controls that were on the old number nine. Compared to the newer engines, it was like the difference between a model "T" Ford and one of today's Lincolns.

"Is it OK if I ride with you a little?" he asked.

"Sure, all you want to." I pulled the throttle open a bit; the old lady groaned and spit a little, but finally she creaked out on to the side track with the three passenger cars.

"Boy, this is something, wait till I tell Dale about this," Roy grinned as we continued on towards the crossing.

I soon discovered what the steel pegs and pulleys were to be used for: a stage coach was positioned on one side of the crossing, without any team of horses hitched to it. They took a rope from the coach and going through the pullets rigged it to my engine, in such a way that when traveling forwards and pulling on the rope, it would pull the stage coach across the crossing in front of me, just barely missing the engine.

Work went on until noon on different camera shots before everyone stopped for a delicious lunch. Then we went back to work for a couple hours more and at three o'clock we were told to put the engine and car in the spur track and tie up; there would be an engine watchman to take care of the engine. We were all given a ten dollar bonus and sent home.

The Rebellion of the New Generation

One afternoon in the fall of that year, I was called for a coast train to Santa Barbara. As I got ready for work, pulling on my overalls over my pants and shirt, I noticed that the overalls were looking washed out and frayed at the bottoms of the legs. I would need a new pair soon, as well as a new cap—the one I was wearing looked like it had come through two wars.

Driving several blocks on the way to work, I stopped for some pipe tobacco at a little grocery store. Behind the counter stood a new and attractive young woman.

"Where did you come from?" I asked her, noting her nice features. "What happened to the old man that runs this place?"

"I live next door and Mr. Webster likes to have a little rest," she replied, smiling, setting me ablaze inside.

"Oh, and what do you do other times when you're not working here?" I asked as she rang my charge up on the register.

"I'm a nurse at the hospital and when times are slow I work here."

"Doesn't your husband work?" I asked, hoping she didn't have one. She looked at me and gave me that gorgeous smile again, then turned to serve other customers. Time was getting short for me so I had to leave; as I looked back, she gave me a beckoning smile and wave.

Driving down Eagle Rock Boulevard and turning off on Fletcher Drive, my thoughts were on the woman at the store. 'Don't get involved, you jackass,' I cautioned myself. 'You know what happened before with Alice. It was hell on earth afterwards and besides you haven't any business fooling around anyway.' I scolded myself as I parked my old car in the company's parking lot.

The 4218 cab ahead malley was almost new, and having Jim Rolls as a fireman, an engineer could not ask for more. The engine would ride smooth and handle easy. What made most steam engines ride rough was the slipping and thrust of the

61

main driving rod, which caused the rims on the wheels to wear out of round. The rims or tires are checked periodically by the round-house force. If the engineer reports rough riding and if the rims are too far out of round, the round-house workers heat the rims to expand them and remove them from the wheels. If they are new enough they will be turned on a very large lathe, trueing them up (making them round), and then they are used again.

The trip to Santa Barbara was extra nice after we had got through the Chatsworth tunnel. I was apprehensive each time we went into the tunnel because of an incident that took place years back. When firing regular on the Coast pool job, I had laid off on this particular trip and a young fireman named Snodgrass, who just hired out, caught my turn along with engineer Jack Dunn, one of the best liked men on the division at that time. When they were about halfway through Chatsworth tunnel, which was one and a half miles long, the engine either started to slip or the wheels started spinning. In such a situation, the engine throttle should be closed and when the spinning or slipping stops, the throttle should be opened again to regain traction on the rail. But on this occasion I think that young Snodgrass became confused, and instead of shutting the firing valve off, he mistakenly opened it up. This caused an explosion of the gasses and oil which in turn set the engine on fire, burning both men up beyond recognition.

As we neared Santa Barbara, the full moon lit the ocean front up and we could see the white breakers for great distances pounding the beaches. The spectacle seemed extra beautiful that night; it was these kind of trips that made railroading a good job.

Santa Barbara had three or four long yard tracks next to the main line. If the switch herder put your train in the yard track, then the engine went back to the round-house. The round-house at Santa Barbara was the elite of all round-houses; it was kept very clean and neat, tucked away between tall palm trees and edged with lawns and flower beds. After tying up, the crew was picked up by taxi, which was paid for by the company, and taken up town to a hotel. If the herder was told by the yardmaster to have the train come up the main line, the train would be stopped at the yard office and the Coast crew would take over. Many trains ran straight through in this manner. That night our train was scheduled for the main line, although we would sooner have gone back to the round-house. Stopping at the yard office meant that the fireman, brakeman, and I would have a long walk up the tracks.

Our train was leaving before I had completed my reports and time slip work. The head brakeman rode on the engine to State Street and got off, leaving the fireman and I to walk to our hotel. As we were walking along the tracks between buildings, approaching the first of three crossings, a new car came to a halt in front of us, blocking our path. Inside the auto was a woman, and by the light of the moon I judged her to be about forty years of age.

"Come on, get in I have a job for both of you," she commanded.

"But lady, we just got off work," Jim told her.

"I don't care, I'll pay you more money. Now come on and get in—I don't have much time."

"Lady, you don't understand, we work on the railroad and . . ." I tried to explain, but she cut me short.

"They told me I could come down here and I would find plenty of help." With that she drove off in a huff. It dawned on both of us about the same time: the lady owned a restaurant and needed a dishwasher.

"Do we look that bad?" I asked Jim Rolls.

"Looks like she thought we were hobos." Jim laughed.

A revolution dawned at that moment, against overalls and coveralls as a standard dress for enginemen on the railroad. It was no wonder that the trainmen fared better than the enginemen; they wore better clothes in their work then we did and did not look like bums. From that day on, Jim and I decided to wear Levis and good shirts, Pendletons, in the winter, and sport shirts in the summer, along with short denim jackets. No more long swaying jackets.

This revolution of ours took hold and spread quite rapidly among the young. We were criticized and ostracized by our elders because of it, but every generation must have its rebellion.

At eleven o'clock the next morning we were called to return to Los Angeles on a manifest train. It meant a fast trip.

"What in the hell have you got on?" Jim grinned as he looked at my hat and new clothes.

"Haven't you seen a cowboy hat or outfit before?" I fired back.

Everything went smoothly going back. I let Jim run the engine from Oxnard to Los Angeles and both of us remarked how smooth everything went. This was until we got to the round-house, where there was a note which read, "You and your fireman contact the road foreman immediately."

"Oh Lord, did we go by a test and not know it?" I asked Jim.

"Hell I don't know. I don't think so," he replied.

"Well, I got job insurance. How about you, Jim?"

"I have too, so I don't care."

The engines' office, where Al Youngs, the road foreman worked, was near the master mechanic's building. The office door was open, as if he was expecting us. He was sitting with his back to us, with his hands cupped behind his head.

"I know who you are, but I don't want to look at either one of you," he announced.

"What kind of a burr have you got in your pants?" I asked abruptly. I knew that I could be fired for such a remark, but what difference did it make?

"You'll think it's a cactus before I get done with you," he growled, turning around and looking at Jim and me.

"Well, what did we do wrong?" I wanted to know.

"I don't believe it, I just don't believe it! Tell me I'm wrong," he said. "I've had over twenty complaints and reports over the phone on you and by God they're right, you're still wearing it!"

For a minute I was unable to put it all together, and then it hit me—my cowboy hat! Jim and I broke out laughing, and then Al joined us until we were almost in tears. After things quietened down a bit, he told us about the phone calls he had received about a cowboy running a train down San Fernando Road. We were then dismissed.

The Attraction

Like a moth being drawn to a light, I had to return for pipe tobacco at the store, even though I knew I had plenty. There she was in a ruffled pink dress with her long wavy blonde hair about her shoulders.

"And what is your name?" was my first question.

"Most people call me Mrs. Miller but you may call me Helen," she said with that memorable smile. "And what do they call you?"

"Just Charlie," I replied. Another customer came in and she immediately attended to him. So she was telling me, in a nice way, that she was married.

"What does your husband do for a living?" I asked after the customer left.

"I don't think he's working now, he's being kept."

"You're not married now?" I was puzzled by her last remark.

"No, I'm divorced. He prefers gentlemen friends over me," she said, downcast and somber. At first, I did not get the significance of her remark, because in those days, gay people stayed in the closet. After a minute I understood. I looked at her again.

"You said that you have two small children?" She nodded. What an atrocious thing for a woman to face, and with two little kids.

"Could we talk sometime off the job?"

"I usually have Friday and Sunday night off and any night after eleven. Stop in if you can." More customers were arriving, so I waved her goodbye..

The world is full of problems; no one escapes having them. My problem at that time was my need to seek out the love and companionship of a woman. I certainly did not like the idea of pursuing other women, but with the situation at home, what else was there to do? Many solutions were offered but no one could tell me what I was doing was wrong. Man was born of flesh and the flesh rules him sometimes, no matter how much he fights against it. Say what you might, the strongest of men loses this battle.

I got friendly with Helen and would stop at her home for a midnight coffee. Talking was as far as things went. Discussing each other's problems created a relief valve for both of us, and in this way we became good friends.

That fall I was cut off the engineers list and went on the Coast Passenger run firing, but that only lasted to the first of the year. After that I was sent once again to Fresno, assigned to the engineers' extra board; it was nothing but a vicious circle.

The stay at Fresno wasn't long as before, only sixty days, and then I went back to Los Angeles on the engineers' extra board. I was glad to see the girls and to sleep in my own bed.

"You are called for a movie special to Chatsworth, on duty 8:45 a.m. You have one hour. Can you make it?" I was sitting up in bed with the phone at my ear. "I'll try," I replied with a yawn, and hung up.

On the road to work, I stopped for pipe tobacco. I thought Helen would be working at the hospital and not at the store, but I was wrong. She was sorting some merchandise on the shelf and was as pretty as ever. The old hungry inspiration flamed inside of me and exploded like a giant fire- cracker. I grabbed her and kissed her passionately in the store, not caring who saw us. Her passion matched mine. "I'll see you tonight," I said, "I'm late for work." I left not daring to think—and without my tobacco.

That day I spent several hours sitting watching rehearsals of a couple of actors jumping off the train and staging a fight, over and over. My fireman watched the boiler pressure closely, keeping the steam below the popping off stage of the relief valve, so as not to disrupt the taking of pictures. Sitting myself on top of the tender I had a commanding view of the action below.

The engine and one coach were positioned by the loading dock of the store house at an open space where all the paraphernalia of motion picture equipment was stored and the director sat with his cohorts directing the action.

While working to make everything ready for filming, the director would say, "Hey, boy," and eight or ten of the workmen would start up like jumping jacks to do his bidding. I really was getting a bang out of watching these clowns jump the way they did, just like trained seals. I kept saying to myself under my breath, "hey boy, do this," and "hey boy, do that," and laughing to myself.

"We're going to run through this once more," I heard the director say, "then we're going to shoot it." The actors did their routine of jumping off the coaches and starting to fight but then it was, "hey boy" this and "hey boy" that all over again, with the clowns jumping up and down. After four more tries the director decided to take a shot of it.

"OK, we're going to roll it now! Everyone quiet please," he called over his megaphone.

"OK, roll 'em," came the command as the actors went through their scenes. Then for some reason I yelled out, "hey boy," to my fireman, "have you enough water in this tub so we won't blow up?" I don't know why I yelled this, it just came out. Everything went into a state of confusion below. The ten or so jumping jacks, leapt up and cried out "yes sir, yes sir." The actors stopped and bent over laughing; the cameramen threw up their arms, and my fireman was rolling in the cab of the engine in hysterical fits of laughter.

The fat little director finally stood up and pointed his finger at me.

"You caused this, you, you. . . " Then he sat down on his fat posterior, wiping his brow with a white handkerchief. Everyone was talking and having a ball, knowing that the director had lost control of the situation. This was until the road foreman, Al Young, showed up.

"What the hell's going on?" he called up to me, and I pointed to the director. I felt a sudden dislike for the director as he and Al held a conference. Then Al Young walked sternly over to the engine.

"Now Charlie, get back into the cab of your engine and be quiet or I see to it you'll get thirty days." Thirty days was the same as thirty demerits. Growling to myself, I went down into the cab and settled down on my seat box.

The director never glanced at me after that, but I got smiles from almost everyone else. When the conductor gave me a back up signal, I looked the situation over, and saw that the little fat man stood between fifteen and twenty feet from the engine, talking to someone, about straight across from me.

In starting a locomotive after it has been standing for some time, an engineer leaves the pet cocks open. These are located on each cylinder of the engine, and are controlled by an air valve in the cab of the locomotive. The purpose of the operation was to let water collected in the piston cylinders drain onto the ground. Opening the throttle slowly I waited until the cylinder of the engine was directly across from Mr. Director. Then I pulled the throttle open wider, and the pet cocks did their duty. Out went the steam and water, kicking up dust and dirt into the surrounding territory. Little clean fat boy was not clean any more; he was dirty little fat boy. Not daring to look at him, I shoved back as if nothing happened. Al Young knew what had taken place but he also knew I was keeping to the rules and therefore he could not rebuke me. But that ended the day of picture taking.

On the way home I stopped by the store to finally get my tobacco. It was already dark that night and Helen had gone home. I didn't want to bother her but the urge to see her became too great, and I gave in. She met me at the door and took my breath away—she was beautiful, all prettied up and smelling like a bouquet of roses.

"Are you going to stand out there gawking all night or are

you going to come in?" she said, smiling. I went in and immediately took her in my arms. What happened next was inevitable between two love-starved people. It was beautiful, clean, and healthy, but the old gnawing guilt, which should not have haunted me all those lonesome years, sprang up inside me. I felt I should not have been there.

"Where are the kids?" I finally asked.

"They're with their Dad until tomorrow."

"You let them with him?" I questioned.

"Why not? He is their father." I could think of nothing to say about that but it sure is a mixed-up world, Then I lay back down besides her and rode off on the waves of ecstasy once again.

Helen and I discussed my situation many times during our long talks.

"You don't mind my situation of being married?" I prodded.

"Not in your circumstances," she replied. "All good men are married in some way and their wives better wake up to what they have. Otherwise there's going to be a great number of divorces in the coming years. Did you know there are five women to every one man since the war ended? I figure these women will have to share a man once in a while." I could see the hurt of her marriage showing through.

I arrived home after midnight really tired. As I lay on the bed I reconstructed my evening with very mixed emotions. My uncomfortable family situation felt like a heavy sentence. I had resolved to stick it out until the girls had grown, but it was about to drive me insane. And what would there be left after they were gone? There was no answer to that.

I thought further of what Helen had said: "There are five women to every man." She was probably right. When working in Fresno, I could stand on a street corner in the city and within five minutes a woman, and sometimes two women, would approach me for an evening outing. They were not hookers, they were just lonely. With pleasant thoughts of Helen, and dismay at my situation, I drifted off to troubled sleep.

Trying to forget Helen and not seeing her was like trying not to eat. It did not work. Our relationship kept on the boil until I received an assignment to Fresno. Then, difficult as it was, I told her we had to stop seeing each other because nothing could come of it. She reluctantly admitted that I was right.

The day after I was assigned to Fresno, an extra board job for an engineer at Bakersfield became available. I bid for it, and got the assignment.

The Toothache

After establishing myself at Bakersfield and marking up on the board, working the Oil City job, the McKittrick, and some helper jobs, I was then dead headed to Mojave, a town in the wind-blown desert. They tell me that the wind velocity is measured by the size of the pebbles it is blowing. It seemed to me that I was destined for dead heads wherever my position might be, but some day I would find how other men eluded them.

I drove to Mojave because it was only to be a one-day dead head. The job would take sixteen hours and was called for four in the morning. Arriving at Mojave, my tooth on the right side of my mouth started to ache a little. It was too early to see a dentist so a little suffering would be in store for me, and it wasn't that bad yet.

Since the end of the war nearly all the work force at Mojave had been eliminated, except for train and engine service. The crew dispatcher office had been relocated to the yard office in the depot across the tracks. There was a bulletin board in the empty round-house stating what job and engine a crew was to operate. If it was not available, it was mandatory to call the yard office on the phone for information. The old teakettle 1721 was a vintage of my grandmother's time, and I hoped it would hold together for another trip.

Troxel, a young fireman, worked hard to do a good job firing the engine, and he did well for what he knew. But he was a slow learner. When he did catch on, he would make a good fireman, and I hoped I would be able to show him a few things to make it easier on him. The conductor handed me some orders and a schedule of work. We were to start at five-thirty in the morning, near Cantel, a station on the Lone Pine Branch. There we were to unload ballast, pick up old ties and tie plates and whatever other material needed cleaning up. We had ten cars of ballast, four empty gondolas, four flat cars for loading old rail on and one flat with a crane, also a caboose.

The grade was steep pulling out of Mojave yard. Through the crossovers and then lined out on the branch proved too much for the old 1721 engine. She just slipped, sputtered, and snorted, not being able to hold the rail. The yard engine would have to shove us out to Chaffee, where the grade wasn't nearly as steep. Each time the old girl jumped, my toothache did the act with her. I told Troxel to keep all 190 pounds of steam in her belly if he could because we needed every bit of it. Most newer locomotives carried from 210 to 250 pounds of steam but these old teakettles only carried 190 pounds. When the switch engine gave us a shove and we started to roll faster, the steam gauges shimmered and vibrated so much that they were was unreadable. Looking at the fireman's gauge, I saw it was doing the same St. Vitus dance as mine. I grinned at Troxel and then went back to my side of the cab. The air gauge location was at the top of the cab, where the engineer could not see it. But it made no difference because it was doing the same thing as the others.

At Cantel, after putting the train away in the siding, we ran to Searles and went around the Y to turn the engine. Then it was back to our train in the siding at Cantel.

My aching tooth was progressing so rapidly that I found it impossible to eat my bagged lunch. And we had nine hours to work before the sixteen hour shift was finished. We were loading old ties and rail that had not been used for many years. The wind started up, slowly at first, then harder and harder with a piercing cold effect, which did not help my aching tooth.

Late in the afternoon I was spreading ballast and trying to see through watery eyes, with the dust blowing in my direction from the dumping cars. It was a good thing I was young and stalwart or the job would not have been finished that day. Finally the work was completed. But as we returned to Mojave, I discovered that I had forgotten my special nut for the independent brake valve. I used it for blocking the valve so the air to the engine brakes would not apply when using the train brakes. Of course this was strictly against the rules of the company, but nearly every engineer used one with the old system of Westinghouse air brakes.

On the way to Mojave I leaned back in my seat, exhausted. The pain in my mouth was excruciating but the work was done and we were on our way back. At least I thought we were, until looking out the window I saw we were hardly moving, even with the throttle almost wide open. I was not able to smell the burning brake shoes on the tires because of the wind blowing ahead of us. I looked up at the air gauge, which showed that thirty pounds had leaked on my engine brake system; the wheels were going around and around in the rims and I had not realized it.

"Oh Lord," I mumbled to myself. "What am I to do? If one of those rims comes off and derails us out here, it will tie up the branch line and my job will be terminated. Little man, what shall I do?" I was referring to the imaginary little man who always sits on my shoulder in an emergency, telling me what to do.

Seeing the ball of waste on the metal holding the long oiler and torch gave me an idea. Shutting the throttle off and coming to a stop, with my gloves and two hands of waste I jumped off the engine and examined the rims. Boy! were they red hot, and also very crooked. Knowing that they would never make it to Mojave in their condition, I picked up a large rock and hurriedly pounded them back into what, in my estimation, was fairly straight condition. It was dark, and I was working by the glow of the rims, which were cooling fast. I did not want them to completely cool until I had them on the rails. I figured that maybe flange against the rail would help straighten them up a bit. Climbing back on the locomotive, I released the train brakes, letting the train move slowly forward. I kept the speed down to ten miles per hour; the old girl creaked and groaned with the flanges screaming against the rails. Holding the engine brakes applied slightly, I hoped that the rims would have a chance to cool down slowly and maybe right themselves more on the wheels. I knew that if we could keep this up for five minutes without cracking the rims, we would make it to Mojave, providing there was enough time left on the law.

I looked for the next mile board, which would give me some idea how far it was to our destination. Troxel saw me looking at him and then at my watch; he knew I was in trouble.

"What's the trouble? Don't we have enough time to get to Mojave?"

"That's what I'm trying to find out. I'm looking for the next mile board." I was trying to keep the engine speed down on the dips in the terrain.

"Well, why not go faster?" he kept asking.

"Troxel, I'll tell you about it later," I replied, as a mile board showed up in the headlight. It was ten miles to Mojave and one hour and five minutes left to work. We would make it, and I thanked the little man on my shoulder.

The next day at Bakersfield, I was really in the hot seat in the master mechanic's office, explaining the events of the previous day to the road foreman, the round-house foreman and the master mechanic. I thought they were going to chew me up and spit me out. I related what had happened on the (Jaw Bone) Lone Pine Branch, and then complained that my tooth hurt badly and could they please hold any investigation off until after I had seen a dentist. They were very good about it and agreed to my request.

The following day, after the dentist fixed my tooth and the pain left me, I called the crew dispatcher to find out when the investigation was scheduled for. No one knew anything about it, and so I reported, and went over to the depot, looking for a magazine to read myself asleep. It was turning dark outside. As I sat on a stool at the coke counter browsing through some articles, Millie from the ticket office touched me on the arm. She was smiling.

"What say you, Millie?"

"Not much, just got off work," she replied.

"Time to go home and make dinner I guess?" I asked.

"Either that or buy a hamburger. When you're by yourself, what's the use?"

"Tell me about it," I replied.

"Would you like to go and have a burger with me?" Millie asked. She was a very attractive woman, about thirty-five, which would put her about two years older than myself. Millie was very meticulous about herself and precise about her work and actions.

"OK. I'd like that, Millie, if you don't mind."

Getting into her car, which was much better than mine, Millie drove out on Nile Street to a drive-in owned by an engineer named Bloomfield. I ordered a hamburger, French fries and a malt, and of course Millie ordered what she wanted. When we both finished Millie asked if I would like to take a drive.

"That sounds good to me but don't lose me, I'm not familiar with Bakersfield."

"How could I lose you in a small place like this?" she asked, starting the motor.

It seemed like a long way out in the country, going by farm lands and irrigation ditches, till Millie came to a narrow oiled road full of chuck holes and ridges. Driving west for a mile or so, she pulled in between some large eucalyptus trees along side of the road.

"What's the name of this road we're on?" I inquired.

"This is Casa Loma," she said, turning the key off and the lights also. Boy, was it dark! Today that road is called Ming Avenue, and we were parked across where the large covered Valley Plaza Mall stands today.

We talked for a little while, then unexpectedly, Millie put her arms around my neck and kissed me. I was not in the mood for lovemaking at the start but that old urge within me was like a rattlesnake ready to strike. We were getting hot and heavy in the car, steaming up the windows and hearing the creaking and groaning of a much-needed grease job on the car. When our lovemaking was about to reach its climax, the surroundings were suddenly flooded with light, and two or three dogs started yowling it up. The car was sitting in the middle of a farmer's yard, and the farmer was at his front door with his shotgun in hand. Never was there such a speedy recovery from an entangled position. Clothes were pulled and snapped on, and at the same time the car started up, with wheels spinning and dust flying. Away we went, expecting any moment to hear the buckshot against the car. Down the road we started laughing, even though the experience had been like having a bucket of cold water thrown on both of us. We knew how dogs must feel when cold water is sprayed them. We were still laughing when I bid Millie good night at the hotel.

Morning came too early when the call boy knocked at my door.

"Mr. Steffes, on duty at seven-thirty. Dead head to Mojave for a light engine back to Bakersfield," he informed me.

"OK," I said, half asleep.

As I showered and shaved, it dawned on me: a light engine from Mojave? I wondered if it was the same engine that I had slipped the tires on.

Eating breakfast at Ted Mills restaurant and having a light lunch bagged, I encountered no acquaintances until Millie came in for breakfast, on her way to work. It was beginning to look like we were latched to each other. When she saw me she smiled and her eyes glistened like stars.

"We meet again, how wonderful!" She greeted me.

"Yeah," I grunted. "I have to leave for Mojave to bring back a light engine. Perhaps the one that I damaged."

"Well, maybe when you arrive back, we can finish what we started last night?" she whispered. I looked at her in a quizzical manner, then I remembered and laughed, nodding my head.

As I rode to Mojave in the company carry-all I tried to figure out how we were going to run that disabled engine back to Bakersfield without derailing, knowing the tires were out of line. I asked the fireman if he knew what engine we were getting, but he did not know either.

At the yard office in Mojave I received orders to run as Extra 3715 west to Bakersfield, which answered my question. Finding the engine watchman asleep on the 3715, I shook him awake.

"What is wrong with this engine? The air pumps are going crazy working like this?" I questioned the poor frightened Mexican, but he didn't know the answer. He only knew that the water and steam had to be kept up in the boiler and he was very poor with English.

While the fireman did his work, I took the oil can and started my tour of inspection. The first task was to find the air leak that made the pumps work so fast. It was not difficult to find. The problem was at the distributing valve below the cab of the engine on the engineer's side. The pipe coming from the valve connecting to the trainline was broken and that made the brakes inoperative. All that held the engine from running out of the round-house was the chain blocking under the wheels. I wondered who in the world would ever leave a locomotive in this condition without telling someone. I looked for a work report but could find none. Because Mojave had no one to repair engines any more, I began to think, if it could be fixed, we could get out of here pronto; but if it couldn't, we would be stuck a here long time, and not get what had been promised me when I arrived back at Bakersfield. This upset me. Glimpsing some flat cars that were stored on a track inside the empty round-house gave me an idea. First thing, call the dispatcher. The phone was busy but finally the dispatcher answered.

"Dispatcher, this is engineer Steffes at Mojave."

"Yeah, what is it you want, Charlie?" he inquired.

"This 3715 has a broken branch pipe from the distributing valve to the trainline. The brakes are inoperative."

"Oh damn," he cut in. "And no one there to fix it. We need that locomotive bad to run up the valley. What can you do?"

"Give me a little time. Maybe I can come up with something that will work to get us there," I informed him.

"OK, Charlie, do what you can but let me know as soon as possible."

Back at the engine I secured an alligator wrench, which is a long handle with a Y at the end. Teeth are notched on the inner side of the Y, and the wrench is used for handling pipe. It's just a cheap version of a pipe wrench. I had the fireman shut off the air pumps, a valve located in the cab. Applying a little persuasion to the broken pipes, the fireman and I removed both pieces. Then we went out to the flat cars, and after unscrewing two air hoses from each end of the car, we took one hose and screwed it into the fitting out of which the broken piece of pipe came, and then took the other hose and did the same thing with it, connecting to the other fitting.

Then came the test, coupling the two hoses together and telling the fireman to turn on the air pumps. The air pressure built up and my idea worked perfectly. Being amazed with myself, I stepped back and someone was right behind me. Looking around, I saw my boss, Levi Franklin, Road Foreman of Engines, standing there. He was the best official we ever had. He was good for the employees and good for the company. Of course he would bellow, rant, and rave but it wouldn't have been Levi if he hadn't—that was his way.

There was not one man on the railroad who would not do the best job he could for Levi. When he went out to pull a test on an engine crew, they were informed as to the place and time and the kind of test it would be.

"I came to see what in the hell is the delay," he bellowed.

"There is the delay." I pointed to the work we had just finished.

Looking at it, he shook his head.

"I sure got a good bunch of young engineers coming up. Say, do you know who brought this engine in?"

"No," I replied, "but I got to call the dispatcher and let him know it's fixed."

"I'll call him, just get the hell out of town," Levi yelled, walking away.

In a few hours we arrived at Bakersfield. At the round-house, a bunch of officials were ready to inspect the engine. Not paying much attention to the group, I wanted to stay as far away from them as possible on account of the pending investigation of me. My first thoughts were that they were going to have the hearing as soon as I had tied up. I went into the enginemen's locker room to wash up and make out the necessary reports The assistant superintendent came into the room. Boy! Here it comes! I thought I was in for it.

"Mr. Steffes, that is the nicest piece of work that I have ever seen on a broken part of a steam engine," he said. "I am going to have it put on your personnel record." I thanked him, and gave a sigh of relief when he left—nothing about an investigation yet!

Assistant road foreman Wheie was waiting for me at the crew dispatcher's office when the fireman and I arrived to finish registering in.

"Charlie," he began, "you did such a good job on that

engine out there and we would like to forget about the slipped tires on the Jaw Bone. But the round-house foreman says you did several thousand dollars worth of damage to the engine so he thinks that you should be disciplined. So how about signing for twenty demerits?" And boy did I, very quickly.

The Decision

Six weeks went by and I was still at Bakersfield when Levi called me into his office.

"The company has an opening for assistant road foreman job at Sacramento. They would like you to take this job," he said.

"I just don't know. Give me a day to think it over," I replied.

"All right, but they want to know soon. Don't forget the Southern Pacific frowns on anyone that turns them down on promotion." I nodded my head and left.

What a big decision to make. Sitting on the edge of my bed at the Quincy, I reasoned with myself. If only someone could help me think this out. Maybe talking to some of the other engineers would help, but most likely their advice would be "grab it," not knowing the other side of things. I wondered if maybe Millie could help me find the answer? I went to the depot where she worked at the ticket office to find out if she was busy after work.

"Come over the house at five tonight. I'm never too busy to see you." Millie told me.

Her house was on Flower Street, not far from the corner of Baker Street. I waited for her to change into something more comfortable, and finally she came out in a see-through negligee. But I wasn't in the mood for that kind of thing at the time. She made coffee and we sat down to chat. Millie knew of my situation at home.

"I had an official job offered me today." I told her. "But it means moving to Sacramento, and Levi wants to know by tomorrow. I don't know what to do. I hate to turn it down."

Millie took some time to think about it. She got up to turn on the music, came back and sat close to me. The aroma of her perfume lingered in my nostrils like a walk in the poppy fields in the early spring. I was intoxicated.

"If you take the job," she finally said, "you'll have to move and then the company might advance you more later and then there will be another move, and another one. You'll probably move many times. How is this going to affect things? Remember you have kids that have to go to school. Another thing, do you want to boss men around or do you want to live and be a friend of men?" Millie had a way of striking at the core of things and working them out.

"Millie, having you say it, clinches the situation. You're right, I cannot take the promotion."

I felt relieved and the tension left my body. That evening I was relieved of other tensions.

Again the Movie Train

About two weeks later a job came up in Los Angeles again and I was glad to see the family.

"Well I see you're back again," Margie said. Then she shrugged her shoulders and walked away. She did not ask how I was, or say it was nice to see me again. It was the same knife-cutting cold reception that I always received. Maybe the wall of self-condemnation and regret that I had built up around myself had a little to do with it, but biting the bullet, I knew I had to continue on. As always the work was piled up around the place, and of course a visit to the in-laws was in order. I didn't mind that; they were good people.

After completing all that is required for normal living, I reported for work and then went to purchase some pipe tobacco. I found that Helen Miller had moved to Tennessee. Another chapter in my life was closed.

I would rather not have been called for my next assignment, but with my luck, what else—another movie train, again at Station Lang. Lang was an excellent place for taking pictures. It was off the beaten path and had a train order office located there, which made it easy to keep track of the mainline trains. It also had a long side track with two spurs leading from it. There was a tunnel at both ends of Lang at that time. Coming downhill into Lang the grade leveled off after getting by the train order office; also, there was one dirt crossing below the office, which was located almost in the center siding.

They had been taking pictures for several days. The train consisted of four open-end wooden passenger cars and the old #5 diamond stack locomotive with wood piled on top of the tender to disguise the oil tank and movie equipment. From past experiences, the company had decided to send an engine watchman out from Saugus at night to keep the old diamond stack alive. On arriving at Lang, my fireman, Coleman Beard, measured the oil and found that the tank was almost empty. Maybe there was just enough to reach Saugus to refuel. This upset the director because it meant that he was not able to get the early start he wanted. If the previous crew had measured the oil the night before and found it low, and had taken the locomotive to Saugus for refueling where it could stay the night, then we could have brought it back that morning. But that is not always the way things were done on the railroad.

We received running orders to Saugus with a restrictive speed of twenty miles per hour and a distance of fifteen miles. This meant about forty-five minutes running time each way, and figuring one hour taking oil meant that the trip would take up two and a half hours, or less if we weren't stuck for any trains. Luckily we made it in two hours and forty-five minutes. Backing the engine on the returning trip Coleman and I had to smell low grade oil fumes all the way to Lang because of some oil that had been spilled on the tank while being refueled.

The director was in an ugly mood on our return. He seemed to think we had been stalling. With his little mind, he couldn't conceive how a railroad was operated, or the amount of time it took to accomplish things. The first shot he wanted taken was of the train running to the East tunnel and stopping just inside of the portal of the tunnel where a white towel had been laid on the ground. I was to stop the cab of the engine at that spot, right at the engineer's window. Stopping the train would have been easy, but Coleman and I had to squat on the floor of the cab while the actors sat in our seats.

Other motion picture studios would put a little make-up on our faces and let us do our own job. At the close of day we were handed ten or fifteen dollars each for our participation and everything went well. But this company would not do that, and it made things very difficult. It was just about impossible to sit on the floor and stop a train at a spot that I couldn't see, or manipulate the brakes or throttle. I made five tries and did not come within fifty feet of the required spot. Finally Levi Franklin climbed up on the engine.

"Why can't you stop this thing were they want you to?" he yelled. "You know the director is very annoyed about your stopping and he's getting very upset with you."

"Horse Mulocka!" I exploded with my favorite expression. "Go back and tell that bastard to get these dummies off of our seats. I can't see the ground, let alone the mark where to stop." Levi knew that I was getting to the boiling point.

"OK, OK," he said, and left to talk with the director. Shortly afterwards we replaced the actors.

"Charlie," Coleman Beard said with his famous big grin, "you don't back up for no one, do you?"

"Nope, I don't especially when knowing I'm in the right," I replied. "My Dad once told me if you back up to a mule he's either going to kick you or bite your ass so don't back up to anyone."

We had made a few moves on the passing track after finishing with the tunnel shots when the movie company's catering truck appeared. They set up long tables with white table cloths provided by the depot and put on a spread of food and drink that wouldn't quit. My stomach told me all about it; I was sure getting hungry. But we worked on the sidetrack until a whistle was blown, then everyone stopped for lunch.

"Well, I guess it's bean time, Coleman," I remarked.

"Yeah, and I'm starved," he replied.

Levi showed up with the conductor; their hands were full of food.

"Did you guys bring a lunch?" Levi yelled up from the ground.

"Hell no, we didn't bring a lunch. What's wrong with eating here?"

"The director says you two are not welcome, but here's a plate of sandwiches you can have." I looked at Coleman and he shook his head.

"The train crew is going to eat here?" I asked.

"You bet we are," the conductor came in.

"I always thought that we were supposed to be a unit and we all ate together? But I see you Los Angeles crews don't hold to that," I said. "I'll tell you Levi, we appreciate your offer but you take those sandwiches back to that little bastard and tell him to use them for toilet paper." I was beginning to get angry. "Isn't there any transportation to take us to Saugus to eat?"

"No there isn't anything available. I'm sorry," Levi apologized. "Now back this train up the sidetrack a little ways, and when we want you, we'll let you know."

Shaking with anger I backed the train, way back, so when they wanted me, the brakeman would have to walk more than a quarter of a mile to get me because they knew no one would be looking for signals.

In a situation like this, the more a person thinks about it, the more the anger builds up. You plan how you're going to get even. In your mind's eye you see yourself tearing your opponent apart and chastising him. But as soon as that feeling passes you feel dejected. Coleman and I both closed our eyes to shut out the reality of it all.

The head brakeman had to walk up to let us know everyone was finished eating.

"I have been giving you signals for ten minutes to come ahead," he yelled at me from the ground.

"Well isn't that too damn bad," I returned to him. "Now get your butt on the front of this thing and ride." There was not very much room to stand on a very little step.

Getting back to the depot again, I was told by the conductor that we were to back up on the main line and then come down the main line making all the smoke we could as we went by the train order office. Mr. Director rode the first open passenger car directly behind the engine. I did not know why he rode there but, anyway, it all fit into my scheme. This director was dressed in the traditional director's clothes of white shirt and pants, hat and shoes. I looked at Coleman, and we both smiled. I think he must have known what I had in mind.

"Get this tub clear full of water, every bit that she can hold,"

I told Coleman. All the modern locomotives were superheated by means of steam pipes doubling in the flues, then going to the cylinders. The process made the steam hot and dry, but these old-time diamond stacks were old soaks; the steam came right off the top of the boiler and then went to the cylinders.

Out on the main line we stopped slowly, then put the big Johnson bar in forward motion, and released the brakes. The train rolled down grade towards the depot.

"Give all the smoke you can until we get by the depot," I told Coleman. We were rolling very good as we neared the depot, where catering people were cleaning the tables. Yelling to Coleman, "work her," I pulled the throttle back and with the Johnson bar down in the corner the engine did exactly what was expected of her: "woof, woof, woof"; she sounded like an old greyhound dog. It worked. Water instead of steam came right out of the stack. Coal-black water spewed for hundreds of feet around. I stopped the train and looked back. Mr. Director was climbing off the passenger steps, dripping wet. All that was visible were the whites of his eyes, the rest of him was black, as was the table with the remainder of the food, and the surrounding automobiles. The train and most of the people working about there were a beautiful, dripping, wet, black. I looked at Coleman and tried to match his big grin, knowing we had both received our reward.

Levi came storming down to the engine, threw his hat on the ground and stomped on it.

"I know what you done. I know damn well what you did," he blasted me from the ground. But knowing Levi, he was having a ball and could hardly keep from laughing. Levi had respect for someone who could figure a way of doing something like that and still stay within the rules.

After surveying the situation, it was decided to call it a day. The director shook his fist at me; just to rub it in more, I waved him goodbye and grinned at him.

Taking the train down to Saugus to be cleaned, we went to eat and then dead headed home. At the crew dispatcher's office I was informed that the motion picture company didn't want me on that job again, and I was pleased.

5. The Home Rule

A regular routine of work prevailed for the next few months, but one day, after being called for a Bakersfield run, the crew dispatcher informed me that I was officially qualified to run passenger. I had run many passenger trains without being qualified to do so, because there were not enough engineers to fill the jobs. So the company used me, and a great many other engineers, in the name of emergency.

Nothing of great importance happened on the trip to Bakersfield, except for beating the average running time by ten minutes. The average had been reduced many times, from sixteen hours to fourteen hours and twenty minutes. The road employees would challenge each other each month to beat the preceding records and very few times a train or engine crew died on the sixteen hour "law."

On arriving at Bakersfield I had dinner with Millie, then went to Quincy for a good night's sleep. But at four-fifteen the next morning the call boy pounded on my door. My first reaction was to kick his butt all the way down the stairs and out into the street. I decided against it and signed the call book.

The restaurant was full because two train and engine crews had been called at the same time. Baker Street in the late forties, day or night, bristled with activity because of the railroad crews coming and going. And of course there were the ladies of the night and the perennial homeless people, as well as the drunks.

Engineer Fritz Iverson, a regular pool man, was called ahead of me out of Los Angeles. Ray Shay was the conductor with Fritz and my conductor was Fuller, a Los Angeles crew working on the San Joaquin district.

Everything went as usual up the Tehachapi Mountain. Watering the engines at Woodford, cutting the short helpers out at Summit Switch. Stopping to eat at Mojave and watering the engines. Then it would be off to Los Angeles via Palmdale, Vincent, and Saugus, including all the stations in between.

At that time, dispatching of trains was done by train orders between Mojave and Los Angeles, and the movement and safety of a train was governed by Automatic Block Signals (ABS) that were actuated by the trains themselves.

Leaving Mojave, engineer Iverson had orders to run as first 804, having right over westward third class trains from Mojave to Saugus and to run three hours late. That would put Iverson out at 11:40 in the morning. I was to follow him, since we were running as second 804. Waiting for Fritz to get off the block so we could proceed behind him, I lit up my pipe and thought how good it was to have a job like this. It took skill to handle those big monstrous trains, especially over the Tehachapi Mountains. Nowhere in the world was there a stretch of railroad like this, and the men who worked it were a close-knit, big-hearted, hardy bunch of men striving to do their work, making the impossible task run smoothly. And that included the dispatchers and all.

Leaving Mojave, everything went perfectly this day. The weather was just right, not too hot or cold and everything fitted together like a jigsaw puzzle. We slowed down at Denis and through Palmdale to let first 804 get past Vincent, at the top of the hill, so as not to stop me on the steep grade up to Vincent on a block signal. Everything worked fine, like a well-oiled engine. Fritz was long gone when we arrived at Vincent. On the way up the hill the brakemen had turned up the retainers on the train so we didn't have to stop at Vincent, where the order board showed green.

In the days preceding Levi Franklin, all trains were required to stop at Ravenna for the purpose of cooling wheels on the train. But when Levi took over the road foreman job, he ran many tests, measuring the heat of the wheels with a very sensitive gauge. It was concluded that the wheel heat at Ravenna was not enough to warrant stopping a train to cool them.

Following Fritz down the hill seemed very easy because he kept his speed even. I would be working on a yellow signal and when I approached a red one, it would turn yellow before I reached it. This happened practically all the way down the hill, making me think the trip was a piece of cake.

But I was still a young person and did not realize that overconfidence was a sign of danger. Following in the wake of first 804 and arriving at station Lang, the brakeman turned the retainers down on the run. Looking back and getting a "high ball" from the head brakeman was the indication that the work was finished. Going through Lang we received a green order board signal, meaning there was no restriction at Lang. But what I didn't know was that first 804 had received orders to meet a train at Humphreys, the next station.

I was traveling thirty miles per hour and on a yellow signal when the little man on my shoulder gave me a warning. Instinctively I reduced the air six pounds in the train line, thinking maybe that was either too much or the wrong thing to do. We were approaching the signal at Humphreys and the siding switch, but for the last two hundred yards they were hidden from view by a small hill, which the track skirted around. When they did come in sight only a short distance remained in which to stop. The speed of my train was slowing but not nearly enough to stop at the signal if it was red, and it *was* red! Boy, I went after the emergency right now!

The caboose of first 804 was standing less than one hundred yards from signal and switch. "Oh Lord," I whispered to myself, getting ready to fly from the engine and yelling to the fireman, who had already left, just as the conductor and rear brakeman on the caboose ahead were taking to the fields. The engine went by the signal as I reached the bottom step of the ladder from the cab, when all of a sudden the train came to a halt, with the nose of my cab ahead malley within ten feet of the caboose of the other train.

Sitting on the rock ballast by the side of the rails ahead of my engine, I was aimlessly throwing stones out in the right-of-way when Ray Shay and his brakeman walked back from their flight to the fields; I did not yet know where my fireman or head brakeman were.

My spirits were at their lowest ebb; I was bitterly regretting my overconfidence, the cocksure disastrous judgment on my part.

"Charlie," Ray Shay grinned, "that was close." I could only nod my head; the shame was too great, it even kept me from talking. Ray was known as a good man and a jewel of a conductor and he knew how to put cooling ointment on a burning hurt.

"Our train is on the move; we must go. Take it easy, Charlie." They boarded the caboose and left. That was all that was ever said or done about the incident, which was a dismissal offense with the company.

The near accident taught me the most important lesson in my life: never assume anything, on train orders, on signals, or, I might add, on people's word. Use the utmost caution and regard everything as negative until you find out for yourself.

The Disharmony

Once again I went to Fresno, this time off the engineers' extra board to augment the extra board at Fresno. It was a very disappointing situation for all of us young engineers, and there wasn't any relief in sight. I realized that something had to be done about it, and resolved to give it some thought.

The next night I drove my car to Fresno. This time it wasn't the old model 'A' Ford but a 1939 Dodge coupe; Margie had a Chevy station wagon for herself. Financially, things were improving, but not devotion. I still had dim hopes, but they were flickering out as the years went by.

I noticed that many diesel electric switch engines were replacing the old steam locomotives at Fresno. It would improve conditions at this place and also the new yard four miles north of town, which had opened since I had last worked at Fresno.

That evening I was talking to a few of the local enginemen at the dispatcher's office. I found out that during the past year, some of the fireman living at Fresno had had to leave for Bakersfield to work as engineers. This was happening with increasing frequency all over the division, affecting the morale of the enginemen and disrupting their home lives.

We could put up with the working conditions because we knew they existed and we accepted them, but this dead heading away from home for many months at a time every year was not acceptable. Although the old time engineers would say "it was good enough for us, it's good enough for you," we thought that was a very biased and narrow way of looking at the situation.

I asked a few of the men around the office whether, if I could come up with some kind of a plan, they would support me. The consensus was that they would.

Lil's husband, Doyle, was at the desk of the Saint Francis Hotel when I arrived.

"Glad to see you back, Charlie," he greeted me. "Lil, come see who's here." Lillian came out from their living quarters, looking as pretty as she always did.

"Hello Charlie, it's sure good to see you. Are you staying with us for awhile?" Lil asked.

"I really don't know, Lil, but the way it looks, maybe any part of a month," I said, just making conversation. Lil was about to walk away, then she turned abruptly.

"I bet you couldn't guess who wrote me?" Her eyes brightened.

Having no idea who wrote her or caring much, I pretended to be interested.

'No, I have no idea, Lil."

"Alice. You know the girl that stayed in the front room by the steps?"

Lil didn't know it, but she had just hit me with a baseball bat.

"Did she have anything important to say?" I was trying to stay calm and appear nonchalant. My insides were ready to explode and my mouth became dry.

"Oh, yes! She has a little baby boy and know what? She named him Charles. Look, here is his picture." He was a beauty, stout and alert with big brown eyes. My insides were churning.

"You know she forgot to give me her return address," Lil said.

"What city was the letter mailed from?" I asked, trying to be calm.

"It's . . . it's from Hawaii," she stumbled.

I signed the register and received a room, then went to bed trying not to think of Alice. It was nice that she let me know. The way she had handled seemed suitable to her way of doing things. I have sealed my lips about this until writing this book; it is just one of the skeletons a man has in his closet.

At exactly five-thirty the next morning, I was awakened by the call boy pounding on my door.

"You are called for a switch engine at the new yard, job number 563," he told me, handing me a pencil to sign the call sheet.

"But how do you get there?" I asked.

"There's a Southern Pacific bus that goes out every twenty minutes. You board it at the depot," he informed me as he left the room.

When I arrived at the new yard I found that job 563 was one of the new diesel jobs. Never having run a diesel engine, I looked around for an instructor or someone to brief me, but no one showed up. I decided I was not going to leave until someone showed me about those blasted things. I waited until it was time to be on duty, when my fireman showed up.

"You know how to run one of these things?" I asked.

"Well, sort of," he offered.

"Well, you're sort of elected to do it. Come on, let's do it." With that we left to board the diesel.

I watched Jim, my fireman, work all morning, doing a good job and teaching me a great deal about the diesel. After lunch I tried running the diesel myself and found it much easier than a steam engine. I became really fond of the diesels, not realizing the enormous role that they would play in the coming years.

That evening, checking over some job bulletins at the crew dispatcher's office, I found a job in Los Angeles that my seniority would let me hold, so I bid on it. Several days later the assignments came out and I was awarded the job.

"I can't release you, we need you here," the master mechanic informed me. I thought for a minute and then responded, "Well, OK, but the company will have to pay me double while I'm here."

"Just what do you mean, double?" he wanted to know.

"I'd rather not tell you why because thinking it over, this is too good of a deal for me to pass up." I was getting myself ready to leave.

"Wait one minute," he said, leaving to go into his office. In the past, this master mechanic had ruled the young engineers with a firm hand; what he said was law, but now I think he was stumped.

"You are released. Go home," he said with a sour note when he came back to the outer office. He did not admit that I was right, but someone higher up than him had set him straight on the phone, and he sure didn't like to be wrong. I looked at him and grinned, then walked away knowing that this might be the last time that I would ever have to work in Fresno.

I had formed my plan of what had to be accomplished when I arrived home. First I would call Joe Ketchum and then Jerry Willey and have them meet at my house. Joe Ketchum had a way with words and was very ambitious. Many thought that Joe was for Joe first but that really was not entirely so. I knew him better than most people at that time and we had lengthy talks on how to better the working conditions for all the enginemen. Jerry had traded seniority from the Los Angeles division to the San Joaquin Division. In doing so, he gained some seniority because the man he traded with was much older than Jerry and was about ready for his pension. This left a nasty feeling with a great many engineers on our division. Having Jerry was a diplomatic move on my part because he had the 'know how' regarding what had to be done.

We arranged to meet at my house at nine o'clock the next morning. I had Margie fix coffee and doughnuts and provide plenty of writing paper and pens. I asked her to stay in the kitchen with us but she said she had other things to do.

"What have you got up your sleeve now, Charlie?" Joe asked me between sips of coffee.

"I have a solution for this aged old dead heading every year to Fresno and you two fellows are the men that can help me put it over. We're living in new times and things should be changed." I took a sip of coffee as I gauged their reaction.

"Can the lecture, Charlie, what have you?" Joe cut in.

"I know the old heads say that they had to go to Fresno for years so now it's our turn. What was good enough for them is good enough for us. Well I don't think that way. My guess is that if their grandfathers ran diamond stack locomotives all the time, they would expect to do the same, but that is not the way it works. Many of us quit wearing overalls because we wanted a change, so why not do the same for working conditions?"

"You still haven't arrived at the point," Joe said. "What do you have in mind?"

"These old engineers are a hard nut to crack," Jerry cut in. "And you need them to help put anything over.

"Yes, that's right," I continued. "As Joe says, we have to

97

have a good plan and here is what I can come up with. At a terminal where there are promoted engineers, they will be used before or ahead of a senior engineer dead heading out of another terminal, with no penalty whatever to the Southern Pacific. If there is not a promoted man available at that point then the company will use the senior man from another terminal."

I stopped to see how they were absorbing my idea, and it seemed to strike the right note. We had a three hour discussion and came up with a program based on my plan. Joe was to type it up and then we would submit it to the Brotherhood of Locomotive Engineers and the Brotherhood of Locomotive Engineers and Fireman. If it was approved it would then be presented to the company for their action.

Several months later both unions passed the proposition and it was sent to the Superintendent of the San Joaquin division, who at that time was Burt Mitchell. He approved it.

The Fillmore Local

What a job it was, the Fillmore Local. Going to work at three-thirty in the afternoon at Los Angeles and fifteen hours and fifty-nine minutes later tying up at Fillmore. The reason for tying up one minute under sixteen hours was because it allowed the crew to go to work again in eight hours, whereas if they took the full time they would be required to take ten hours rest.

With conductor Joe Leftner everyone did as he said. Joe was a hard working man and if he told a brakeman to do a job of switching out cars he expected it to be done exactly the way he instructed. Even if the brakeman found an easier way of doing it, Joe would make him do it over the way he had been told. Joe addressed everyone as "Mr.," and his instructions to an engineer was very formal and precise. As long as the rules were lived up to, everything would go well, but if there was any infraction of them, look out.

At Fillmore there weren't any hotels available so the company had taken an old camp car that was used in 1890 for track workers. The wheels had been removed, a little carpentry work had been done, resulting in windows, screen door, a toilet, and a wash stand. The toilet was put in new, way before my time. It was the type with a flushing tank near the ceiling with a chain pull on it to flush it out. If we wanted to wash or shave, we used a hand basin, but first we had to go outside to the faucet, fill it with water, then put it on the potbelly stove to heat. The beds were furnished but each person supplied his own bedding. It was not the best of conditions but had been in existence for many years, and, as it was said, "what was good for the old heads, is good enough for the new ones." Being a little cautious about lice or bed bugs, I gave the mattress a good spraying before using it. Everyone ate in the town restaurant.

I was doing some plumbing at home about two weeks later after being on the job and not getting my rest that day. I should not have gone to work tired but I knew that my experienced fireman, Clyde Cochran, would run the engine for me, and this would give me relief from staring at signals in the dark all night. But when I arrived at work I found that Clyde had laid off sick and that about made me sick. You never know what to expect until the job is on its way and you're leaving town— then it's time to size up the situation. That's what Henry Bock, an old engineer, once told me and I found him so right many times. My situation was bad tonight; my fireman was a new man and had never been to Fillmore, and probably did not even knew where the town was located.

We managed to make Saugus and did some switching that

was always required there. As usual Joe allowed us to have something to eat at the Saugus Cafe, and instead of getting some rest on the engine, I joined the crew at the restaurant for coffee and pie. Glancing at my watch, I saw it was two o'clock in the morning. Six more hours to work—if only I had not come to work! With three kids coming up it was almost mandatory that I had to make money because of the lean year at Fresno. After finishing our meal I went back to the engine, taking water for the fireman, thinking that it would revive me a little. It did for a short while. After the watering of the engine, Joe Leftner handed me our running orders as the brakeman lined the switch to the Santa Paula branch for us to come off the siding. Long before my time, this branch was actually the main line up the coast from Los Angeles.

Our first stop would be Piru, where we would do some switching. It was about twenty miles away, and with very slight water grade downhill. At Piru the switching would take several hours at the packing sheds and then we would move on to Fillmore, another eight or ten miles farther down the branch. There we would do some more packing shed work and then tie up. If by any chance we were finished before being relieved by the crew going to Montalvo, the fireman would have to stay on the engine, and see that the steam and water were right for the relieving crew.

We left Saugus with forty-five iced refrigerated cars; our speed at that time was twenty miles per hour. Five minutes out of Saugus the head brakeman was sitting on the sandbox with his head on his knees snoring up a tune, drowning out the rattling of the engine. And after setting his fire to a drifting throttle, the fireman seemed to have many friends down this track because he was nodding at everyone he knew although it was pitch dark out. He must have had good eyesight. I grinned to myself, let them be, let them be.

The air brake rule said that a reduction of six pounds of air is required but under this condition; we would be sitting still at the first blow of air. There are several ways to bring a train like this down the hill. One was to work a heavy throttle and set and release the air, causing an according action with the train, but that would being old Mr. Conductor out of the caboose fighting mad, so that was out. The second way would be to use the bridging methods, but I wasn't very good at that so that left me with either screwing the feed valve down a few pounds or using the lap position on the brake valve, letting the leakage set the brakes slightly, then putting the handle on running position and getting a slow release. I chose the latter method that night. Everything went fine until I started to nod at my friends along the right-away, and worst of all I forgot to light my pipe.

After only a short period, maybe fifteen minutes—although it seemed like an eternity—I woke up with a hell of a start. The train was standing still! Having the brake valve on a lap position, the leakage stopped the train with the air gauge showing fifty-five pounds of air.

The snoring was going into symphonic movements by now and the fireman didn't have any more friends to nod at so he was resting his head against the cab window with his mouth open in a gargling position. I stuck my head out the cab window and there, not very far back, two electric lanterns appeared along the train. Quickly I thought, 'Boy you better do something quick or else get your rear end chewed out so bad that sitting down will be impossible for a week. Shaking the head brakeman and the fireman awake, I grabbed the long oiler and motioned the brakeman to follow down on the opposite side of the engine than that which Mr. Conductor and his cohorts were walking up the train.

"Spot your lantern on what I'm trying to do," I said to him, climbing up on a driving rod and starting on the procedure of oiling the inside oil cups in the back of the driving wheels.

"What's the trouble?" the brakeman asked.

"The old man is on his way up. Just do what I tell you and I'll explain later, OK?" The brakeman finally got the drift of what was going on and about that time the old bulldog came around the front of the engine. I had my head in between the driving wheels and the head brakeman was trying in vain to hold his light where it should be.

"What is the matter here?" The voice was rough and husky. It really surprised me that he didn't use the word mister; maybe he was out of breath from walking. Pulling my head slowly out from my cramped position, I looked down on the almighty creature standing below me. He did not seem so big standing there, so I thought maybe I should push it a little further.

"If you have some difficulties in seeing the trouble I have here and what I'm doing maybe you better go back to the caboose and let me take care of this myself. I have enough problems here." I did not realize how rude this must have sounded, but he cleared his throat and gave a grunt to the rear brakeman.

"You heard the man, let's go back to the caboose."

From that day on, things went along fine, and I was not called mister anymore.

The Boy Scout Special

One nice morning in late spring of the same year, after vacating the Fillmore loco for the extra board, a call came for me to run a Boy Scout Special. I was to pull twenty empty passengers coaches to Chatsworth, then go around the wye with the engine and return to Northridge depot, pulling the train into the house track for loading of Boy Scouts. Northridge at that time was not a very large place, just a great many walnut orchards and such, but they did harvest seven to eight hundred Boy Scouts from in and about the outlying areas of the district. That morning five train loads were called to pick up Boy Scouts between Santa Barbara and Los Angeles for a Boy Scout Jamboree. I have long forgotten the destination but I do remember all those shining happy faces as they came from all over to get on the train. I watched their mothers and dads bid them goodbye, telling them, "stay warm and change your socks." And the scout master assuring the parents that everything would be all right.

Troxel was firing for me on this trip and he had acquired a new calabash pipe, the one with the curved stem, which fitted his style.

"Troxel, that's a good-looking pipe, but why the curved stem? I asked him with a laugh. "Are you going to rest it on your chin when you get tired?"

"No, no, I just like it," he sputtered out, with more water than words.

I was still chuckling to myself as we climbed on the 4324 passenger locomotive to await our departure and orders to Los Angeles. The conductor finally emerged from the office with the orders.

"OK, line us out," he yelled to the brakeman, handing me the orders, giving us a straight shot to the big city.

"Troxel, this looks like an easy trip for us," I remarked. "What you going to do with all the money you're going to make this trip?"

"Oh, I have lots of room for that. The missus will see to it," he assured me.

We left the house track and got out on the high rail. I made my running air test, then put the reverse down in the forward motion more than was necessary, to make the locomotive bark a little louder, so the little scouts would think, "Boy, are we traveling!" The reverse gear was in fact not a reverse gear at all. It was a small handle affair sitting on a half quadrant with notches like a gear holding the mechanism in place, where the engineer wanted it to be.

We passed siding Raymer at seventy miles per hour. Next was Hewitt, where I started to use the air because farther down the track to Burbank Junction a yellow signal was showing up. In those times, smog was virtually unknown so the distance of vision was much greater. As we approached Burbank Junction the tower held the signal red. I had the train speed down, and was ready to stop at the signal. It turned green. Kicking the brakes off and easing the throttle down so that short sassy strokes of steam came out of the stack, we rolled through the restricted speed of the tower and made sure the complete train was through the plant (tower) and on the double track before increasing speed to fifty miles per hour. Usually the conductor would let the engineer know with the air whistle from the train to the engine that it was condition green to proceed, but sometimes they were busy and forgot.

The double track between Burbank and Los Angeles consisted of many grade crossings. Automatic crossing gates were being installed as rapidly as could be expected but there remained many wigwags in use. It was imperative that the engineer keep a sharp lookout at all times along this stretch of track because of the great volume of traffic, so the steam whistle was continuously blowing.

Resuming my speed at fifty miles per hour, I suddenly

realized that something ahead of me was very wrong, but it was too late for me to avoid it. A twenty-one ton caterpillar tractor was being unloaded on the bank of the railway right-of-way. The tracks were eight feet higher than where the unloading was taking place. The cat was being backed off a trailer parked with its rear against the dirt bank, which made a good ramp for unloading. Because of the noise of his machine, the operator never heard me coming. My hand froze on the whistle cord, with my other hand on the brake valve. My body was tense, and things flashed before my eyes in that split second that no modern day computer could equal. These flashes are gone as fast as they appear—then another inexplicable force takes charge of your actions. The things I did in the next few seconds were amazing. Under normal conditions I would not even have tried them, but at that time they proved to be right.

I hit six inches of the bulldozer scraper blade with the front of my engine. As the operator spun the cat around, it swung all of the twenty-one ton caterpillar into the side of my locomotive, ripping it to pieces and doing great damage to my engine. One side rod was ripped off and it about took my side of the cab with it. I pulled my body in and away just in time or I would not be here today. The swinging cat did not remove my seat and the back part of the cab was still intact.

Just before the collision I had put the train in emergency, going the speed we were. As the flying debris cleared up I glanced back and saw the cloud of dust the baggage car was kicking up. Immediately I knew the car was derailed and could pile up any second. I thought of all the little kids riding the train. Many would be killed or maimed for life, and they had put their trust in me! God, this cannot happen. I thought. The tragic thing was that these kids had their windows open and were waving at people as the train went by.

I kept the throttle wide open and my engine brakes off so as not to have any slack between the engine and baggage car, and, hopefully, not any slack between the baggage car and the passenger car. I desperately hoped that maybe the train would stay upright until it came to a halt. We traveled another four hundred and forty feet to the next grade crossing. Surely, when the wheels of the baggage car hit the crossing this would be the end. I looked at Troxel, who was white as chalk and slobbering, with his pipe in his mouth. Then I glanced back at the baggage car as it hit the crossing, jumping up two feet or more. Everything was happening so fast I took everything in at once. When the car jumped up, a miracle happened. All six wheels of the first truck, which were the only ones derailed, rerailed at the crossing! The draw-bar between the locomotive and the baggage car slipped, leaving the engine free to proceed down the track on its own. I was later told that such a thing would happen only once in a thousand times.

The train came to a nice stop, but we were still going very fast because the grade from Burbank Junction to Taylor Yard at Los Angeles was downhill. Once, when several boxcars on the storage track at Burbank started rolling after some boys released the hand brakes on them, they were traveling an estimated seventy miles per hour by the time they reached Glendale, a distance of six miles.

The yard master was notified of the runaway. Figuring to halt the cars coming down the outbound mainline, he ran a switch engine out and told them to wait until they saw the cars coming, then travel in the same direction and let the cars bump into them gently and then brake to a stop.

The runaway cars came in view. But it did not happen like the yard master figured it would because he had miscalculated the speed the cars would be traveling. The poor engineer on the switch engine could not get his engine going half the speed of the cars in what little time he had after they came into view. The impact of the two forces were like a baseball player hitting a home run. The runaway cars were derailed, causing great damage, but the switch engine was demolished, killing the engineer, fireman, and the switch foreman. All of these thoughts were going through my head as we rode the runaway engine. The air reservoir tanks had been damaged or ripped from the locomotive at the collision point. Without air to actuate the brakes or air reverse I could not reverse the engine and stop. It seemed like our fate was sealed. If we jumped, our chances of survival were nil. Poor Troxel, I thought, he will never know what it's like to be an engineer. Then, like a guiding light, a voice whispered in my ear, "the steam reverse." Frantically looking for the right valve in the cab—there were many—I found it tucked away from view. It was scarcely ever used. With every ounce of strength I could muster I tried to turn it. Finally it turned a little, and then a little more, until it was wide open. The engine came to a spinning-of-the-wheels stop. With the throttle almost closed we started to back up.

"Troxel, tie the tender hand brake. I can't stop it from rolling either direction entirely," I yelled at him, and he complied instantly.

I was shaking with relief or fright or maybe shock, not knowing exactly what had happened. But one thing I knew— Troxel will live to be an engineer. Telling Troxel to stay on the engine, I walked back half a mile to the train, still shaking. But the walk steadied my nerves a bit. The most amazing thing was that when all the excitement was happening, I remained calm; it was only when it was over that the shakes got to me.

I reached the train but there wasn't anybody out and about; none of the scouts could be seen. One scoutmaster was standing at the vestibule doors looking on with bewilderment and confusion.

"Where are all the little scouts?" I asked him.

"They are all on their knees praying and giving thanks for their deliverance and for having such a good engineer to bring us through all this," he told me.

Tears swelled in my eyes and I was very close to bawling. I was glad no one was close to see me. Someone appreciated me, but I knew that without that superpower, that little man sitting on my shoulder, and which I knew to be God, the Supreme Being, I wouldn't have been able to do anything.

The conductor was surrounded by a crowd of clamoring people. I wasn't in the mood to answer any questions and tried to back away, but I backed straight into Jim Canty, road foreman of engines—my boss.

"What happened, Steffes?" Jim always called me by my last name. I related my version of the accident.

"But after you broke away from the train how did you stop the locomotive?" he inquired.

"With the steam reverse valve, using steam to reverse the engine."

"I see," he said. "You did a good job, but how much damage is done to the locomotive? Can it be run to the yard?" Jim kept firing questions at me.

"No," I replied. "It will have to be towed in with a switch engine. The air tanks are ruptured and the right side rods are loose and one missing. There isn't much left of my cab on my side."

"OK. You've told me enough, we'll take care of it. You better return and see if Troxel is OK," Jim told me. He wanted me to leave so I would not talk to the press. That was all right with me, but I was a bit put out that Jim didn't ask how I felt.

He seemed to assume that engineers had the constitution of a mule.

The conductor caught up with me on the way back.

"I'll make out the accident report and send it over so you can copy it," he told me.

"Thanks, but how did the operator of the caterpillar come out?" I asked.

"He was killed. They've taken him away and there wasn't a scratch on him, but he was busted up inside," the conductor informed me.

"That's too bad. One minute you're alive then the next it's all over. Neither of us knew each other or knew that we would meet at the same place and one of us would kill the other," I mused almost to myself. "It is like that in peace or war. Ironic as it might seem, but that is the way it is."

Arriving back at the engine, I saw that Troxel was not moving. He sat like a wooden Indian, staring at the boiler head. I surmised that he was stunned and in shock. I explained to him what had taken place at the train and that we would be towed in with a switch engine. Nothing seemed to interest him, not even his pipe. Then I knew he was in some kind of a trance, but I didn't know how to get him out of it. I looked at the water glass and saw there was only a half of an inch of water left and steam was down to one hundred forty pounds.

"Troxel!" I yelled, shaking him. "Get some damn water in this thing and bring the steam up to where it's supposed to be."

Troxel suddenly came to himself. He shook his head and moved to put on the water injector, and proceeded to build a larger fire. Then he filled his pipe and put a fire in it. When he did this I knew he would be all right.

It was not long until a switch engine came and took us to the round- house. It was the end of a day that would live with me for the rest of my life.

Every Man's Dream

I began to dream about building a house on the desert property. Maybe that would bring Margie and me closer together. It would be worth a try. I gathered some plans together and thought about what the best one would be for that environment. I wanted a house that when built would stand any kind of weather or stress. I found a suitable plan by Frank Lloyd Wright and submitted it to Margie. She looked it over, and halfheartedly thought it might be all right. Margie never really voiced her opinion or offered any suggestions, many times leaving me without any idea of what she really wanted.

I decided that this was the plan to use. It was for a three level house. Three nice-sized bedrooms and a bath above a large garage and washroom. There would be steps coming down from the bedroom halfway to a large family dining room which was off from the elaborate kitchen and entrance hall. Next to that was a master bedroom and large bath. From the entry hall and family room was a huge sunken living room. It was a very elaborate plan, with the outer wall of concrete building blocks and rough hewn redwood boards and bats. The heavy shake roof matched the decor of the blocks, being chartreuse, and the redwood brown.

I made arrangements with my Mom to borrow ten thousand dollars to buy the material. But I would have to do the work myself because it wasn't too long after the war and there were not many tradesmen around.

Driving over the Angeles crest highway, a twisty climbing road fifty miles from Los Angeles, to Little Rock between trips on the railroad, I thought that I should be able to finish the place in three to four years. After buying a used pickup and the necessary tools for building the house and hauling material, I was set.

Reporting for work after a little time off, I was called for a Bakersfield run. Vince Cippolla was firing for me, and he was a promising, talkative young man. Vince did his job perfectly and as long as he had someone to listen while he talked, he was in his element. Some of his conversation was interesting and useful, but . . . ! One thing though, time didn't drag with Vince along.

The head brakeman was a tall slender boy with a likable personality. With his long legs he was fast. An engineer never had to stop a train for him in lining a switch to head into a siding. All that was required was slowing a train down enough for him to run ahead of the locomotive, and he would have the switch lined into the siding before the engine arrived at the switch.

"What name do you go by?" Cippolla asked him.

"Jackson," the brakeman replied, and they started a lengthy conversation which I didn't want to be involved with.

Returning from Bakersfield to Los Angeles we all ate at Mojave. No one really liked to eat there because of the treatment that the crews had received during the war. The proprietors of many restaurants had banded together and informed the Southern Pacific and Santa Fe Railroads that the patronage of the train and engine crews was not welcome. The company then established an eating place for their employees in a converted building located in the yard across the tracks from the depot. The company supplied cooks from the dinning car pool of the passenger trains and they were the top chefs of the time. The waitresses were hired locally and paid a dollar an hour more than they received in town. This created a shortage of employees in the town, and the unobliging

111

merchants complained again. But this time it was to a deaf ear. During the war most food was rationed, especially meat, but the company went to the government and gained permission to obtain first grade meat, and plenty of it, for the working staff. Boy, we would get the biggest juicy steak that was available. But it wasn't too long before the public started to come over and eat at our place, and that ended it all.

Leaving Mojave after having ham and eggs, we had time to make Lancaster for the San Joaquin Daylight. As the train pulled out on the high rail leaving Mojave, the morning sun danced on the glistening rails in front of us as if it were saying, "come catch me." Of course, like the pot at the end of the rainbow, no one has ever been able to do it. The cab ahead mallet locomotive gave the engine crew a greater view of what was happening in front of them. Also, when going through tunnels with such a large steam locomotive, the heat and gasses, as well as the smoke, was kept to a minimum. Cab ahead malleys were used entirely on the mountain districts for the Southern Pacific. Stack ahead locomotives were used in the valleys or territories where there were no tunnels.

A conversation was going on between Vince and Jackson on the subject of the improvement and safety of steam locomotives. Especially when it came to engines blowing up, Vince had a line of talk that would convince a Rabbi to take up the Catholic religion and preach it in the synagogue. So convincing was he that the poor young brakeman would hardly look at the boiler head of the engine.

At the mile board of Lancaster, I reduced the trainline air six pounds for the initial set of the brakes. Then I told Vince that I was easing the throttle down and then recharging the train line air, hoping the train would ease down to walking pace by the time we arrived close to the siding switch so

Jackson could use his speed to line us in the siding. Everything was working perfectly, and I was surprising myself by seeing how well I could imitate the older, experienced engineers, until all at once the boiler belched forth a loud report like a small cannon, filling the cab with steam.

Jackson did not stop to use the ladder down to the ground, even though it was a good six feet. He just jumped and landed running for Lancaster Highway, a distance of perhaps one hundred yards. Boy! I thought to myself, "If only a football scout would have seen the speed of this man, he would have been drafted for their team."

On this section of the highway there were many cement culverts for drainage. The openings were rectangular, between eighteen inches and two feet high, depending on the terrain. It was a most amazing sight to watch Jackson dive head first into the first culvert he came upon, not worrying about snakes or the likes. Vince sure did a fine job of converting him about steam engines.

Both Vince and I knew what had happened. A flue let loose in the boiler was letting water and steam escape, putting the fire out. This was the end for this engine. Walking over to the culvert where Jackson had taken refuge, it finally occurred to me that his action was from the war days when he fought in the Pacific theater against the Japanese.

"Come out of there," I called to him. "It's all right, only a flue let go." By that time the Highway Patrol had driven up and wanted to know what the trouble was. After hearing my explanation, the patrolman went away laughing. Jackson was frightened almost to death. Pleading with him didn't convince him that it was all right to leave his sanctuary.

The conductor, catching a ride from the caboose in an automobile, came to find out what the trouble was. The lad being in the culvert didn't seem to bother him much.

"Number 51 is standing up at the depot for some time," he told me.

"We have first to get Jackson out of the culvert," I insisted, with some agitation.

"OK," he fired back at me, and like a sergeant he yelled at the lad: "It's all clear Jackson, get the hell out of there on the double." The stern voice did the job—out he came, dirty and a bit scratched up.

I admired the conductor for the way he handled the situation; he probably had experience in the war himself.

"Is the engine completely dead?" the conductor asked, not wasting any time.

"Yeah, it is. About the only thing left for us is to have 51 cut their engine off and try pulling us into the siding," I suggested.

"Looks like that's it," he said. "I'll let the dispatcher know what the trouble is and then I will have to walk up to the depot."

"Here comes the operator in his car, he'll take you back," I pointed to the telegrapher who was driving up. Jackson went along with them to help do the work.

After a short time the two locomotives on number 51 came down the main and coupled into our disabled engine. The Daylight always had a road engine and a helper out of Los Angeles.

They took several tries at starting our train after the brakes were released and eventually it began to move. The old 4449 would spin her wheels and then settle down but would keep the train on the move ever so slowly. It took almost twice the power to start a train as it did to keep it moving after starting.

Fifteen hours later, tired and dirty, we arrived home. All-new crews came out from Los Angeles with plenty of power to pull us in and we had to deadhead home on the same train.

But that was railroading and the pay was good.

The Van Nuys Incident

I spent the year of 1950 going to my property on the desert and working on the extra board. I finally learned how to avoid making so many deadheads out of town by bidding off the extra board to a lesser job like a switch engine on the division some place, and then bidding back on the same job that I had previously had. In that way I would go to the bottom of the deadhead board. It worked very well and some engineers that I knew scarcely ever made a deadhead working this scheme which was not according to Hoyle, but sometimes one must fight fire with fire.

"You are called for 10:00 p.m. on duty on the Van Nuys loco," the crew dispatcher informed me over the phone. "Merl Harper is your fireman."

"What's wrong with Beardon? Is he sick?" I asked.

"That's what he said."

"OK. I'll be there," I said, hanging up the phone.

It was an old saying around the railroad that Beardon was responsible for the booming population in San Fernando Valley. Very early in the morning except Sunday, when the job did not work, as he returned from Canoga park to Burbank Junction on the branch line going to Chatsworth, Beardon was whistle-crazy, as loud and as hard as he was able to blow it— it could be heard miles and miles away. It was said that he knew every rabbit and chicken crossing, as well as the road crossing, dirt or paved. So he never let up on the whistle and many people were roused from their sleep at about four-thirty in the morning. Because it was too early to get up and too late to go back to sleep, we figured that it accounted for the increasing baby population.

115

Arriving at the dispatcher office, I found out why Beardon had laid off. A diesel switcher was called for this job and not knowing anything about them he marked off. Many older engineers had the same thought, the consensus being, "They are just a flash in the pan! They won't last." How wrong they were.

I did not have an instructor ride with me because I had run the switcher before, but this was a road switcher with a nose protruding out in front and toilet inside. Can you imagine a toilet? Another innovation of modern science. Boy, we must be getting soft. On the steam engines we used the sand box and then shoveled it with the sand scoop into the fire-box, or if you were stopped you found a discreet place behind a tree or bush.

At the beginning I ran the diesel, showing Merl Harper how to operate it, telling him to make sure to use sand on the rails when stopping so as not to slide the wheels because the company had not run the weed control car out on this branch as of yet and the weeds were high, making the rails very slippery. Merl caught on very quickly about the running of the engine because diesels were easier to operate than a steam engine. I turned the running job over to him and watched him for awhile. He did an excellent job and he knew every spot to stop and switch on the branch, since he was Beardon's regular fireman

"How do you stand the old man?" I asked him.

"Oh, the old fart is harmless, if he would just leave the damn whistle alone. I usually do the work going out and then he blows the whistle all the way back," Merl told me.

The farms and ranches in San Fernando Valley were losing ground to houses and industry, but many still remained and the railroad did a very good business on the branch. Leaving Chatsworth after going around the wye with the engine, we

116

were running very late. This job was bulletined to start at four p.m.

I told Merl I could run the engine so he could get a little rest, and promised not to hang on the whistle for long. We had thirty cars and a caboose on the way back. We had to work for a couple more hours, after spotting some box cars and flat cars of dry wall material along the way back. It was nine-thirty in the morning, a very beautiful sunny day, when beauty suddenly turned to tragedy. On a right-hand sweeping turn in the track, overgrown with weeds and grass, a little child, no more than two and a half years of age was playing by the rail. The baby had been trying to climb over the rail on my side. I immediately put the train in emergency. Even as slowly as we were going—twenty miles per hour—the engine slid on the grassy rail like a skier on water, even though there was sand on the rail. We hit the little fellow. Even today I hear that thud and get the same sick feeling I had then. Hurting or killing someone stays with you all your life. It sort of engraves itself in the everyday pages of your life.

Stopping three cars after hitting the baby, I jumped up and left the engine, running back to where the child laid. I expected to find it mutilated but no, the good Lord had not found it necessary to take its life. The baby was unconscious but still breathing, as it lay beside the track on the grass with a cut on its little head where the front step had hit it. Picking it up and holding the little tyke in my arms, my eyes were swimming in pools of water. Why? I thought. Merl and the head brakeman had gotten there by then.

"Go to one of these houses and call for an ambulance and then try to find out who or where the parents are," I ordered.

It didn't take long for a crowd of people to assemble and then the mother came running and screaming.

"What have you done with my baby?" she cried.

"What was your baby doing out playing on the railroad track?" I asked, and about that time the ambulance and the police showed up.

I told my version of what happened, then I left and went back on the engine, letting the conductor take charge of the details.

That night, reading the newspaper, I found that the report was nothing close to what really happened. But the mother admitted that she was looking at the television, a new contraption that had taken a hold of the country, although radio stations were saying it would not last. Many people were not sold entirely on it as of yet. How wrong they were! The paper also stated the little baby had been playing in the streets a few days before and was almost hit by an auto, while the mother was mesmerized by the boob tube.

Finding out later that the baby was going to live, I was very relieved and slept for fifteen hours.

Things went fairly well for the rest of the year. I managed to have the foundation poured for the house and then laid the building blocks, making sure to watch where the electric outlets belonged and also making sure the bond beams block and steel were at the correct place. I insisted that one should be placed halfway up the wall in addition of the top one. It took seven months to finish laying the blocks between trips. A regular mason could probably have done it in three or four weeks, but none were around, so I did it as good as anyone, making it straight and level. I was proud of the job and what I had accomplished, not knowing very much about laying blocks to begin with.

It was March of 1950, and after making a trip to Bakersfield and tying up at ten-thirty in the morning, I stopped at the depot to purchase a magazine. A bunch of my friends were congregated in front of the superintendent's office.

"What is going on?" I asked.

"Well," one replied, sounding a little sour. "It's about time for Fresno to ask for engineers and we all are slated to go. We want to know what happened to the Home Rule. We all decided we're going to quit if we have to go this year. Most of us just got back on our feet financially from last year. What the hell are we working for?"

"Yeah, I can make more selling apples on the street than going to Fresno," Bob Powell chirped in. Many similar comments came from the crowd of fourteen men.

"By gad, Charlie, you started that Home Rule, why don't you go to talk to the man?" Kenny Osborne asked.

"OK," I said. "If it's all right with the rest, how about Hector or Trusty, maybe you, Bob Powell?" I was trying to evade the situation, but I knew it was my baby so I was elected to see the old man.

Just as I was about to open the door, out came Burt Mitchell. He was a medium built man, fast and wiry with a quick way of talking. He was also a good superintendent and would help anybody that he could.

"What's the trouble here?" He grinned, looking at the group. "You fellows calling a strike?"

"No, Mr. Mitchell," I blurted out, trying to gain confidence. "We're about to quit if we have to go to Fresno this year. The boys, including myself, can't make it anymore. We just get out of debt and then it's back to Fresno."

"What happened to your, what you call it?" he inquired.

"Home Rule."

"Yes, that's it. Doesn't it state in there that a terminal uses their engineers first?"

"It sure does," I said, "but nothing has been done about it."

"There hasn't?" Burt came back. "All of you stay right here, don't leave, I will be right back. I sent that to Frisco a year ago." Burt turned and went into his office.

A buzzing discussion started between us. "I suppose it will take another year now," Kenny Denson remarked.

"Well if it does, I'm leaving. I was looking for work when getting this job," Osborne remarked. There were many sighs and clearing of throats and standing on one foot and then the other in that long fifteen minute wait. But finally the door opened.

"All of you go back to work, you have your Home Rule as of today. Some nincompoop up in the city filed it away and about lost it." Burt smiled and turned to leave, as yells of success filled the air. There would be dancing in the streets that night.

Eventually the Home Rule was adopted over the whole system and used as a pattern on other railroads as well. I went home feeling much happier, thinking and feeling good about the small part I had played in bringing it together.

Mumps

Seniority climbed very fast that year, enabling me to hold a Bakersfield Pool freight run in the later part of the year. The house was not moving along as fast as I would have liked, but it was shaping up nicely. The pool run lasted a few months. Then I was bumped and went on the Santa Barbara pool run, where I was less likely to be bumped off the job because there were many engineers younger than me in terms of seniority. So I accomplished much more on the house the rest of that year.

I had a telephone installed in the old trailer that I was using while building the house, and I made arrangements with the crew dispatchers at Los Angeles to call me collect when getting first out on the pool. Then I immediately drove to the city, which took an hour. Many times I was on duty when I arrived and if not I went to bed until I was called.

The average trip to Santa Barbara was six hours and after my tour of duty, I would go directly to bed. Sometimes we doubled back to Los Angeles; then I would have to rest at home before going to the desert.

In the Spring of the following year the diesels were getting very popular on the mountain run to Bakersfield, although there were still a large number of steam locomotives left. Knowing that they were here to stay, I bid back on the mountain run, hoping to catch some of the diesels, and also took a course on diesel locomotives from the I.C.C. people. This helped me understand the mechanics better. Four engineers younger than myself were regular on the run, so my chances of getting bumped was lessening. Also the thirty-six hour or more layover at home gave me more time to finish the house.

Charoline, my middle daughter, came home one day from school not feeling very well. She had a sore throat and swelling around the neck. We found that she had the mumps, even though she had been given shots for them when she was three years old. But at least this meant that she got over it quite rapidly. However, not many days later I began feeling bad, with a sore throat and swelling around my jaws. I did not say anything to anybody. I thought that being strong and healthy from working on the house in the sun and clean air of the desert I could shake the thing in a couple of days

The next day the phone rang early in the morning. Before answering I was thinking about laying off sick. That would have been the correct thing to do.

"You are called for train number 51, the Daylight to Bakersfield and return on number 60 tomorrow. You are on duty 6:40 a.m." Never having had the pleasure of pulling the Daylight before, it would be hard not taking the call. So with a fever and feeling bad, I went to work. I had a very good fireman, Harold Hunter, a tall grinning and laughing fellow older than myself but younger in seniority. Harold bumped his way through life but he had his virtues. One time, after knowing him for some time and when he wasn't married. I fixed him up with a cute little redhead who lived next door to us in Los Angeles. Her husband had been killed in the Korean War, leaving her with a little girl that my oldest daughter would babysit sometimes.

Harold went dining and dancing with her, then took her home. Several days later I asked her how her date turned out.

"He was a gentleman, we had a nice time," she told me. "But he was too much of a gentleman. When getting home he walked me to my door and kissed me and I asked him in for a cup of coffee and you know what else! He said no. He was too old for me and that wouldn't be right. So here I was panting in my pants ready for bed and he left."

She was too hot to trot for me also, so that's why I stayed clear of her, and besides, it was too close to home.

Running the train as it wound its way up through Soledad Canyon, my thoughts were of Jockey Franey, a regular engineer on this job. A couple weeks before, when he was going into the same curve as we were approaching now, he coughed and lost the bottom plate of his false teeth out the window. He tried to grab them as they fell but to no avail. Jockey stopped the train immediately and walked back over halfway along the train to where he thought the false teeth should be. And he found them, too, picking them up undamaged. As he went back to his locomotive, the conductor, hanging out the vestibule door, asked him what he should put on the delay report.

"Tell them I stopped to find my china teeth that I coughed out the window of my engine," Jockey replied, a little perturbed. And that was just what the conductor put on his report. I have no idea how the *Bakersfield Californian* got wind of it but the headline in their paper read, ENGINEER STOPS PASSENGER TRAIN TO PICK UP FALSE TEETH. The incident also made the national news, through *Time* magazine.

Arriving at Bakersfield, and coming down to a stop in front of the depot was probably one of the biggest thrills of my life, even though I felt very sick. If I had gone to the doctor then instead of going back to Los Angeles the next morning, maybe things would not have been so hard on me. But no, the next morning found me climbing up the ladder on the smooth running 4294 mallet with my groin hurting. At Los Angeles, as I climbed down the ladder of the engine it felt like I had a basketball between my legs. I ended up in the hospital, asking the doctor what was wrong with me.

"You have the mumps and they have gone down on you a very acute case," he told me. "We'll transfer you to the contagious ward at the County Hospital."

For three weeks I lay there. It was like a dungeon in the dark ages: no windows, and cold cement floors in the basement that were swabbed with buckets of water and then switched with a dirty gray mop every night. And open ceilings where all the pipes, big and little, hung, supplying the much better part of the hospital upstairs. The only thing separating the beds was a folding cloth screen that was only used when the doctors came.

It was a wonder that each contagious person did not contact

the diseases from all the others. Maybe they did, because a great many dead were removed from there. The doctor on my case, a little fat fellow, was good but he couldn't resist inviting every doctor in the hospital to look at me and that irritated me. This went on until a woman doctor appeared on the scene to view the spectacle. I sat up in bed and said "no!" and after that it all stopped.

For a short while at the hospital it wasn't sure if I was going to come out a man or a eunuch. I was relieved when I realized that I was still a man.

The Red Letter Day

Neal Seeds was my fireman on our way to Bakersfield. We were called early in the morning and left the "A" yard at six in the morning with a steam locomotive cab ahead 4240. With a good start and a real good crew, I thought this was going to be a very good day. How wrong I was—it turned out to be a red letter day.

First the tower operator at Burbank put us up the coast main line by mistake and a coast train left the yards right behind us. By the time I stopped with my eighty empty cars at Burbank, we were half through the plant heading up the main line for Santa Barbara. Things came to a halt. We were not able to back up on account of the many crossings at the back of me at peak hour traffic, and also because of the coast train coming up behind us. To continue ahead I would have to send a flag out for protection to the next signal, which, being red, indicated that some train was either coming or going ahead of us. On a closer look, a headlight appeared in the distance, leaving Hewitt. Immediately the head brakeman went out flagging. Our train had at least four crossings blocked and the coast train behind us had many more. Without any phone close by, I had to send poor Neal walking back to the tower to inform the operator that when the flag was far enough out, and could stop the approaching train, I would pull up in the clear. From then on it would be up to the conductor to figure out what moves to make.

The approaching train happened to be the Lark, the most important passenger train the Southern Pacific owned, a businessman's train that ran between Los Angeles and San Francisco. I once had the opportunity to tour this train. I hadn't seen anything like it in the world. It had a beauty shop and barber shop, a cocktail lounge car second to none anywhere, and the dinning car was so plush it made the Waldorf Astoria look shabby. I was told by one of the porters that the company had their own call girls traveling on the train for the convenience of the passengers. Stopping the sacred cow as we had done would not go unnoticed. Actually this constituted a mainline meet, but I could not help it. Knowing that the Lark had stopped, I pulled the train up to the siding switch to ease some of the congestion at the crossing behind. I told the brakeman to get the tower man on the phone located nearby and let him know that the Lark would go down the pass track and out on the inbound main line to town.

As soon as the passenger train left the side tack and cleared the tower, the coast train came up the pass track and went on to Santa Barbara. Then my head brakeman climbed up the ladder of the malley, telling me that a switch engine was coming out from Taylor yard to pull us back so we could continue on to Bakersfield.

The road foreman and a trainmaster drove up in a company car.

"Oh, here's where we catch it!" the head brakeman warned as I put more water into the boiler. The two officials came up the ladder to the engine. I got that awful feeling in my stomach. Who was going to get the axe now? Me or the tower man?

"Well what the hell is your story? Didn't you see that you were lined up the Coast?" Jim Canty inquired.

"Yes," I said looking at him and trying to keep my composure. "But my speed was thirty-five miles per hour. The approach signal was green and the signal was green for the coast, so by the time I set the air to stop, the train is halfway through the plant. What else was I to do?" (The signal approaches at Burbank Junction are much improved today.) After listening to my interpretation of what happened the two officials looked at each other with searching eyes. I believe they had some idea they could trip me into a situation where they could place the blame on me.

"We're trying to cover this thing up," Jim Canty finally admitted. "The tower man has only a few months to go for his pension."

"I figured you guys were trying to pin this on me," I grinned, as Neal Seeds opened the door, returning from his long walk up the train.

"Well, hell, what's thirty demerits? You can work them off in a year." Jim made a mistake, not realizing that I had a witness, Neal. But I thought, "if it saves a man his job, what the hell!"

"OK," I replied. "If that is all I'll get, do it that way but you and the rest of us will know why I'm doing it." After this, they left the engine.

"What was that all about?" Neal asked.

"Boy, what a mess things are in back there," he said after I explained. "Traffic is tied up for miles and miles. I guess you know that we have to wait until a switch engine arrives to pull

126

us back over the crossings?" I nodded my head.

The coast train was leaving for Hewitt to use the siding, letting the coast Daylight number 99 that was coming up the siding behind it at Burbank go by. Of all the firemen, it had to be Vince Cippolla, firing on 99 for Ennis Brown, who pulled alongside of us and stopped waiting for the signal to clear (turn green).

"Are you lost or can't you find the right rail to run on? Maybe you like the coast better?" Cippolla joked. I was not in the mood for bantering but I smiled anyway so as to make his day. The signal went yellow and Ennis pulled out for Santa Barbara.

One hour later we were on our way to Bakersfield, or as far as sixteen hours would let us get, given that six hours had already elapsed. We arrived at Saugus and took on water and orders, then started to pull out slowly to pick up the brakemen who were inspecting the train's running gear. Saugus had an eastbound and a westbound siding. The westbound siding was controlled by the operator at Saugus and the eastbound was manually operated. The sidings were located at two different places, one at the west end of the Saugus district and the other one at the east end. At the end of the westward siding stood the depot and train order office; from then on the track curved to the right, going to Vincent, and also started its ascent. After confirming that the crew was all aboard, I opened up throttle a few notches and then, having a green signal at the west end around the curve, opened the throttle wide.

But we hadn't traveled a distance of thirty cars when the train line went into emergency! The conductor, Red Griffen, pulled the air, opening the conductor valve in the caboose and so stopping the train. I grabbed the train orders and feverishly thumbed through them. The very first one we had received said that we had to meet the Extra east 4249 at Saugus, and we were to hold the mainline. With all the delay, I had overlooked the order entirely. If there had been no delay, the meeting with this train would have been up the line somewhere, but as it was I had a bona fide mainline meet. In the early days it was known as a "cornfield meet," but it also made the perpetrator liable to punishment by dismissal.

Recharging the train line with air, I took a little time, then whistled three blasts on the steam whistle, letting the train roll back behind the signal. Neal and the head brakeman were both upset, knowing that they were involved in this violation also. The signal showed green as we backed behind it, noting that the 4249 was still not on the circuit. But the conductor was standing with his legs spread out, looking at us with a big wide grin on his round, baby red face. Red Griffen looked much younger than all the rest of us, although he was the oldest man on the crew and a darn good conductor.

"Don't say a word," he said, grinning as he ascended the ladder. "This guy will not be here for another ten minutes. And that wait at Russ is going to hurt us a bit anyway. If I know Hank Oswald, he'll take all the time he is given." Hank was the conductor on the work train that we had orders on.

We felt better knowing that we weren't going to get fired. Twenty minutes later we were on our way. At Ravenna we took on water, with Hank and his train in the siding. Our tour of duty ended at Mojave because of all the delays.

It was there that we received the bad news. John Oswald, Hank Oswald's brother, had been killed on a curve west of Russ. It had happened after we met him and his crew at Ravenna. The work train went out on the mainline and set a flat car of heavy machinery on the house track adjacent to the mainline. John instructed the other brakemen to put the engine back on the train while he secured the flat car with its hand brake, which was necessary because of the descending grade. The air on the car of machinery had been bled out of the brake system so it could be kicked up into the house track. John rode the flat and tried to tie the hand brake, but it didn't hold. He tried once more and it still didn't hold. and by this time it was rolling through the mainline switch and on down the hill. Hank and his crew members called for him to jump, but John continued to try in vain to get the brake to take hold. John Oswald met his death when the car of machinery left the rail. He had been trying to save the company money.

More and More Diesel

The diesels were coming in larger numbers. The young liked them but the old heads hated them: they were a flash in the pan, they would not last, nothing could replace steam, and so on, was their cry. But it was all in vain. They knew and we knew that diesels were here to stay. The railroads were clamoring for diesels throughout the United States. The company held classes because diesels were arriving faster then the officials could qualify the employees. I had been previous qualified so they did call me several times to ride with another engineer. But I told the dispatchers not to call me for the instruction job anymore so that ended that. It took over two years for all the engineers to become qualified.

The first diesel locomotives, used primarily for road service, were covered wagons (as we called them), because the engine and cab were enclosed, so that when an employee walked back along these engines, he was not subject to the wind and rain or smoke and gases from the engine. Even their first appearance was a masterpiece, but comparing them with today's engines is like comparing a model "T" Ford and a

Lincoln.

It has been many years since I ran one of the first covered wagon diesels, but I can recollect how they were. I was informed at the time that a diesel motor was good for one million miles before it would need any care or overhaul. The fireman's job required him to walk through the units and on each one there was a large oil filter with a crank affair that cleaned the oil filters that had to be periodically turned. Also he checked the load-meters, making sure that all units were doing their maximum power. In the electric cabinet compartment behind the cab of the engine, there was a conglomerate of heavy wiring and big air electric relay valves. The young engineers coming up today would surely laugh at the crudeness of it, but like anything else, a baby has to be born.

The operation procedures of a diesel are very different to those for a steam engine—the two are as foreign to each other as the United States is to Russia. An engineer had to develop a whole new technique in handling a train.

With steam, the practice was to keep a train stretched out to avoid slack action when stopping, because of the six inches of slack between each car. The maintaining valve was not built into the brake valve to take care of the air leakage throughout the train, but each engineer had other ways and means of maintaining the air in the train line. Even if it was contrary to the rules of the company, we did very well in our own way.

Now the diesel was a different dimension. The rules we learned still form the basics of today's operations. I remember learning to bunch the train and going into dynamic braking, which was done by first using the engine brakes gently until most of the train was bunched, then using the electric dynamic brake, a handle on the control stand for that purpose, which reversed the current of the electric motors on each axle, making them a dynamo. The more excitation the engineer gave them by the lever, the more holding power was achieved, and in conjunction with the air brakes a heavy train could be brought down any grade.

On the first covered wagons, nothing was automatic. The engineer had to keep a vigilant eye on a gauge in front of him telling him when to make a transition manually, which was accomplished by using the transition lever and throttle at practically the same time. Many of the trains were torn apart by this practice, although it wasn't long before automatic transition became standard.

In retrospect, the coming of the diesel meant that working conditions were so much better than with steam locomotives. The skill that steam required from an engineer is gone, as well as the lonely wail of the far off steam whistle that once could be heard across the land. We have lost much of our heritage, but that is part of progress.

EPITAPH OF A STEAM ENGINE

HERE I SIT WITH GHOSTS OF THE PAST AROUND ME WAITING TO BE DISMANTLED. I HAVE DONE MY JOB WELL AND PULLED WITH EVERY OUNCE OF STRENGTH I HAD UP MANY MOUNTAINS, ACROSS THE PRAIRIE AND THROUGH THE DESERT SANDS. NOW I WILL BE GONE LIKE THE GHOSTLY WAIL OF MY WHISTLE ACROSS THE LAND.

* * *

One early morning, the phone rang, calling me to work.
"What train did you say?" I asked.
"You getting a duck-y," the caller replied.

"A what?"

"You know! A duck-y, a lu-lu."

"Wait a minute," I said with a little dignity. "I am on the pool freight board, not the extra board."

"We know that, Charlie." Frank Dwyer came on the phone. "But the extra board is depleted and besides this is a diesel passenger train going out there, and you would have to be an instructor even if we had an extra board man."

"OK, but who in the hell was that on the phone before?" I asked.

"Oh that's a young fellow breaking in, just out of school," Frank told me.

"I guess I'll have to learn the new kind of lingo they use now days," I said, and Frank laughed. "What time on duty, Frank?"

"You're on duty at five-thirty this morning and your train is at the top end of the A yard."

I was figuring on laying off and taking the family up to the desert because the kids were out of school for the summer. But they would have to wait until I returned, which would only be until tomorrow.

The journey to Saugus, where we arrived a little after seven in the morning with seven cars and two diesel units was quick and easy. The operator put our train in the westward siding. We pulled up within a hundred feet of the crossing west of the depot, stopped and told the fireman to tie the units down and isolate each unit. Then we could go over to the Saugus Cafe and have coffee. As we were walking across the street. we saw the motion pictures crews arriving by the numbers. A high tower had been erected near the post office. I assumed it was for the cameramen to take shots from high up. As we sat at the counter and ordered coffee, the topic of conversation was the movies that were going to be made today. It was something about killing the President.

"And guess who is playing in it?" the little waitress asked.

"I have no idea," I replied. "Who?"

"Frank Sinatra," she beamed.

"So?" I shrugged my shoulders and drank my coffee and left, with the fireman still chatting with the waitress. As I climbed on the engine I noticed some autos parked in a space between the depot and the crossing. I didn't pay much attention at first, sitting in my seat on the locomotive. Then I happened to look down at one of the autos and I saw two people just below me doing a little lovemaking. Boy! this time of the morning! That guy must be quite a stud. I was hardly able to believe what I was witnessing. Just then my fireman came through the door from the engine room after checking things over.

"There sure is a lot of activity going on cross the street," he informed me. "They have cameras up on that tower they built and on the roof of the restaurant and some along the street." I nodded my head—my poor fireman didn't know how much activity was really taking place.

"Where is Sinatra?" Someone was calling on a megaphone. "We got to make a take, find Sinatra, somebody." The megaphone and its mouthpiece trailed off in the distance.

Looking down at the increasing activity below me, I saw that the car was vibrating and shaking with an undulating motion. Glancing at my fireman I was about to mention what was taking place below us, but then decided to keep it to myself. It would be between the stud down there and me. The quavering of the auto slowed down and the young stud twisted around with a satisfied grin on his face, revealing two of the most radiant blue eyes I ever looked upon.

After making several long runs through Saugus and getting

133

orders to run to Los Angeles, we were finished for the day. I was glad; I was tired of movie trains.

The House

After returning from the movie train I went with my family to the house on the desert. I had three weeks vacation coming and was able to split the weeks up. My plan was to take one week now and two weeks later, which would help me with the completion of the house. I had the roof on and shingled. I was in the process of putting bats on the twelve inch redwood boards on the bedrooms above the garage, so if I could get that finished, and the windows in their frames, this trip would be a good boost towards finishing the house. Perhaps I could get the kids to clean and rake up some of the junk around. Margie was cleaning out the trailer, which was plenty dirty.

I had built a scaffold up to the second floor to work on the bats and for installing the windows. So the first thing I started to work on was the bats on the second floor. Two of the kids cleaned and raked while Charoline helped me on the scaffold. It seemed that she always took the place of a son that I never had, being at my side all the time. Work progressed very well until Charoline and I were standing in the center of the scaffold, putting up the last bat. With a creak and a groan, the scaffolding broke and both of us fell with it. I grabbed Charoline and tried to protect her as much as possible by letting her fall on me. After we hit the ground I was sitting on my rump with one leg straight out, which Charoline was using for a bench, while the other leg was tangled up somewhere else. It must have been a comical sight because Charoline stood up laughing, and unhurt. I was grateful for that, but my leg hurt, along with other bruises and some strawberries. When I stood up it took awhile before the landscape stopped

134

tilting. But the tongue-lashing from Margie was worse then the fall.

After hobbling around for the rest of the week putting in the windows and then planning the kitchen cabinets, I was ready to return to my job.

Earthquake

I was at home and in bed when it all happened that July morning, the 21st, 1952, at eight minutes to four in the morning. My bed shook as if someone was trying to wake me and my little house creaked when the earthquake hit Tehachapi and was also felt in Los Angeles. I thought to myself, 'someplace must have been hit hard,' as I turned over in bed and went back to sleep, dismissing the quake entirely until two hours later, when I was awakened by the blasted phone. It was Dwyer calling me for a work train.

"A work train?" I stammered. "I'm a pool man."

"We know that but you are the first out on the pool and no extra men," he informed me. "Maybe you haven't heard. We've had an earthquake, all of Tehachapi is destroyed and the mountain is in very bad condition. You're going to get a trainload of ballast for Mojave. I guess you better be prepared to stay a few days."

As I had breakfast I listened to the radio account of the quake. Tehachapi, Bakersfield and Arvin had all been all hit hard. There was no report on road conditions or of any damage to the railroad, but when I got to the crew dispatcher's office, rumors were flying fast and thick. Coleman Beard stood waiting for me as I arrived.

"Can't see why you couldn't have gotten us a diesel," he jokingly complained, "instead of this old malley the 4218."

"I think you're the unlucky bastard; I always get a diesel

with the other fireman." I laughed, being glad to have Coleman for a fireman, for he was one of the best in the pool.

After picking up the train crew and caboose at the top end of the "A" yard and leaving for Rosco, later known as Sun Valley, we were to pick up twenty-two gondolas of ballast from the rock plant. At Burbank Junction we received an order: On account of the earthquake, you will run at restricted speed and be preceded by a motor car, looking out for any obstruction that might hinder safe passage.

The ballast was ready at the rock plant and we were informed that the track to Saugus was clear. We made our way through San Fernando and on up to the Newhall tunnel, which was one and a half miles long, with the crest of the grade two thirds of the way inside the tunnel from the San Fernando side. Inside, the tunnel was lit up by a string of electric lights hanging on the walls. After entering the portal on the San Fernando side there was a slight curve, making a blind spot for a hundred feet or so. Then it straightened out, making it possible to see a great distance ahead.

Entering the east portal, we arrived at the point where I could see straight track. A motor car sat on the rail with a crew of track workers working in the tunnel just beyond it. When they saw and heard me coming the track workers scampered everywhere. I used the emergency on the train but it was too late to save the motor car. We hit it, dividing it up into many more pieces that it had originally started out as. Luckily, no one was hurt, but someone was crossed up on their instructions. The foreman asked me not to make any delay or accident report; he would cover it up so no one in his group would be fired, and I agreed to that.

At Saugus we received a message that the track had been inspected to the top of the hill at Vincent and everything seemed to be in good condition. So so we left for the top of the hill and all the way to Mojave.

Waiting for word from the roadmaster that it was safe to proceed up the mountain to Tehachapi, we had something to eat at White's Cafe. Engineer Mobely was married to the woman who owned the place so many of us ate there, even though we had been shabbily treated during the war. Engineer Mobely said that he was not in on that escapade of not wanting the railroad employees' business.

I had a cup of steaming hot coffee to my lips when it struck again. A jolt and then came a wave-like motion, making the coffee in my cup come alive, spilling on me and the counter. Customers stood up wide-eyed, looking at each other for some kind of assurance.

"Sit down folks, it's only an aftershock," the brave waitress called out loudly, trying to calm the situation. The patrons reluctantly sat down but with nervous feelings. Coleman and I left for our train across the highway, not saying much about the incident.

Shortly after the tremor, the conductor climbed on the malley and gave orders to me.

"At Tehachapi, we will put all but four cars of ballast in the lime track and then the roadmaster will let us know where he wants them dumped," he informed me.

"Is everyone ready to depart?" I asked.

"Yeah, but don't exceed twenty miles per hour, it's in the orders." I nodded my head. Pulling up to the top end of Mojave yard, the herder came out from his shanty and waved a high ball, indicating the switches were lined and we could continue up the hill.

The town of Tehachapi lay in shambles. Several buildings were standing with their fronts lying in the streets, looking ready to crumble. So far, damage to the railroad tracks was not bad, but down the mountain all the way to Bakersfield the damage was astronomical. All sixteen tunnels had been damaged to a greater or lesser extent. Some were caved in, others were twisted out of shape. The water tanks at Caliente and Woodford had all been demolished. The entire track system had to be repaired. Tunnel five was so damaged that a shoe-fly would have to be cut around a mountain and a temporary track put in until the tunnel could be repaired.

Work for the rest of the day was slow and confusing because no organization could be put into effect on account of all the conflicting reports. That night, before going back to Mojave, I asked the trainmaster where we would stay. There were so many homeless people in Tehachapi, I thought they would probably take up all the extra rooms. He assured me that they had reserved a room for all of us.

Tying up at Mojave and after making out the necessary reports, Coleman and I went across the tracks to the train-master's office to see if he had found a room for us.

"Yeah, we got you a room, you'll have to share it, but it has two beds," he informed us.

"What are we, some stepchild?" I came back. "I understand the train crew each have a room to themselves."

"Well, that's all I could do. You two know each other and they don't so I thought it would be better this way."

"OK. I guess I can stand Coleman snoring."

"I don't think I snore because I never heard myself," Coleman grinned.

What a room it was! Something out of the middle ages. It was one of the first two-story buildings ever put up in Mojave. It was a wonder that it had stood up in the quake. We had a large room located on the second floor, with a well worn tongue and grooved pine floor, and an ancient dresser with two full sized iron beds, each having a lumpy mattress. On the dresser sat a large white china bowl and a china pitcher full of water. I started to look under the bed for a pot.

"Charlie," Coleman said, reading my mind. "You go down the stairs and out in the back for that."

"Boy, they're sure modern," I joked, putting my suitcase down on one of the squeaky beds. The one good thing about it was that the two large open windows, reaching almost to the floor, faced west and so caught the evening breeze, cooling the hot room. The hotel—I have long forgotten its name—has long been torn down. In the prewar days the place was a haven for whores and miners.

If you were a drinking man, there were many bars in Mojave, and girls to take your money. But if you did not drink it was quite dull, and Coleman and I were in for a dull evening. After we had eaten at Whites, we took a walking tour of the town. We came upon a hardware store where a small crowd had gathered, watching a television set in the window with a speaker outside. Many stores did this at that time. Television was very high in price in its infancy, and this put it out of the reach of many people's pocketbooks. People would gather and bring folding chairs and popcorn and the likes.

Standing until my feet hurt, I told Coleman it was past my bedtime and that I was going to the 'flea bag' to retire. He told me that he would be along directly. I did not hear him when he came in the room to bed that night, but I remember the dream I had. The boat I was rowing started to bounce around and was scraping on some sharp rocks on the bottom of the ocean floor. And then it seemed like someone was driving a motorcycle on top of the waves, which were getting real rough. The figure on the motorcycle was yelling, "Jump, jump!" I tried to jump but the sea was too choppy for standing up in the boat. Again the motorcycle went by and the guy that was riding it happened to be Coleman. Just about that time the boat hit a tree! In the middle of the Pacific Ocean?

As I woke up my bed hit the far wall and was making its way towards one of the open windows.

"Get up, get up," Coleman was yelling. I rolled off the bed before it got half out the window, then I looked around to see what was happening. We were having one hell of an aftershock and it lasted for a long while.

"Let's get dressed and get the hell out of here," I yelled to Coleman, thinking the building was going to go. It didn't take much persuasion on my part—he already had his shoes on before anything else. We raced down the stairs four steps at a time. Reaching the street, well away from the buildings, we breathed a resounding sign of relief. All of the townspeople were awake by then and were buzzing around like ants. The best place for safety, I figured, would be the wooden depot. No matter how it might twist or turn or gnash and grind, it would stay up. But when we arrived at the waiting room, it was already full of people. Some were sleeping on the benches and others were milling around holding crying kids. This was no place for us, we decided. The next best place would be the round-house. Not wanting to stand around the rest of the night we climbed on our engine, chasing the engine watchman out, and sat there until we fell asleep.

Morning came too soon. I opened one eye and looked about. My head felt like a bowling ball hitting the bowling pins. The taste in my mouth was atrocious and my beard stubbled and black. I was just feeling grimy all over.

Coleman was still sleeping on his seat box with his head tilted back, resting on the backrest. Having his mouth wide open was an invitation for several flies to enter it. But about the time one had its nerve up to do so, Coleman would snort or spudder and the poor fly would flutter off only to come back to try again. I thought about waking him but decided against it. So I let him sleep with the flies testing each other again, as I wondered which one would zoom in first?

I climbed off the engine and went to the old round-house office, but could find no one there. I tried the old bunk-house, but it had been padlocked for quite sometime. I had hoped that we could take a shower and shave somewhere but so far no luck. Everything was deserted; there was only the stirring of the wind, waiting to claim back the land for the desert which it finally did—today there is nothing there except a few tracks and sage brush. Going back to the engine, I found Coleman awake and spitting and sputtering—the flies must all have decided to zoom in at once. We looked at each other and began to laugh. What a frightful mess we must have looked to each other.

"What we going to do, boss?" he asked me.

"I don't really know, but the first thing for sure, I'm going to find some place that we can wash and shave, even if we have to break in a door or lock."

"I'm with you," Coleman replied.

We found what we were looking for at the other end of the round-house, which had been a locker room for the mechanics. The door was already open. A hot shower and a shave made us presentable again. Next we had breakfast; the quake didn't stop the restaurant from opening. Some dishes and glasses had been broken but business continued as usual. Having eaten a good breakfast, Coleman and I sat sipping our coffee when the call boy found us.

"It seems that Bakersfield wants the work train service," he

141

began. "So you fellows will have to deadhead home."

"On what?" I inquired.

"I don't know, you'll have to find that out at the yard office."

"OK," I replied. "Tell them we will be there as soon as we've finished our coffee." Later we went home by carry-all, ending that escapade.

So devastated was the railroad between Bakersfield and Tehachapi no one would even predict how long it would be before trains could operate again over that territory. Actually it was three weeks and two days, from the start of repair work to the running of the first train on this stretch of territory. It cost the Southern Pacific several million dollars, but D. J. Russell had a way of squeezing it out of the railroad to pay for this emergency without hurting the stockholders.

While the work on the hill was being done, all rail traffic was diverted up the coastline. This didn't bother me because the rest of my vacation was scheduled at this time, so I scooted off to the desert house.

Unbelievable Truth

Three weeks went by fast as I worked on the house. I was on the painting stage, and hating every brush stroke. Going back to work was a relief. The road to Bakersfield had just opened and the first train I caught was #55, an M. M. & N. special, as we called it (Mail, Milk, and Nuts). It was a good train, consisting of two passenger cars and nine baggage cars, designed for old men who had the patience of Job. All that was required was to jog along at a leisurely pace, stop, and start again, at any whistle post or station, even where there wasn't any, and it took all night. And worst of all we had a cab ahead malley steam engine for power.

Before leaving the Los Angeles Union Passenger Station I talked to Slim Watson, the train conductor, who happened to be a very good friend of mine. I said jokingly, "Slim, if you see any forlorn, good-looking women back there bring one up, I need the company. Looking at those firemen all night, doesn't turn me on."

"I'll sure do that, Charlie," he said and grinned.

It was about time to leave so I climbed up on the malley 4207 and waited for a high ball from Slim Watson. I don't recall the fireman's name because he worked out of Bakersfield on this job, but I do remember that he was darn good and also a promoted engineer.

We stopped at every place imaginable along the road, and even some places not imaginable. If a section man wanted off at a certain place all he had to do was tell Slim and he would pull the whistle cord, notifying me to look back, and Slim would give me a hand signal with an electric lantern. This train carried a lot of mail. At various points along the way there were large yellow wooden boxes with heavy, slanted medal lids which had cables and counterbalances attached to them so the mail attendant could raise the lid to put canvas bags of mail into the box.

"Who in the hell gets this mail? I don't see any town around," I said to my fireman.

"Oh, there's a place out in the boondocks that you can't see; someone will come get the mail. We also pick up mail from them," he explained.

At some places where the train didn't stop, but where a station such as a train order office or such was located, the mail bags were strung between two steel arms that extended from a post. The mail attendant would reach from the speeding car with an iron contraption attached to the side of the mail car and snag the mail bag. One time I had a big brute of a fireman named E. Taske. Thinking that the mail bag was a train order hoop, he put his arm out, tried to grab the bag and almost broke his big arm.

There would often be a long wait at Saugus because it was the hub for many little towns and settlements, such as Newhall, where Bill Hart, the old cowboy actor, had his large ranch. Also, the freight shed had merchandise to load and unload: small farm equipment, refrigerators and the like. My pipe felt warm in my hand in the midst of the cold of the night, as I looked back at the rush of people hurriedly going about their duties. My eyes were watering from brisk night air that always seemed to prevail around Saugus no matter how warm the day might be. This type of climate was good for farming all through the Santa Clara Valley. But how that farm land would be destroyed within the following forty years or more, when all the land was taken over by the subdividers bringing in scores of people. The farmer is like the American Indians; he is shoved back and back and his land taken away until there will be no more good land to till. Then what?

Slim was emerging from the group bringing someone with him. In the darkness and against the lights of the depot I could not see who it was but as they came closer, I was sure that it was a woman. I was about to drop my pipe because I could not believe Slim had taken my earlier comment seriously. I told the fireman to watch the running time at the stations and stay on his side of the cab. On the cab ahead steam locomotives the fireman and engineer could not see each other unless one or the other stood up; there was so much equipment between them.

"I have someone who wants to ride the engine to Palmdale with you, Charlie," Slim called up from the ground.

144

"Fine, send her up," I said, and up she came, using Slim's gloves on the ladder. Slim introduced her to me as Jackie Welch. I stood up and invited her to sit down in my seat. She had brown wavy hair with a very pleasant cute face and a smile that would win anyone over. She was small in stature and shapely.

Boy, this was an entirely new experience for me. It was an engineer's hopeless dream to have at one time in his career a woman sitting on his lap while he was running a train. But that was an impossible dream. I had only been kidding with Slim, but now he had called my hand and I had to see it through. I looked at her. She must have been thirty years of age. She was well dressed, wearing slacks, a beautiful blouse, and a jacket. The excitement showed in her dancing eyes. It was tremendous. I guessed that very few women had ever experienced something like this. Her eyes were sparkling brighter than jewels as I took her soft hand, sat down on my seat and invited her to sit on my lap while I ran the engine. Jackie did not seem to mind, and anyway, there was no other place to put her except on the empty brakeman's seat over by the fireman, and I was damn sure wasn't going to let that happen.

After leaving Saugus I explained all the features of the engine to Jackie and let her blow the horn. On the malleys we had an air horn for road crossing and steam whistles for communication to crews. After a while I put my arm around her, just to support her back. She looked at me and smiled.

"You know," she whispered softly into my ear, "I thought all engineers were old but you're hardly not much older than me."

I smiled and looked at my watch then pulled her closer to me. The smell of her cologne, its fragrance, sent me spinning into orbit. Not being able to stand it anymore, I softly kissed her luscious lips, and she kissed me in return. For one brief moment, there was no train, no engine, just her and I together, spinning through the night air like ballet dancers, until reality returned. The blood racing through my body was like a geyser, uncontrollable, and Jackie had the same feeling. I knew it by her heavy breathing.

"You know we have a stop at Acton?" The voice came from my fireman. It was like an ice cold shower.

"Yeah, I know," I replied, hardly able to talk. Acton was only a short distance and it was only one of those yellow boxes. I used the train air quite heavily but stopped exactly on the spot. I could not have done that again in a million tries.

The next stop would be Vincent at the top of the hill, then it would be down to Palmdale, where Jackie would leave me. On the way to Vincent, I asked if I might see her again. We kissed again with the same intensity as before, and my thoughts spun through my head—this is not real, running a passenger train and making love. I told myself I must be dreaming.

"No," she whispered in my ear. "I have commitments and I'm sure you have. No one like you would be running around loose." I nodded my head to that. I did have commitments.

Leaving her at Palmdale was a very hard thing to do, for her and for me. We waved goodbye as she walked away into the darkness. To me she was a like a lightning bug; she lit up my life for an instant and then was gone.

"Did you make out?" my fireman asked on the way to Lancaster. His inquisitiveness could not be restrained any more. Making out was a new expression for having sex. That disgusted me—a perfectly beautiful experience being tarnished by that kind of talk. It made me feel like puking up, but I realized that it was only natural for him to ask a question like that.

"No." I tried to find words but there weren't any. "You come over here and run this train for a while." I knew that he was a promoted engineer and thought that a little diversion of work might stop his inquisitive mind and give me time to think.

The return trip home on train #56 the next night—the same kind of train that I ran to Bakersfield only with a different fireman—was uneventful. But I was still troubled by the events of the previous trip. My fireman, nicknamed Blackstack, a diamond in the rough, must have thought, 'where in the hell did this moody bastard come from?'

The troubles of my married life seemed to get more and more perplexing as time went on. Where in the world, and how, did I fail myself and those around me? I had tried so hard to hold things together by building a house, hoping that would bring Margie and I together. But bit by bit it was breaking up. It seemed like all that held us together was a rope of sand. I did not blame Margie any more than I blamed myself. Margie was a good woman and in her way she tried also. But the years were slipping away and the longer we went on, the more agitated the situation became. I tried to avoid situations like the one on the last trip to Bakersfield, but only being a mortal man, with that built-in, God-given, beautiful, wonderful, and cursed urge that all men have in their souls, what else could I do?

Getting off duty and hurrying to my house in the desert, I knew then why I had built it. It was a covenant not only to keep my family together but also for myself. Part of me was there and always would be. When I wanted to clear my mind and soul, I would sit and address the emptiness of the house, which was then nearing completion. Some people might think that I was daft in the head, but actually I was having communion with the blessed spirits around me and the unseen spirit of what I had created. My house was as much to me as an artist's painting was to him. Sitting on a box in the living room that night, I addressed the spirit that watched over my masterpiece.

"I have won; you are built. You have the strength and fortitude and will stand forever." My voice boomed throughout the house. "Nothing shall knock you down nor shall you grow old like us mortals." I gazed at my achievement and was pleased. Outside, the wind was softly murmuring to itself, as tears of compassion swelled within me for all the years of hard work. Almost every man has a dream to build his own house exactly the way he wants it. The wind grew stronger until it was moaning, and a voice came out of the wind into the house: "I shall stand long after you are gone, but your spirit shall be in the shadows of the thoughts of anyone who shall enter hereafter." I knew then that I had a covenant with my house. There are those who would believe that I was a psycho, but this was real. Many strange things happened in my career on the railroad and this was no different.

As I traveled back to Los Angeles the weather was closing in for a good rain. But I felt much better. Sometimes it is best to sweep the cobwebs from the mind; otherwise you can't see the forest for the trees. When I arrived home, a call was already there. Another passenger train, #59, and coming back on the Daylight #52. This was a premium job. I put on heavier clothing on account of the change of weather, remembering how cold it turned coming over the mountain. At Los Angeles the weather could be mild, but up on the desert and mountains, blizzard conditions could set in.

J. A. Baker, a very fine fireman, was to work with me that night. The biggest surprise came when the power was released to us: a four unit diesel, and with the new radios installed in them. But usually they did not work.

"However," I told Baker, "we have a windshield wiper and a warm heater." Baker grinned, knowing he was going to have it easy that night.

By the time we arrived at Vincent, the wind was blowing so hard it made the snow fly in a horizontal direction and we were headed into it. The visibility, with headlights glaring against the snow, was no more than two hundred feet.

"How deep would you say the snow is, John?"

"I would say seven to eight inches," Baker replied.

"I guess you're right because its just over the top of the rail, but if it continues, there will be a foot or more by morning."

I was thinking about my house only twelve miles away from Vincent, and wondering if by chance I had left a window open? By this time we were going through Palmdale.

The snowstorm had increased its velocity but the wind had stopped blowing by the time we went by the mileboard for Lancaster. Now visibility was only seventy-five feet, slowing the train down to a walk. As we neared the station Lancaster I was peering for the signal that was not too far from the depot. It would give me a landmark of where we were. With the cab heaters on full it was not any too warm.

"John, is that valve to the heaters on full? It's not any too warm in here."

"It's on full but there's subzero weather out there," he reminded me as the signal came in view. It was a bullet light type signal and the snow had stuck on the lenses. But I recognized a yellow cast showing beneath the snow: the signal showed yellow. What a night for a freight train to be heading the side track! Drifting slowly down to the depot I tried to get the operator on the radio. Finally he answered.

"This is the operator Lancaster. Go ahead train #59."

"This is the engineer on #59. We came in on a yellow signal. Have you any freight trains on your circuit coming here to meet us?"

"No, I sure don't," he responded, "Maybe the weather has fouled the signals up."

"Let the dispatcher know that the signals are covered up with snow," I told him. "Maybe if we can't see them, we'll have to stop and climb the masts to uncover the snow to see their indication."

As we made the station stop, the conductor pulled the whistle cord. Looking back, it was impossible to even see the end of the locomotive.

"Baker, try and find something to scrape the snow off the signals with."

"I already found something," he replied showing me a small piece of tin. That's the sign of a good fireman—when he is ahead of you in thinking.

The snow started to build up on the windshield as we left the station Lancaster. We proceeded with the utmost caution and finally arrived at the signal. Not being able to identify the color, we stopped.

"Well John, here is your chance to try out that tin," I told him, and he climbed the mast. The signal was showing red, we discovered. After John returned he was just about frozen.

"I'll clean the next signal," I assured him, whistling out a flag because this was a block signal territory and rule #99 had to be applied. I opened up the crank down window; the sub-zero wind and snow streaked across the inside of the cab, making me close the window immediately.

I looked out the side window and saw the poor head brakeman in his passenger uniform, wearing a light jacket and no boots, sloshing through the snow.

150

"Wait, take my coat," I yelled to him. Mine was much warmer than his. Accepting the coat, the brakeman walked on. When he got to the signal, someone stepped out from behind it. The brakeman must have been frightened, because he knocked the man down with a blow to the jaw. After the fallen man got up there was quite an altercation between the two of them. Finally the unknown man took a key out of his pocket and unlocked the box at the bottom of the mast; the signal went green. He was a young trainmaster who was new on our division. Climbing down the ladder with fury building up inside of me, not needing a coat, I ran to the signal.

"You saw what he did, he hit me!" the trainmaster shouted.

"Not until you hit him first." I was thinking fast to protect the brakeman. "And it's too bad it wasn't me—you would still be laying down in the snow. You ought to be real proud of yourself pulling a stunt like this on a night like this. Now get yourself away from here so we can get our train rolling." I glared at him and he glared back.

A young trainmaster trying to make a name for himself. But he would be watching for me, now that I had apprehended him and it would work both ways. Back on the engine I waited for him to step across the tracks to his car, then called the flag in from behind, with the air horn. I bet his ears still hurt from the blast. That was not the only result of his foolish actions: his car was stuck in the snow and he had to stay in it all night. By morning he was almost frozen when they found him and rushed him to the hospital. I think that was the end of his career because he was never seen after that.

When the flags were all accounted for we continued our trip, well behind schedule. The temperature dropped below zero at Tehachapi, which was rare. The blizzard continued, and we were reduced to walking speed in many places. When

I was able to travel at normal speed, the snow that lay on the ground above the rail, which was increasing by the minute, would fly up as the diesel plowed through it. Much of the snow landed on the windshield, and together with the falling snow, rendered visibility down to zero. As we made a station stop at Tehachapi, the radio came alive.

"Dispatcher to engineer Steffes on train #59, come in, please." Grabbing the receiver, I was glad to talk to someone, because the stress was getting too heavy for us both. Baker and I were wet and cold from cleaning snow off the signals. John started to complain about his eyes, which were suffering, after hours of peering into the snow, straining to see ahead.

"Dispatcher, this is Engineer Steffes."

"We know you're having a bad time. Do you read me?"

"Yes, I read you. Sometimes you fade out but we understand you. Go ahead, dispatcher."

"The mountain is closed down. We want you off the mountain with those passengers. The board (C.T.C.) here shows all the switches are lined for you and all the signals are in green position. The superintendent says that you are absolved from any irregularities that might happen."

The transmission started to fade away, so we started down the hill. At Rowen the snow was still falling, but I began to see a very slight let up in the intensity of it as we approached tunnel #8. Entering the tunnel was like lifting a curtain. Visibility returned; there was no headlight glare against the blinding snow, which was a relief. Inside the tunnel was a curve and it was there I saw them. I sat straight in my seat and put the train in emergency. The six steers were milling around in the narrow tunnel, holding their heads high, their big, wild, frightened eyes looking for some escape. The barbed wire fencing along the right of way must have snapped in the bitter cold and this poor bunch of scrawny cattle had came through and taken refuge in the tunnel.

That split second after putting the train in emergency, a thought flashed before me, of a time long ago when Engineer Virgil Newbill had hit a steer at Cameron as he crossed on the way down to Mojave. The locomotive and a number of passenger cars had been derailed. The locomotive turned over, killing Virgil.

Hitting the cattle in the tunnel was like striking a cue ball on a billiard table. It made a bump each time the engine struck one, and I prayed we were still on the rail. The horrible sight and sound of the bawling cattle was bad, but the stench proved unbearable. The train came to a stop with the engine barely out of the tunnel. It was my duty to inspect for any damage done to the locomotive and to make sure it was still all on the rail. I was holding my breath on account of the stink as I looked for any damage. I could see none, and all the wheels remained on the rail. I met the conductor at the rear end of the four unit diesel by the end of the tunnel, who was walking up to see what the trouble was. I told him to stay where he was because of the awful blood and chopped beef. I climbed up the ladder of the last unit and went through each one to the warm cab, by which time I was nearly frozen. I tried to reach the dispatcher on the radio but with no success, on account of the mountains which hemmed us in.

When finally we arrived Bakersfield, it was daylight and rain was pouring down. A valley engineer took over at the depot that morning for his assignment of running on to Fresno. How many officials greeted me for interrogation, I lost count. Each one had to have an account of what had happened, and none of them gave any credit to our efforts. Finally I said that enough was enough, and we would continue when we were rested.

A month later, the rancher who owned the cattle that had been killed in the tunnel gave a bill to the Southern Pacific railroad for ten of his prime steers. Boy, I hope he was paid.

6. The Ugly Divorce

Some months later I put the finishing touches on the house. I was pleased, and my kids were pleased. But Margie did not say, one way or the other. Again, I never knew what pleased her. I was in hopes that this home would bring us closer together, with her being closer to her folks. But only time would tell.

We made the move that summer during my vacation. It was painful for the kids. It was, 'what about my friends,' 'what about schools,' 'are the schools any good up there,' and a hundred other questions of how and when. By the time the move was made and things settled I was exhausted. I knew that there had to be curtains and such, but surely three girls and a grown woman could do that.

I continued to work on the pool freight job to Bakersfield, taking my calls at my new home in the desert. If it was necessary to stop and rest before driving home after a trip, I could stop and rest in my old room at Mom's.

Winter came and things started to get hectic. Margie found so many little things to complain about, and the harder I worked the more she would find things to irritate me with. I did not have my little house outside to sleep in as at Los Angeles; Margie would not sleep with me, and when I was home she would sleep on the living room couch. Maybe I was restless or snored? Instead of improving, things got unbearable, and I began to feel the stress of the situation wearing me down. There were times when, driving over the mountain, to or from Los Angeles, the temptation to end it all by driving over the brink and into the deep ravine was strong. Beads of sweat and trembling would come upon me when those thoughts took hold. But I knew that I had to see that my girls were taken care of until they could fend for themselves. I decided that something had to be done or else sometime, when things were at breaking point, my darkest thoughts would win out. I made an appointment with Margie's female doctor.

While waiting in her office, the shakes and the sweats took hold of me so intensely and severely that I hardly could talk.

"Have you the flu?" the doctor asked.

"No," I said trying to gain control, and finally telling her the complete story.

"I have witnessed this for a long time between you two and I was hopping it would work out," she said. "Now you can see a head shrinker [her name for a psychologist] but he can't do anything more than I can for you. Your situation is very acute and you alone will have to do something about it because if you don't you will end up in a rehabilitation center in less than three months and you will be there a long, long time."

"You mean that I have to leave my family or have a nervous breakdown?"

"Yes, and maybe more."

"But what about my kids?"

"Yes, what about the kids," the doctor continued. "They have a way of growing up. Sometimes it is much better when disharmony starts in the home to call it quits. Then the healing process for the children begins quickly, rather than them having to live in years of confusion and turmoil. I'll give you some pills to help you, but it's up to you to decide what you do. You are going to have to leave her or become a pill addict, and you won't get the pills from me.

Leaving the doctor's office I was stunned, and confused about what course to take. Going to my Mom's place I took a pill and lay down on the bed in my old room, closing my eyes to think. For twenty-four hours sleep engulfed me. Upon awakening I wanted to return to sleep and keep the world away from me.

Sometime later, I told my Mom what the doctor had told me. She nodded her head, saying that she could have told me the same thing, but she knew that I had to find it out by myself. All these trying years—maybe I was wrong, but one hates to give up and in my dilemma, I forgot to see the forest for the trees.

Knowing that I would be seen as the bastard in this whole situation, I decided I had to make my moves in such a way that the least amount of pain would be caused, to anyone. I had been faced with many things in my life, but nothing that compared to this. After many hours of deliberation, weighing all the pro's and con's, I decided to tell Margie of my decision: we should temporarily separate, because it was useless to go on. I would tell that she would get support money, as much as I could possibly send her, and she wouldn't have to worry.

When I confronted her with my decision, she cut me down immediately. I was glad the girls were not around to hear the language that was being used.

"I knew you wanted to get me up here to get rid of me," she accused me.

"That is not so," I returned. "I worked hard building this place for you and the kids, but you never been a wife to me in

157

years and you know it."

I was going on to tell her what the doctor had told me but she cut me short.

"Now get out and never come back," she said. I did just that, with only the shirt on my back and a pair of pants that needed washing.

The divorce came next. It was ugly; even the word is ugly. It left me bitter and solemn, and I became the bastard to many. Even to my kids, but they didn't know what had really happened. I had to watch myself around people, so as not to talk against Margie. They would frequently ask, "And what will Margie do?" They never asked me what I would do.

But soon all that was behind me, and the awful spells of affliction and sweating disappeared. In wanting to keep everything, I had lost it all—all but my sanity.

I did not contest the divorce. The court ordered me to pay $225 a month child support and $150 alimony, making a total of $375. And I was to make the payments on the house for one year, which had to be sold and the profits split 50-50. That was very high in that time. My earnings were between $600-700 a month. By the time the IRS was finished with me and I had paid my expenses away from home (at that time the company did not pay these) there was not much left for me. Sometimes I had only one meal a day, and many times I would not have eaten at all had it not been for Mom.

I felt dejected and lonely. My house was gone. Starting out with nothing was not so bad, but people look down their noses at a man when they know that his wife divorced him and that there were three kids involved. All these things made me feel like an outcast, living around the fringes of humanity, trying to find where I fitted in.

158

The Passenger Business

On the San Joaquin Division two extra passenger assignments were created for the overloaded passenger business. Many senior men forgot to put a bid on one of these jobs, but I did so and got assigned to one of them. I held the position for several weeks before being bumped. I remember one incident while on this assignment going to Bakersfield on #59. One evening, Larry McCune was firing for me. Larry was a gentleman and a quiet person; a good fellow to work with.

"Charlie, tell me, is there a nude woman at Sylmar, like they say there is?" Larry asked me at the round-house when we were preparing to go to work. I laughed and nodded my head.

"Yeah, Larry, there sure is and she'll probably be there tonight."

The very attractive girl in question would be out near the tracks at night, nude, with automobile lights shining on her. She waved as the train went by. I suspected that someone back in the olive trees was taking pictures of the whole action. There had been much speculation about this but I don't think anyone really knew. Sylmar is located on a long curve, skirting a large olive orchard.

Arriving at Sylmar on time and slowing the train down to ten miles per hour, I looked back at the train before making the curve. The head brakeman and the conductor both had their heads out the vestibule doors and electric lanterns ready to spot the girl. They knew why I was slowing down, being out for the show also. The running time that was lost could easily be made up going up the mountain from Saugus.

There were two headlights on a diesel passenger engine. One was the regular headlight and the other was called a Mars headlight, which oscillated in a figure-eight pattern. It was used for warnings at crossings, but an engineer could stop the

movements with a switch and put it in any position that he desired. So I put it to shine on the ground and to the right. The stage was set and I had Larry come over on my side of the engine, the side on which the girl would be, and wind the window down behind me. As we arrived on the curve, there she stood, naked as a newborn baby, illuminated with automobile headlights. Combined with the lights we had shining on her, it was lighter than day. I had my window open to watch the show. Larry had his entire head out the window of the door, not believing his eyes. The girl was beautiful, with her right arm up waving at us. The tan on her perfect body was the most desirable color. She had a coquettish, flirtatious air about her and a smile that went with it. This was not the first time that I had seen her, but it was the first time I ever saw a man's eyes bulge out so far that they could have been scraped off with a stick.

I recall another incident in my passenger days while running the coast train #75 the Lark. This was a businessmen's train, before the airplane became popular. Travelers would board at Los Angeles or San Francisco at night, have a good night's rest and be ready to do their business the next day and return the following night. The Lark was considered the most beautiful train on wheels at one time. As I mentioned before, I was able to walk through it one time and it was plush, with barber and beauty shops, dining cars, cocktail lounges and sleeping quarters, mostly all roomettes. It was also rumored that girls of the night were furnished on this train; of course this was only a rumor.

Everything was going fine until leaving Seacliff, a siding along the coast between Ventura and Santa Barbara. I decided that a drink of water was in order so I got out of my seat. On returning and sitting back in my seat my jacket pocket tangled up with the automatic brake handle and gave it a pull. The brake valve went into emergency. Seeing my blunder, my heart flopped. This should never happen to this train. I put the handle in lap position before the fireman had a chance to notice. We came to a stop rather roughly.

"We must have a dynamiter in the train," I said, winking at the fireman. A dynamiter is a term used for an undesired emergency application of the air brakes.

"Yeah," he replied, looking at me doubtfully.

When the air settled down, I recharged the train, whistled the flag in and we started on our way. But that was not the end of the matter. For a long time after that incident, I was writing letters to different officials. On one occasion an official wrote me and wanted to know what happened because the stop caused a gentleman to accidentally spill his drink while in the lounge car. His companion's mink stole had been damaged and she wanted a new brassiere because that had been damaged too. My guess was that the old boy was so drunk he just poured the liquor down her boobs trying to have a feel. Then when she objected, the rest of it went on the mink stole. The company replaced them both to keep goodwill.

I also learned that because of my unscheduled stop, a gentleman who was using the toilet wet all over his two hundred dollar trousers. I never found out whether the company paid up on that one.

Another time in my passenger train experience, I was pulling the Portland train #59, Los Angeles to Bakersfield, with a four unit diesel. Upon arriving at Mojave at ten-thirty that midsummer night, I learned there had been a severe thunderstorm near Cameron in the mountains, ten miles west of Mojave. A cloudburst had caused great damage to the tracks so that night we were marooned at Mojave.

"How about going back to have pie and coffee?" I asked the fireman.

"No thanks. I think I'll stay on the engine and rest," he replied.

Walking back along the dark and quiet train, with only the soft murmur of escaping steam once in a while coming from the steamline running through the length of the train, I encountered the conductor, Ted Percell, close to the depot.

"We'll be here for a long time the way it looks. We may have to return to LA," he told me.

"OK, but how about going across the street and having pie and coffee?" I inquired, and he was agreeable. As we were walking around the north end of the depot a lone person stood in the semi-darkness. I guessed he was sizing things up. On coming closer to the person I saw he was slender in build, in his late forties, and with a jaw full of chewing tobacco, which he was spitting in the dust of the depot. If I recall correctly he was wearing a black brimmed hat.

"Good evening," I said.

"Good evening," he replied. Spinning around and taking a closer look at the gentlemen, I saw it was the actor, Ronald Reagan!

"Aren't you lost? What in the hell you doing here?" I asked.

"Well," he started slowly, "I was on my way to Sacramento. I must be there by tomorrow for a meeting; I'm campaigning for Shell."

I was not much into politics and did not know who Shell might be or what he or she was running for.

"That's too bad," Ted chimed in. "Maybe we can figure something out for you."

"How come you don't fly to where you're going?" I asked. He spit out his tobacco while I loaded my pipe and lit it.

162

"Say," Reagan said. "That smells pretty good. Let me try some of that to chew." So I handed him my tobacco pouch.

"Well," he said in his slow manner. "I really don't care to fly." But as we all know, in later years, he took to flying. And substituted jelly beans for tobacco.

The three of us talked for over an hour on different aspects of the government. Reagan brought out many things that were going on in the government that should be corrected.

"Why don't you run for governor? You seem to know what's happening up there," I urged.

"I don't think that I would have a chance. Whoever heard of an actor being in politics, let alone in the State Capital?" he said, sheepishly.

"Who ever heard of a wood splitter being a President?" I asked. "We need a change in this state," I continued. "You run and you'll make it.

In the course of our conversation, Ted had gone back into the depot. Now he returned.

"Mr. Reagan, I have a ride for you to Bakersfield. Then you can catch the Greyhound bus to Sacramento. There is a brakeman driving to Bakersfield. By going around Oak Creek Road, he can by-pass the flood." Ted was always good at fixing things up. I guess that is why he was promoted to a higher job later. Ronald Reagan rode away with the brakeman.

I have a postscript about this incident.

Some years later, when I joined the Antelope Valley Search and Rescue party, which was part of the Los Angeles County Sheriff Department, our duty was to patrol the fair at Lancaster each year. This particular year the new Governor, Ronald Reagan, would be coming on a visit. The unit was fully informed of their duties by Captain Jack Bones.

"Everybody shall be in Class A uniforms and will be at

attention when the Governor drives in." Jack went on and on about the regulations.

When "D" day came I laid off from my job to be at the Fair. My post was way in the back and to one side of route that the automobile used for bringing in the Governor. Being a new recruit in the outfit, I was probably conspicuous—in my haste to be at the Fair I had forgotten my hat. Waiting around was dull because the procession was an hour late. I was lighting my pipe and strolling about to keep up my circulation, but not getting far from my station, when the Governor came in through the gates, riding in an open top limo. I tried to scamper back to my post. The Governor told the driver to stop, and then he motioned me over to the car. I went over with a little embarrassment.

"Charlie, how are you?" he greeted me. I was stunned to think that he remembered me.

"I'm just fine, Governor, and see, I told you you could make it." I grinned. He shook my hand and smiled and then waved the driver on.

I walked back with pride to where I should have been. But looking about at the other men, I saw they had looks on their faces like I had just committed a crime.

"How come you know Reagan?" Jack Bones asked. Later I told him about the Mojave incident. There is one thing Reagan has—a good memory.

One of the highlights of my passenger experience came when Coleman Beard, my fireman, and I, pulled the San Joaquin Daylight #51 to Bakersfield with the vanishing steam locomotive #4449. We lost running time coming up the canyon to Vincent because the company had taken off the helpers on trains #51 and #52. This was part of the movement towards doing away with the much-needed passenger service in the United States. It was a sad to see the big corporations planning the destruction of the passenger train service throughout the country at that time. Only the employees working in close connection with the passenger business could see what was happening. Patron support never wavered, even though the railroad predicted that it would. People only stopped using the railroads when the service was cut, ticket offices closed, and the number of passenger cars greatly reduced on the regular trains. The head of the Southern Pacific Company, D. J. Russell, was no different from the rest of the big moguls. If the government at that time had not let these unscrupulous men in positions of power exploit the railroads for their own gains as well as for those of the stockholders, we would still have beautiful, fast passenger trains, profitable and competitive, today.

Going down the hill from Vincent I noticed that the lock had not been snapped shut on the speed recorder box that sat on top of the speedometer. I opened the box and removed the pencil lead that registered the speed and mileage on a tape at any given place. Coleman watched and grinned, nodding his head in approval.

After making a station stop at Lancaster, we received a 'high ball' to leave. I started the train gently and then opened the throttle wide. Boy! did these yellowbelly steam locomotives run smooth as silk. There was nothing like it in the world—the feeling of power under your command is something unexplainable. I realized that the diesels were superior to the steam but the romance of running the last of the passenger steam engines that were built was terrific.

The track leaving Lancaster was straight as an arrow for twelve miles, with heavy rail and good ballast. So I let her purr like a kitten with a clear stack as we gained speed every second. We were doing ninety-five miles per hour in nothing flat and so did the miles flash by. Coleman glanced at me grinning, his eyes snapping like fire eating up a log. Then it came to me: What a daredevil fool I am with all these people behind me, their lives entrusted to my hands. With this flashing in my mind like a neon sign, I came to my senses as the 4449 started to roll sideways and weave a little. The speedometer showed well over one hundred miles per hour. By my watch we were doing a mile in thirty-four seconds—about one hundred and ten miles per hour. Going through Rosamond I set the air because one mile and a half up the grade there was a slight curve. I slowed the train to normal speed. With the excitement over my forehead dripped with perspiration. Coleman gave a sigh of relief. Of course, safety should have been the order of the day. I replaced the pencil in the recorder and locked the box.

The Past and the Future

The saga of the steam locomotive was a thing of the past now. Gone into the dusty pages of history, but never to be forgotten. The romance and the glory of this time will always live in the hearts and mind of the American people.

The new diesels were becoming more automatic. They had other features as well, like the maintaining position on the air brake valve, refrigerated drinking water, and the radios on the cabooses, which made it possible for the engineer and conductor to communicate. Little did we realize that the diesel was the beginning of the replacement of employees. Nor did we know that we were entering the sunset of the golden years of railroading.

The steam locomotive had long been retired that early Spring morning when I received the call for a light engine to

Bakersfield.

"And what is the engine number?" I inquired.

"We don't know yet, Charlie," Frank Dwyer replied.

Andy Smihula smiled as I came into the dispatcher's office. He was always smiling; it fit his name. He was a big Irish man with the most even temper of any man going. His smile today had another twist to it and I soon found out why.

"How do you like what we're getting today?" he asked.

I looked at the call board and then stepped back in amazement, hardly believing what was there.

"Smiley," I stammered, "this is Sunday and you are supposed to believe, but this can't be true. Is there a diesel of that number?"

"No, not that I know of, but there is a steam engine numbered 2914 and that's what we're getting," Andy went on to tell me.

I threw my hands up. "What in the hell does anyone want with that old pile of junk and where did they get it from?" I exploded.

"They dug it out of the bone pile, you know that tail track along the river," Frank Dwyer said, leaning on the counter, grinning.

"So that's why you didn't give me any engine number when you called me this morning? You were afraid that I would have marked off and I sure would have. Look at the money we're losing by not having a diesel." I complained. We were paid by the weight on the drivers, the weight for the 2914 being around 186M against about 876M (M=1000.)

"The company knows that you're a good steam engineer and that you can get it to Bakersfield." Frank was feeding me full of bull.

"Horse monocky," I returned. Monocky is my own coined

167

word for something else. Andy and I went out to the turnout track and there it stood, patiently waiting. There was quite a crowd about her because a live steam locomotive was a rare sight. It had been a long time since one sat on the turnout track and of course curiosity drew workers from all the shops to witness probably the last steam locomotive to leave Taylor round-house. Before leaving I inquired whether any water would be available. I knew that many water spouts still remained intact but the question was how many contained water. We found that water was available at Saugus, Vincent, Mojave and Tehachapi. We figured to take water at Mojave and if we did not eat en route maybe we might have a good trip. But after getting our orders we found a restriction of forty miles per hour maximum speed dampened that expectation.

Leaving the yard I practiced on the whistle, because it might be the last time ever. I tried to imitate hogger Nelms but that was impossible; no one could do that. But I must have been doing fairly well because many people stopped to watch us pass by and a great many followed.

"Smiley," I called across the cab. "I feel like Pied Piper and his flute, with this whistle. We have quite a crowd following with their cameras." Andy laughed and shook all over.

At Burbank Junction we received a message to smoke the engine slightly going up along San Fernando Road, because there was a picture company doing a skit. As we progressed I began to think of how much money this was costing me. Then I reminded myself not to get like some of the others around, who were turning into money hogs.

"Andy, what do you suppose the company wants with this old relic in Bakersfield?"

"Perhaps it's going further than Bakersfield," he replied.

Meeting the regular amount of trains on the way out of

Mojave, we were a spectacle to each and every one. Leaving Vincent we found that the retainer on the tender had been disconnected, making the tank brakes release the same time as the engine. This made my drivers' and tank brakes smoke severely. Arriving at Lancaster we received a message to check the engine over for fire. That was how much we were being scrutinized by the public on this trip.

After stopping and checking the engine over, and then leaving Lancaster, a parade of autos over a mile long followed us on the highway paralleling the railroad. I played a tune on the whistle and told Smiley to smoke her up a little now and then.

"We have something running hot on this side of the engine," Andy said as we approached the hill at Rosamond. Going over to his side of the engine and climbing down the cab ladder, I detected a smell of hot metal with smoke coming from the drivers of the locomotive. I knew instantly what it was. The cellar packing was gone on driver #2.

"Damn," I exploded harshly. "We sure have trouble." I stopped the engine and while Andy obtained his flagging equipment, I looked about for dope sticks to pack the cellar, realizing that my chances of finding them were very slim. Andy had already left on his flagging errand and a crowd of people was collecting. I was about to give up the search when in the most unlikely place I found the sticks. Someone had stuck them in the empty first aid kit. Climbing off the engine I found myself amongst many people wishing to help, so I asked them to find some blocking for the wheels because I would have to crawl under the engine, which was on a slight grade. I did not trust the air brakes. After many rocks and wood blocks were obtained a young man of about twenty-eight, clean and well-dressed, volunteered to crawl under the engine

169

for me. I thanked him but told him that it was too much of a job to drop the cellars and put the sticks in, not knowing much about it myself. Scrumming under the engine between the two wheels proved to be difficult, and luckily I happened to be thin or it could not have been done. Everything that I touched burned my gloves, it was so hot. My gloves were old and full of holes, so it didn't make any difference to me. But when we were tied up at Bakersfield I put in for a new pair, and just like the rancher and his prime cattle, I received a fine new pair of leather gloves.

Doing some quiet swearing to myself, I finally finished the task and had one hell of a time turning around and looking out between the openings of the wheels into the face of a highway patrolman.

"Do you need the hook and ladder to help you out?" he inquired.

"No, I got in here and I'm coming out," I told him and by that time the crowd had swelled to perhaps forty people. The young man who had wanted to crawl under the engine for me was there when I oozed out from beneath the engine. He helped me to my feet, and his cute little wife was standing by him.

"How would you like to ride on the engine with me to Mojave?" I asked, trying to dust myself off after standing up. A murmur of approval went through the crowd.

"I always wanted to ride on a steam locomotive," he said hopefully. "You really don't mind?"

"No," I laughed and motioned for him to climb aboard the engine. He readily did so, after telling his wife to pick him up at Mojave. With the whistle I called Andy in from flagging, and while he was walking back to the engine there was time to show my passenger the different features of the locomotive.

Andy's arrival sent the crowd scrambling back to their autos, so they would be ready to keep pace with us.

I let my passenger off at Mojave and while Smiley filled up the thirsty water tank, I oiled around the engine as a crowd of rail fans gathered around. After finding the place where the retainer pipe was disconnected on the tender and repairing it, we were set to go. Looking around at the large crowd of people from all walks of life, I realized how really important our heritage was, not only of steam engines but everything else. I believe it is even more important today. Looking at the face of the crowd, we waved goodbye, amidst shouts of laughter and some tears. It was a shame that the death of the steam locomotive had arrived, but as in all things, progress must continue.

I feel ashamed today that at the time of running that obsolete locomotive to Bakersfield, I had growled and complained about the meager little money lost in wages by not having a diesel locomotive. Little did I realize that was an historic run. Today that engine 2914 sits in the museum at 3801 Chester Ave., Bakersfield.

Upon returning to Los Angeles the next day conductor Harry Cross and his fine crew and I went back on a pickup and set out train which was called a local. It was not a train one might choose, but with a good crew it could be made bearable. Bill Olney, the head brakeman, a good friend of mine made the trip enjoyable with his dry old humor. Bill had Andy laughing all the way home with his stories and of course he amused me also, although I had heard many of them before.

There were many cars to set out and pick up that trip and the day was getting short for working hours. Also, the passenger train schedules would further complicate things. We had one car to set out at Roscoe to the rock track.

"Charlie," Bill said as I started slowing the train for the set out. "I'll drop off Andy's side and get the switches, cut you and one car off then after you pull down we'll shove the car in the clear on the lime track. While I'm tying the hand brake on the car and lining the switches, you can recharge the train. Then I think there'll be time left to make Burbank Junction for the Owl #57."

Bill had three switches plus a derail to attend to. Burbank Junction was a little over three miles farther down the road and if we didn't make it for #57, then we would have to head into the siding here for them and also stay put for train #52, the Daylight, coming behind us, and die on the sixteen hour law.

Everything worked according to plan until I was ready to shove the car into the lime track. Bill came on my side and gave me a big stop sign. He had cut the engine off the train but in all the confusion and hurrying had left the car still there. Going back and getting the car cost us valuable minutes. When the train was finally ready to leave Bill came back to the engine with a very red face for his blunder. Andy and I were about rolling on the floor of the cab laughing, and that didn't help anything.

"We're going to be a couple of minutes short but we're going." I said and after receiving a 'high ball' from the caboose, I let the speed increase rapidly to several miles faster then the allowed limit. We rolled into Burbank on the double track, not quite thirty seconds on the Owl's time. But he was not there anyway.

Before leaving the dispatcher's office I looked over the bulletins, and, finding a coast pool freight job open, I placed a bid on it. The summer weather at Bakersfield had started and was reaching 105 degrees. Santa Barbara was in the 80s and besides, I liked to do a little fishing in the kelp beds from a row boat. One time I pulled in a thirty pound halibut. Not being able to take him home I gave him to a restaurant, and received a free meal in return. Ocean fishing relaxed me and took the edge off things. Sitting there mostly on the wharf fishing, I could think and sort things out. I used to ponder over the blunder I had committed, wasting fourteen years of my life when I should have cut it short by at least ten years. Then maybe the kids would have understood better. And I had also wasted Margie's life. Maybe she might have found someone compatible—who knows? Now I was at the start again, building up my finances and taking a new turn in life, perhaps a bachelor's life would be better? But no, that wouldn't be for me; I just wasn't cut out for it.

On about the fifth trip, coming back from Santa Barbara on a freight job, we were instructed to pick up some cars in a spur at Raymer, located in the San Fernando Valley region. Bill, my fireman, was running the engine at the time. We had four jeeps (four small valley units) and I had just started to relax when old man sun poked his head up over the horizon and about blinded me at six o'clock. I stood up and stretched a little, but still kept a close look out for the traffic on the crossing that we were working over. The high front walk-in nose prevented the engineer from viewing the complete road crossing, so both sides had to be observed at all times. The newer diesels came with the low nose, making the forward view unrestricted.

Picking up the cars from the spur, and back on the train with the necessary procedures, we were ready to depart for Burbank Junction. Bill was pulling out slow because the rear brakeman had walked up the train for a distance, inspecting the running gear, so we had to pick him up on the caboose. Arriving at the road crossing, Bill was blowing the horn quite loudly. His hand froze on the whistle handle as he stopped the train and looked back.

"A kid on a motorcycle hit the third unit back," Bill yelled at me. I hit the ground running. Three box cars back the motorcycle lay in a tangled mess and just beyond the shoulder of the crossing, someone was trying to get up from the ground. When I got there, I found a young man about twenty years of age. He was still conscious.

"My leg, my leg," he moaned. As I took a closer look I felt sick at my stomach. The lower part of his leg was missing just below the knee and he was bleeding profusely. No one was around and I knew something had to be done instantly or he would die. Luckily I had two clean red bandannas in my back pocket, a throw-back to the old days when we used them for handkerchiefs until they wore out. Tying them together and getting down on my knees, I tied them around the man's leg just above where it was severed. It stopped the bleeding but the gruesome task almost made me pass out because I was also covered in blood. Bill finally showed up and when he saw the situation, he backed away and threw up, which made matters worse.

"Get some help Bill," I ordered. Bill ran off while I stayed with the lad, trying to keep him quiet, rolling up my jacket and putting it under his head to make things a little more bearable for him until help arrived. Only a few people stopped to see what had happened, and none of them offered any kind of help. They just went back to their cars, turned around and left. Finally a Highway patrolman showed up and immediately called for an ambulance and wanted to know if we could cut the crossing.

"Yes," I said, "but first find the man's belongings." I pointed to his leg, not wanting to mention it while the lad was in shock.

"Did you tie the tourniquet on his leg?" the officer asked.

"Yes," I replied.

"Well you did a good job; it saved his life. Can you tell me what happened here?" he asked in a nice way, and about that time Bill came back again.

"Bill, tell the officer what happened."

"I was running the engine for the engineer," Bill nodded at me," and we had just picked up some cars off the spur track and were fixing to leave. Pulling out slowly, I whistled the crossing and the wig-wag was working. When crossing the intersection, I glanced down the road and saw this motorcycle coming at fast speed. I thought he was going to stop. The closer he came, the harder I laid on the whistle but I guess with the noise of his motor, he didn't hear me and he didn't see the train until it was too late. When he finally realized that he was going to run into the engine, he laid the bike down, trying to turn but it was too late." As Bill spoke the officer scribbled it down on paper.

The ambulance came thundering up with sirens screeching, and about the same time the conductor arrived from the caboose. After a search they found the injured man's leg under the train and the ambulance took off. It seemed like everything was happening at once. The operator from Northridge drove up in his car with orders for us to meet #99, the coast Daylight, at Hewitt, and then run ahead of all trains to Los Angeles yard. The Daylight took siding for us at Hewitt. Boy. that was the first time that train took siding for anyone.

Bill didn't want to run the engine anymore because he was sick, but so was I. To decide the matter, we flipped a coin and I lost. Leaving Raymer and picking up the head brakeman, whom I sent out flagging against #99 earlier before getting orders, we took off for Los Angeles yards. Arriving there was a relief. Going into the long relief track just below Glendale tower and down to Fletcher drive, I glanced at my watch. We still had three hours to work before the sixteen hours were completed and I thought to myself, 'I came over here on the coast to have the short hour trips.'

Receiving the 'high ball' from the herder, which was the yardmaster authority to continue down into the yard and the track would be clear to the other end of the yard. One third of the top end of "A" yard was on a long left hand curve as a train entered. Usually all the tracks except one or two remained full, and we were using one that was supposed to be empty. All of Los Angeles' yards were built on a water grade they following the Los Angeles river. So when coming in from the north an engineer had to hold his train to a speed of six to eight miles per hour.

The view ahead, between tracks full of cars, was not very extensive, especially with the kind of long nose diesel we had going around the curve.

"Stop the damn thing!" Bill yelled and disappeared some-where—I think it was out the window. I was not yet able to see anything because of the curve, but instinctively I put the train in emergency. It is the last thing I remember. The next thing I was conscious of was how cool the sheets were and how quiet it was as I lay in bed. At first I thought that maybe I was in the old club house at Indio and the sheets were not quite dried out. But then I remembered that it had been torn down years before. I wiggled my toes and fingers. They all worked so I was in one piece. Sitting up in bed I tried to figure out where I might be. Putting my hand to my head I found a lump as big as a goose egg and it was hurting badly. Then it came to me that I was in a hospital. While I was sitting upright a hook-nosed nurse came bustling into my room.

"And how are we today?" she squeaked. "We must not be sitting up, now, we must lie down."

"Well, we ain't in the mood to lie down," I told her resentfully.

"But the doctor said. . . "

"I don't give a damn what the doctor said." I cut her short. "Suppose you get *we* out of here and find the doctor and send him to me." She stormed out in a huff, with hawk-like piercing eyes expressing her anger. As I looked around I had that awful feeling in me about hospitals, which dated from the time I was in for the mumps. I decided this was no place for me. Looking in the closet I found my clothes, and feeling for my wallet discovered that it had not been disturbed. I dressed in a hurry and slipped out the door and down the hall. By the time they discovered my absence, I would be a face in the crowd.

I boarded the first bus that came along, and after many transfers, I finally made my way back to Taylor yard. When I arrived at the crew dispatcher's office and looked at the calendar, I found that two days had been lost somewhere.

"Do you know," Dwyer excitedly asked, "that they are looking all over for you?"

"I came down here to bid off this Coast job. It's a jinx to me and I'm going back on the hill," I informed him. Never did I return to the coast, even when I could have the Coast Daylight #99 and #98 regularly or on Amtrak.

I was turning to leave when Ray James came in the door.

"Well!" he said in his dry manner, "If it ain't the switch engine pulverizer. How do you feel?"

"Outside of a bump on my head, I'm fine," I replied. "Tell me Ray, what happened? All I can remember is hitting something." I knew he would tell me the truth after a little joshing.

"You never saw such a mess," he began. "I still don't know how you ever came out alive. Your lead unit was sideways to track when it ended up. Those cars that your engine hit on either side in turn hit others next to them, just like a bunch of dominoes—one knocked down and they all fell. Of course they got it all cleaned up over there now." Ray stopped to have a drink of water from the fountain. I began to think about his words, 'all cleaned up over there.' How long had it been since the accident? Looking at the calendar again, I then realizing that three days rather than two had passed.

"You ought to see that switch engine. It crumpled up like a paper bag and your control stand was in your seat. It was a good thing that you dove for the floor or you would be six feet under right now." Ray stopped to wipe his mouth. "You know!" he continued, "No one was hurt but you. Everyone else got away."

Somehow Smokey Snyder, road foreman of engines found out that I was at the crew dispatcher's office, and he came bustling into the door, out of breath.

"What in the hell you doing here? Smokey asked me. "Don't you know that the police are looking all over town for you?"

"I don't know about that but they're not going to get me back in that hospital again," I said, determined.

"But when they catch up with you, they will put you in there," he insisted.

"They will play hell, Smokey, I won't go."

"Charlie, if you don't go back and let the doctors complete their examination to find out if you're OK you can't come back to work. That's not my ruling, that's the company's."

"Well, from what Ray tells me maybe I won't have a job

anyway," I informed Smokey.

"I don't know about that. The yardmaster put the switch engine up wrong. . ." Smokey realized the mistake he had just made, and cut the sentence short.

"If it's not my fault, then I have the company where the hair is short, don't I?"

Smokey could not answer; he just looked at me. All this time Ray James was grinning with his eyes twinkling and shining. To him it was like a bitch bulldog watching two males fighting over her. I cooled the situation by telling Smokey, "you tell whoever it is to call off their dogs and I'll go to my own doctor and have an examination. If I'm OK, he will give me a release to go back to work."

Smokey didn't say anything as he left the premises. I was feeling bad talking to Smokey like that because he really was a remarkable person.

"You should have told him that you're going to retire on what you're going to get on this deal. Boy! I'd like to be in your shoes." It was Ray talking, but the idea of bringing any suit against the company was far from my thoughts. I liked my job and I also liked the Southern Pacific Company.

After taking a week off I went to my doctor and he found everything in fine shape. I took my clearance to return to work to the crew dispatcher's office. The clerk shook his head and said that he could not accept it.

"You better accept it or I'll retire on what it will cost the company if I go to court," I told him. He immediately got on the phone to somebody and all I could hear him say was "Yes sir, Yes sir." He then turned to me.

"OK, you are on the board, Mr. Steffes."

7. A New Life

Business continued to flourish in the following years on the railroads. The lumber mills in the north shipped many train loads of lumber down the San Joaquin Valley and also on the coast route. Besides that the expansion of trailer on flat cars, known as piggy backs, was going full blast, along with the containers that came from the ships which were loaded on flats. Then there was the dead freight and this combined with the perishable food products. The Southern Pacific Transportation Company, as they called themselves by then, was getting fat on the hog. The employees were happy and their relationship with the company was at its peak. Train and enginemen were a proud bunch of men and were glad to acknowledge that they worked for the Southern Pacific. The conductors brought in more business in one day then all the new Stanford graduates could muster in a year.

However, the fatter the hog, the more he eats and the greedier he becomes. And that was what was happening to the Southern Pacific Company. A new breed was showing up on the horizon. A new breed that forgot who laid the golden egg. They were fresh out of Stanford and did their railroading in the San Francisco coffee shops. Unfortunately the new breed managed to put many of their ill-informed ideas into practice.

Many of the old regime remained in power for a while, but the bunch of new grads rightly assumed that the old war horses would soon be gone and then they would run things their way. And that is what they did—they ran it from a first-class railroad making good money to the poverty-stricken railroad it is today. And as a result, the relationships between employer and employee is at its lowest ebb today.

Shortly after going back on the Bakersfield pool, I was called at Bakersfield to return to Los Angeles. Arriving at the dispatcher's office early I went to the master mechanic's office, where I thought I might be able to get a safety pin from one of the women who worked there. My pocket had a hole in it and my money or keys were always going down my pants leg. At that time I wore slip-on dress boots, so much of the time the items would go into the tops of the boots, and I had to take them off to remove whatever had fallen into them.

Bud Day was the office manager. He was a nice fellow but a little cocky in manner. He greeted me as I opened the door and stood by the counter.

"What can I do for you, Hogger?" Bud asked. Hogger was a nickname for engineer.

"I'm in need of a safety pin," I replied.

"A safety pin? This is a railroad not a dress shop," he grinned at me.

"I know that Bud, but you have women working here and they usually carry some around." The female employee who worked behind the counter began to giggle.

"Mary, see if you can fix Charlie up with something," Bud called to one of the women and then turned and went back into his office. Mary was by far the prettiest girl of the bunch. She had long wavy brown hair, green dancing eyes and her lips were very red and pronounced, the kind that set me afire. Her

face was oval and she had a well-shaped and well-dressed body. The kind of body that invited me to bed. I was dreaming of course, but I liked what I was seeing.

"Let me see what I can find," Mary said, fumbling in her purse. "I don't seem to have a pin. Do any of you girls have a pin?" she asked. They all shook their heads.

"All I have is a needle and thread. Maybe you can sew it?" She looked at me in a quizzical manner.

"But I can't sew. Can't you do it for me?" The others started to giggle louder.

"Go on Mary, sew it for him," one of the girls urged. By then Mary had begun to blush.

"Well, come into the master mechanic's office and take your pocket out and I'll see what I can do," she said. As I followed her through the door into the office I looked at the grins and smiles on the faces of the other girls. From that I guessed that Mary was not married.

"Where is the boss today?" I asked.

"He won't be in today, he's out on the road," Mary answered, getting her needle and thread ready.

"Let me see your pocket," she ordered. Pulling my pocket out I felt a little ashamed of putting her in this position. But the smell of her exotic perfume sent many small electric shocks through my bloodstream.

"You know this is not the way this should be sewed?" she said.

"What is the right way?" I inquired.

"The pants should be taken off and the pocket sewed on the outside of the pocket."

"OK, let's do that," I agreed, and started to unbuckle my belt.

"No, no," she said hurriedly. "We'll just do it this way," and then she started to sew on my pocket, but she finished too soon. "I sure thank you and I don't know how to repay you. Perhaps we could have dinner my next trip up?" I stammered, trying to find the right words.

"There's no need for repayment, but if you'd like to go out to dinner sometime, stop in next trip and then we will see."

"I sure will," I promised.

My engine was a four unit covered wagons, and the nose of the lead unit was sitting in front of the office. My fireman, Joe Niemeir, had his head out the window and was watching me come out the office door. In his hand were our orders. He had all of the work finished because I was late.

"What's wrong, you get waylaid on your way down here? I know you ate the same time I did and left the restaurant ahead of me," Joe said with his gray-blue eyes twinkling.

"Naw, I had a hole in my pocket and one of the girls in the office sewed it up for me." I kind of passed it off.

"Oh, yeah, a girl sewed it up!" He grinned and looked at me with that same twinkle in his eye, and then left to go back through the units for something.

Putting my suitcase down and getting out my clipboard and timetable I found that I had forgotten my lunch. I looked down from the cab window and spotted a vending machine with food in it standing by the master mechanic's door. After purchasing what was available, I turned to climb back on the engine. As I did so, Mary came out of the door and silently handed me a note. Then she turned and went back into the office. Joe had been watching the exchange, so I stuffed the paper in my pocket.

The switch herder was trying to gain our attention at the outbound track switch for us to come ahead. When coupling up to our train in the yard and waiting for an air inspection, I read the note, which read: "If you would like to have dinner with me when you come back, my telephone number is ..." I put the note back in my pocket before Joe took notice.

Struggling up the mountain to Bealville with a heavy train, we were stopped on a red signal on the mainline. I stopped the train behind a dirt crossing and we were waiting for a train coming out of Cliff. In this procedure my head brakeman rolled our train back for a few cars inspecting the running gear; then he would cross over the track to roll the incoming train for any defect as it went by.

Sitting and waiting, I happened to look back and saw the brakeman hurrying up to the engine.

"Charlie, there is a transient in the first gondola with his stomach cut wide open," he yelled, looking up at me from the ground. "He's holding his guts in with his hands. He won't live long if he doesn't have medical help."

"Just a moment," I told the brakeman, reaching for the radio. The new radios sometimes worked but most of the time they did not. However, this happened to be a good time.

"Extra 6133 east calling the dispatcher at Bakersfield, come in please."

"Go ahead extra 6133 east, this is the dispatcher Gaylon." Everyone knew "Pop" Gaylon. Not only was he the best dispatcher but he was also known for teaching his boys and nephew that worked there to do a first class job.

"We have a transient on the train who's had his stomach sliced open by another transient. He has been robbed and left to die. Also my head brakeman reports that he is still alive. What shall we do?"

"I'm going to hold you there until we get an ambulance and the sheriff to take care of the matter. Charlie, aren't you by that road crossing that goes down to Caliente?"

"Yes, we're stopped in the clear of it. Over and out."

The more I mulled over the situation the more alarming it seemed to be. If this butcher had stabbed this old man and robbed him, what would he do to us later?

A Santa Fe train came down from Cliff and went through the siding by us. Then a S.P. train followed him. Finally the ambulance and a sheriff arrived. Before we could continue on our way, another S.P. arrived from Cliff. Back in those times, when trying to start a train, an engineer would call his helper engines and let them know that he was going to start the train. Then he would release the air on the brakes. When the brakes were fully released on the caboose the conductor would notify all the engines on his train. The helpers would shove against the train while the lead engine came out on his throttle to run six. Then they all hoped, with a little prayer like, "O God, I hope this bastard starts."

Sometimes, if the train did not move, I would come out another notch on the throttle and feel a strain on the engine. Then it would be back to run six. A train could be easily broken if not handled with kid gloves. One main reason for this was that at that time many lightweight draw-bars from the war days were still in use. The knuckles used in conjunction with the draw-bar were also a factor. These were always called the "weak ones." I have seen knuckles broken and in the break of the metal an outline of a wrench or a bunch of bolts and nuts that had not been quite melted into the molten metal before it was poured into the mold.

Traveling through Woodford at the great speed of eleven miles per hour I called the dispatcher. This time the chief dispatcher, Uhal Pierce came on the radio.

"What is your problem extra 6133?" he asked.

"We haven't any problem as of now, dispatcher," I told

185

him. "But we don't want this murderer on the train. We are afraid that he might do harm to one of us. Would you please have the law shake the train down at Tehachapi?"

"Go to Summit Switch and when you stop your train, the people there will take care of things. Now let me talk to the conductor.

"This is the conductor on 6133; go ahead dispatcher."

"Do not cut your helpers out until the authorities tell you they are finished at Summit Switch, understand?"

"We understand perfectly dispatcher, over and out." The conductor finished the transmission.

"Now why couldn't they have told us that earlier?" I asked Joe and the head brakeman, who normally sat in the last unit so he could watch his train. But I could see why he did not want to be back there by himself with that scoundrel running loose.

"Well," Joe answered in his slow way of talking. "Maybe the sheriff wanted to get a description of the guy from the one they took to the hospital before they took any kind of action." What Joe said made sense.

By three o'clock that afternoon we were going through Tehachapi, with only a couple more miles to Summit Switch. I eased the throttle off so the helpers could shove the train. Then it would be bunched, making it easier to cut out the helper engines.

Upon arriving at the Summit siding, we saw, on both sides of the track, uniformed men with rifles standing twenty feet apart stretching for over a mile, waiting for me to stop.

"Holy cripes!" Joe exploded. "They must have the whole National Guard out today." And that was the only time in my career I ever saw anything like it.

Between Mojave and Tehachapi it was double track territory. The dispatcher held all opposing trains at station Warren by train orders until we arrived. After stopping the train I was surprised to learn how many freeloaders were riding on it. I wasn't able to count them but it was a considerable bunch the guards gathered and took away.

When traveling through Mojave we received a message with the train orders that the man that the authorities were looking for was in the bunch that had been taken off the train, as well many other wanted men. We were relieved to hear it.

The Krauts

The next trip turned out to be a dilly to Bakersfield. The call came early in the morning for train #2/803, engine #9002. The engine number puzzled me, but maybe it was a mistake by Frank Dwyer, the crew dispatcher. When I arrived at Taylor round-house there were more officials running about than flies on a hog. As I registered, I asked who the fireman would be.

"No fireman today, Charlie, there is none available," Frank told me. It shook me a little. Then I remembered the agreement between the brotherhoods and the railroads, stating that no new fireman would be hired. The firing jobs would be phased out gradually, rather than being abolished all at once. This was another epitaph in the pages of history.

"This engine number, where did it arrive from?" I asked Frank.

"Oh they came specially for you, Charlie," Frank assured me. "Right from Germany. They are called the Krauts and I'm sure you'll like them. I've been told that they run on hydraulic fluid, instead of electric."

"And no fireman to enjoy all of this," I growled.

"But think of all the money you're going to make," Frank grinned.

"Yeah, in a pig's butt," I replied, turning sharply and leaving for the turn out track. Arriving there, it was like a three ring circus. I watched all the gray flannel suits and blue flannel suits climbing up and down the ladders into the diesel. It reminded me of when I was a child and had received a stuffed monkey on a gadget which did tricks when it was wound up.

The German engines were nicely made, heavy and had somewhat of a German look about them, although they resembled our diesels also. They consisted of three units with a dynamometer car on the rear end. This car measured everything that the diesel engines were operating, good or bad. I waited my turn to use the ladder to climb aboard. In the cab, which was somewhat like ours, many officials were crowding around, leaving only standing room. I eased my suitcase down while they all looked at me as if to say, "did you have an invitation to come aboard?"

I looked at them, and seeing that they probably had taken up residence, I decided this wasn't going to be.

"Get," I said, and they all seemed to evaporate. When the cab emptied out I opened the windows to let the cigarette smoke out. I knew my pipe would smell bad enough, but not as bad as stale cigarette smoke. Sitting in the engineer's seat I looked over the control stand. Just when I was about to get up to resume my duties a tornado came through the door from the engine room.

"Damn it, don't you touch anything, not a damn thing and get out of that seat, you understand?" Jim Canty, the Los Angeles Road Foreman of Engines exploded.

"Are you addressing me?" I asked, puzzled.

"Yes, you damn right I am," he said, getting red in the face. I figured that some of the higher officials had dressed him down because I chased them out of the cab. But as an engineer

188

I had the right to do that.

"Take your hands off of the control stand," Canty ordered.

"Now damn it, Canty, I was called on this job to be the engineer here. I didn't hire out yesterday and you talk to me with respect, and with a decent tone also. I will not touch your damn sacred cow, you can take it from here, but those donkeys back there are not riding up here in the cab, understand?" He understood because from then on he was very nice to me. Maybe I was too hard on him because he got it at both ends, from his peers and then from me.

Sitting on the fireman's seat I watched the blundering mistakes of my superior. Then Canty would ask me about a certain grade condition or speed restriction. I told him very quietly and waited for more mistakes, but nobody disturbed us in the cab. Arriving at Newhall tunnel and tipping over the crest of the grade in the long tunnel, Canty did not ease off on the throttle as the train gained momentum. We shot out of the tunnel, going like hell.

"We must be doing downhill, that right, Charlie?"

"Hell, yes we are going downhill and if you don't get a hold of them, we're going to end up in that ditch over there," I bellowed at him, pointing my finger to the drainage ditch along the track.

Coming to the slight curve a little way below the tunnel, the engine rocked like a cradle before Jim was able to slow it down. I guess letting him go that far without telling him to use the air was my fault, but when he finally acted he used too much and almost came to a stop. I was certain he was going to tear the train in pieces.

"Get out of that seat or you're going to be in a mess in a minute," I told him, and he gladly relinquished it to me.

Shutting the throttle completely off I bunched the train with the engine brakes holding the head end from running out as I released the train air. Then I just hoped for the best. Luck was on our side.

"Here's your seat back. You're going to run this baby to Saugus where you get off," I told him when I knew the train was safe. Canty meekly sat down just as the caboose came out of the tunnel.

"Steffes, what in the dickens are you trying to do? Kill us? You knocked over the stove and you almost killed the rear man," the conductor shouted over the radio. Only silence followed, but after a few seconds Jim picked up the radio and called the caboose.

"This is Jim Canty talking. I was running the engine when this all took place. The general office mandate was that I run this engine for testing it. I am sorry for the inconvenience that it caused you but this is the very first time that I have been over this territory."

"We thank you for that, but Steffes should have instructed you better than he did." So I had it back in my lap, but I admired Canty for his acknowledgement.

Saugus loomed up ahead of us. We were to stop there and let the Los Angeles Division officials off and take on the San Joaquin bunch. The group stood in front of the depot, and if my memory serves me right, a light mist was in the air. Levi Franklin and Buck Brewer were both looking up at the engine as we rolled on. Also in the crowd of dignitaries, I detected Brick Waggner, District Road Foreman of Engines. Buck Brewer was to take Levi's place after Levi took his pension. Brewer was a gem of an official, as was Levi.

The crowd was astonished as we zipped by and stopped twenty cars further on. I was grinning all the way. Jim Canty made his exit on the opposite side of the engine so as to avoid anyone noticing his red face and to escape the playful ridicule.

Buck had the orders folded in his mouth as he climbed on the engine.

"What's the deal, can't you stop this outfit where it belongs?" he greeted me.

"If I had been running it I would have."

"We all know, Charlie; we heard on the radio in the depot what was happening."

"Buck, when I went to work, he told me not to touch anything or do anything, so I didn't." Buck looked at me and shook his head.

"I'm sort of new on your division and Levi is riding back in the dynamometer. I would really appreciate any help you can give me," Buck said to me. What a difference between officials, I thought.

"San Francisco ordered that the local officials run the engines so they could evaluate these German locomotives," Buck went on. "But I believe you fellows would be far better than us."

"One thing you might put in your notes is that there isn't any maintenance valve on the air brake system," I said.

"No wonder the air was so low when it arrived here," Buck remarked.

"And one more thing about these German engines. When they are in dynamic braking I am told that it is accomplished by restriction of the hydraulic fluid. This makes it extremely hot and that in turn reduces the holding power. Why don't they incorporate a refrigeration system to run the oil through before being used again?" I asked.

We started up the hill. Before we got to Vincent, Brick Waggner came up from behind to see how everything was working, but he only stayed a short while.

"Just how would you take this train down from Vincent to Palmdale?" Buck wanted to know.

"You really want my opinion or do you want to know what the rules say?" I asked.

"The way you would do it. I know how the books say."

"Well, Buck there are three ways, pinging, bridging, or turning the feed valve back. Down this hill I would use the feed valve. It acts the same as a maintaining feature on the new brake valves." After telling him that and seeing that the order board was green, I said, "I must go back and ring my sock out." That was the expression for using the toilet.

Going up the steep grade out of Mojave, someone came in on the radio from the dynamometer car.

"Buck Brewer, stop up here on the steepest grade and then start. We want to find out how much draw-bar pull it takes to start this train."

"You want me to break into, is that right?" Buck asked.

"Well, let Charlie do it, he is more familiar with this territory than you are." Buck looked over at me and shook his head.

"They would want me to do something like this. Maybe they're right, you better run it."

"No, Buck you run it," I said to him, because if he didn't it might set a precedent. "If I can help in suggesting something, that will be all right. If there happens to be a break into I'll take the blame."

"OK, Charlie, you tell me where the best spot is to stop."

"You see that curve up ahead?" I pointed out a long right-hand curve. "Well, when the engine is on the straight track after the curve, stop there and be sure to sand the rails in doing so."

When we got to the predetermined spot, Buck eased down

and set the air, closing the throttle off and setting the engine brakes. We came to a nice stop. Buck looked at me and I nodded, smiling. "You see Buck, nothing to it, you've done the same thing on your division a hundred times."

"Yeah," he said, getting up for a drink of water. "But not with all the big brains riding behind me." He pointed with his thumb and twisted his mouth in defiance. "The proof is in the pudding, and that is getting it started. Call the caboose, Charlie, and tell them to let us know when they are released on the brakes." I did as he asked.

"Caboose to the head end of second 803, the brakes are releasing," came the report.

"OK," I repeated. Buck came out to run three on the throttle and then released the engine brakes. He gradually opened the throttle a notch at a time, and the train started to move.

"All moving back here on the caboose." Buck and I both gave a sigh of relief.

Starting that train made Buck Brewer's day. In the old days, many draw-bars and knuckles were strung along this right-of-way from break intos, until the company enacted the grade signal, indicated by a yellow "G" on the signal mast. This allowed a train to proceed by a red signal without stopping; an engineer would slow his train and follow another train up the mountain. This eliminated many of the dreaded incidents that consumed so much time.

"You are elected to run this train the rest of the way to Bakersfield because you can do a much better job than the rest of us," Buck told me. "No one will come up here and bother you, that I will promise and I'll see to that. By the way Charlie, thanks." With that Buck left, but I wished his words of thanks could have been framed. It was the best I ever heard in my life.

Having the mainline all the way to Bakersfield, we made a

record trip. Climbing off the engine on getting relieved, the Bakersfield Californian newspaper crew, complete with photographer, greeted me. The staff writer asked me what I thought of the German engines.

"They're a well-made engine but it in my opinion that they are not as good as the ones made in the United States." I don't believe my remark made the papers, but it was true, and the German engines never caught on much in the United States.

Mary

In my room at the Quincy, I washed, shaved, and tidied up a bit. From my wallet I took out the little note, which I treasured, and went down to the telephone. I let it ring once, twice and then a third time. I began to figure that maybe Mary was not at home. But just as I was deciding to hang up someone answered "hello." Then there was a pause; somehow my words would not come out.

"Is this Chucker?" said a female voice.

That was a new one, no one had ever called me that before.

"Yes, this is me," I finally found the words.

"I knew you were coming!" the voice said excitedly, and I knew it was Mary.

"How did you know that?"

"Why everyone knew where your train was, all along the way. This was a great event and of course when I found out that you were the engineer, that made it much more interesting."

"Well what do you know," I replied. "How about that dinner date?"

"Oh, yes, but you're coming here for dinner. It's all fixed."

"But I have no way of getting there and I don't know where you live."

"Don't worry, I'll pick you up in fifteen minutes. You stay

at the Quincy don't you?"

"Yes," I answered.

Mary drove me to her home on Shalimar Drive. At one time it had been a large stable for horses but Mary had made it into a very nice and beautiful home. It had even been featured in the home section of the newspaper.

I will never forget the little round table set for two with a hanging light above it making it an exclusive place, just for dining. The food was cooked to perfection.

"This food is fit for a king," I told her.

"Well you are, you are king here for the night." She had a way of saying the right things. After eating, we talked way into the night and then she drove me back to the hotel.

A week later I was able to come up at the right time and we went out to eat. This time it was a little more casual than before, and not long after that I was seeing her every trip, regardless of what time it was. Our relationship grew stronger and turned into an intimate and flowering romance which we both enjoyed. Mary needed things done to her place, such as a better heater. So I bought and installed a new heater that hung from the beamed ceiling. It had a large blower incorporated in it that kept the place much warmer. Driving to Bakersfield between road trips, I was able to accomplish a great many things and it was really nice. The rewards were great.

Playing Chicken

One day, working back to Los Angeles, I was running the Piggy Back train, a nickname for Trailers on Flat Cars. This premium train held a passenger train schedule. I had a fireman that day, Jess Pound, a big, burly, slow talking person who thought before he said anything. But what he did say deserved a hearing.

195

"This is the way to railroad, Charlie, all trains should run like this," Jess said to me as we left Sylmar for San Fernando. The scheduled time for #60 to be at Sylmar was 7:52 a.m., and we ran as 2/60, running six hours late, putting us by Sylmar 1:52 p.m. Looking at my watch I saw we were right on time.

"That's right, Jess, but you tell the company that and see if they will listen?" I replied.

The speed going through San Fernando at that time was thirty miles per hour until the engine crossed the main crossing where the depot stood. Then it went back up to sixty for passenger. Further down the track to the next crossing and on the left stood the city's high school. Some of the students were getting out. Beyond the school was a wide wash with a trestle for the tracks to cross over. On one side of the trestle a walkway of two twelve inch planks was provided for work-men to repair and maintain the tracks.

Whenever school was let out, there was always a large bunch of students along the tracks and crossings, so I would blow the whistle long and constantly. They would usually scatter, but on this particular day, three boys on the trestle were going to play chicken. "Chicken" was the way the kids amused themselves. Each tried to outdo the other on some dangerous trick. But this was a new one, trying to outrun a train doing over fifty miles per hour and climbing.

Setting the air and closing down the throttle, I tried to stop the train from hitting the three young black boys who were running for their lives over the walkway on the trestle, which was only six or eight feet above the sandy bottom of the wash. One lad lagged behind the others and I would have hit him if he had not jumped off into the sand below. But the other two kept on running.

My air gauge showed below the equalizing pressure,

meaning that any more reduction would be useless. My emergency was gone because I had used the air in slowing down for the street crossing. In those days there was not an emergency available until the train line was fully charged. Today, with the advance of technology, the brake valve (I have been told) always has an emergency.

"Why don't those damn fools jump?" Jess yelled.

I was not being able to answer. We hit them. I will never forget the sickening sound of the thud of their bodies at the moment of impact. If they had only started a few seconds sooner they would have won the race because they only had ten more feet to go.

Coming to a stop twenty cars further down the track and I looked back. I couldn't see anything because of the dust but I found out later that the boys had not been decapitated; they had been thrown to each side of the rail. All Jess and I could do was to look at each other and shake our heads in bewilderment as we waited for the police and the ambulance to arrive.

Things like this stay forever with an engineer, or anyone riding with him in the cab of the locomotive. Even today I have dreams and mini- nightmares about accidents in the past, and of running an engine down the highway instead of on a track. Somehow I cannot put it all together but doctors tell me that it is a throwback to earlier events in my life—the imprint the accidents and tragedies have made on my mind. Maybe so. Certainly these events, and the later dreams, put lots of gray hair on my now bald head.

The Flood and the Important Decision

A year passed and Margie had not sold the home. I was not going to force the issue as long as she took good care of the girls. My sister finally bought Margie's half of the house and

I could pay her back in installments. It was a long time before I went to see the house. It was clean and in good shape. But this time the house did not talk to me. There was nothing but dead stillness only broken by my footsteps, so I left quickly without looking back. A sore must have time to heal, and besides, I was close to being called for work.

My lonely, sour mood followed me to work. Knowing that my company would not be appreciated in the cab of the engine, I took with me my mini deck of playing cards and put my flat-sided suitcase across my lap, making a table for playing solitaire. Running the engine and playing cards, kept me awake and alert. From then on it was my pet hobby.

As we arrived at Mojave that early afternoon, huge ferocious dark clouds covered the Tehachapi mountains. These mountains were the start of the southern end of the high Sierra range that skirts the eastern side of California. The air was still and sultry at Mojave and gave off an eerie feeling. I slowed the train speed down because we were coming in on a yellow signal.

"Operator Mojave, calling number 803." The operator was calling us on the radio.

"This is engineer on 803," I replied.

"There seems to be some signal disturbance up the hill but we are going to let you go anyway," he informed me.

"Yeah, I came in here on a yellow and the pot up by your office is yellow and it just went green, operator. Thank you, over and out." Hanging up the radio speaker and preparing to scoop up the orders, I looked at a Santa Fe train standing in the yard, which had just come down off the mountain and was very wet.

"Must be raining pretty hard up the mountain," I remarked to the brakeman.

"Well you couldn't prove it by the looks of things down here, it's so dry," he replied.

The first signal leaving Mojave was in green but the next one further up showed red. It was then I surmised something was wrong because it should have showed yellow if someone was going up the hill ahead of us. Because all the signals going up the hill were grade signals, I could go by them without stopping, but if anything were to happen—like a rear-end collision or getting on the ground from a broken rail or such—then I would be the fall guy. I went by the second red signal and went around a loaf of a hill and then went into a reverse turn heading for Cache Creek, which was only a dry wash. The wind came up blowing so hard that it slowed me down to two miles per hour. About then spits of rain hit the windshield. Getting on the radio I asked the operator in Mojave if anyone was going up the mountain ahead of us.

"No, the mountain is clear all the way to the top," he informed me as the rain began to come down in torrents. Visibility dropped to zero because the wipers could not operate fast enough. It was just like someone was pouring a bucket of water on the windows. Peering through the curtain of water, I saw the bridge appear just ahead. It was then the little man on my shoulder said, "Stop." And I did, with one unit sitting on the bridge.

"What in the hell you stop for?" the fireman asked. "We can make it," he insisted.

"In a pig's ass," I replied. "Look down and then look ahead of you."

The wash below us was a mass of tumbling muddy water full of debris, and it overflowed onto the bridge, covering the rail. The rain let up for a moment, enough for us to see further up the track, where the right-of-way led between a cut in the terrain. The cut was about eight foot deep but never in my experience had I witnessed so much water. Large boulders and uprooted Joshua trees, and a mass of other rubble, was coming at me in a three foot high wall. On top of that tumbling water came another wall of water further back.

I looked at the other two men in the cab, who by this time were in a frenzied state of mind, with wild eyes. They were looking to me for reassurance. I hated to think what condition we would have been in if I had arrived ten minutes sooner. I called Mojave on the radio.

"Is there a train coming up the hill behind us?" I asked.

"No, not yet, but a Santa Fe is about to leave."

"Hold him there! Because I am backing out of this mess to Mojave. We're about to go under."

"What do you mean?" The yardmaster came on the radio.

"The track is washing out beneath the engine and there's a wall of water coming at us four to six feet deep at Warren, and Cache Creek is over the top of the bridge. Hold that Santa Fe because I'm backing up to Mojave. This track is washing out under me now."

"This is the caboose, Charlie. The rear brakeman's been out tying down some hand brakes, so back up where you're ready. Over and out."

"OK," I replied. Backing up a long train is a tricky job, especially downhill. After you are certain that the brakes are released you must let the train roll back a few feet at a time until the conductor informs you that the train is on the move. Then you hold the train with the dynamic brake and air if necessary. Another way is to use the air on the train and shove back against it but in this case I preferred the first way. As we rolled back, the ballast and track disappeared under the water for fifty feet or more.

Congress had just passed a new law restricting the time employees spent working out on the road to twelve hours a day. The railroad companies were to have two years to gear up for this law. In the interim, a fourteen hour law would go into effect immediately. After we got back to Mojave, I stayed there for that period of time, after which we were deadheaded to Bakersfield by carry-all around the Oak Creek Road.

I did not want to wake Mary up at two-thirty in the morning, so I went to bed at the Quincy. But rolling and tossing on the bed was all I could accomplish in the way of sleep. Sitting up on the edge of the bed and lighting my pipe, I then realized what my trouble was. Other times when getting to Bakersfield, Mary and I would go out or go to her house and talk, or do something even more enjoyable. like going to bed. I looked at the time and saw it was eight-thirty in the morning. Mary would be working now at her assignment in the chief dispatcher's office with Uhal Pierce, a very slender man with straight grayish-blond hair combed from front to back. Uhal knew his job well and with the assistance of Pop Gaylon, they kept a good eye on the dispatchers working in the office.

I took a hot shower, shaved and took my best outfit out of the closet. I brushed it and put it on, then left to eat a little breakfast and think out the scheme that was bouncing in the back of my head. Finishing up my breakfast, I headed for the chief dispatcher's office.

"Good morning everyone," I said as I went through the office door. Mary looked up and I smiled at her. By this time nearly everyone knew we were dating.

"I have Mary working hard, so what do you want?" asked Pierce in his dry, quizzical manner. I hesitated for a few seconds. 'This is it,' I said to myself. 'I am ready to do it—after all, I am forty-four years of age and I am not going to live by myself any longer.'

"If you deadhead me back to Los Angeles tonight or when my turn gets first out, I will take Mary to Las Vegas and get married," I blurted out.

A bomb going off could not have caused more excitement and commotion than that. Both men in the office stood up and the dispatchers from the operating room rushed in.

"You will what?" Pierce fired back.

"She has tomorrow and the next day off and it will work out just right," I said. The assistant chief dispatcher, Pop Gaylon, twirled around in his chair. "You marry Mary! Why, she's too good for you." he said.

"I know that but I want to marry her anyway," I replied.

"Does she know it yet? Have you asked her?" Uhal Pierce inquired.

"No! But I am now," I shot back.

"How do you feel about this, Mary? Do you want this, this diesel fumes to be your husband?" Pierce asked Mary. She was sitting with mouth wide open and eyes dancing. No one ever proposed to a woman like this before, with an audience such as this.

"Well, I thought it was coming, but not this way or so soon," she replied. But Mary knew I meant what I said.

"I was going to buy a new dress for the occasion," she continued. "Chucker, if you'll have me, I will be more than happy to be your wife." Everyone in the place cheered and whooped it up until the superintendent, Bob Robinson, came into the office to find out what the commotion was all about. When he found out, he joined in the festivity.

"There's nothing wrong with the dress you're wearing, Mary. After all, I'm going to marry you, not the dress," I told her, and everyone cheered some more.

202

"OK, I'll dead head you," Pierce told me. "But you better have a marriage license when you get back because if you don't you'll never get another dead head out of me."

Mary and I were married at Las Vegas at midnight that night. On the way back the next afternoon we stopped at the house in the desert. Of course Mary fell in love with it.

It was decided that I would stay on the pool job and once a week drive to Mary's house from Los Angeles.

8. Trying Times Without Help

Very seldom did I have a fireman; they were getting phased out rapidly. Some of them, if they did not have too many years with the railroad, were severanced out with two years pay. Engineers working without firemen received more pay but it was much better with a fireman at that time. All the firemen left were promoted engineers, and those that could not hold a job as an engineer were cut back as a fireman and went to firing passenger. But the day of the passenger jobs were coming to a close.

Once in those days, glancing through a magazine, I read that the Southern Pacific was becoming the most overstaffed official corporation in the U. S. I noticed this was very true. It was a regular saying among the men out on the road that a trainmaster hid behind every bush and signpost along the right-of-way, and if it wasn't a trainmaster it was a nine-day wonder, a Stanford graduate who knew nothing about the workings of a railroad.

Mary related to me that one day, while she was doing some filing, and the door to another office was open, she heard D. J. Russell, the president of the Southern Pacific, say to our superintendent, "We have a good railroad, it's making money for the stockholders. Now all we need to do is get rid of the human element." That was how much that man thought of his fellow man. In my observation, this was the start of the decline of the Southern Pacific Company. Russell's idea to overstaff the officials came mostly from the efficiency experts that he hired. Also, the trainmasters and suchlike were required to attend classes on how to handle employees. This was brought to my attention by someone who took the class but decided not to continue because he could not bring himself to treat his friends the way he had been instructed to do. Russell wanted the employees to be afraid and bow down under official pressure, but this never worked. All that his regime accomplished was to kill the goose that laid the golden egg. I was thankful for the old guard that still dominated the rules in San Francisco, but how long would they last, I wondered?

The round-house was all that remained at Mojave; all other buildings were being taken down. It was like entering a morgue when I went down to the round house with my power to pick up some units to take with us for Bakersfield. Without a fireman, I had to do all the work myself. I hoped that the units would be in one set so I would just have to couple up and do the necessary electric and air hose connections. But that was not the situation. The units on my list were buried in the middle of three different consists. I figured it would take me about two and a half hours to accomplish all that had to be done. I could halve that if I could secure help from someone. I called the yardmaster, but he told me there was no help available.

"I've been on duty over eight hours and I'm going to go over to the restaurant to eat because there is a lot of work for one man," I protested.

"You can't eat. You never notified us of your intention to eat."

"I was never notified of all this work until arriving here

either," I pointed out. "You raise horses don't you?"

"Yes, but what has that to do with this?" He was becoming indignant.

"You feed them in the morning and then about nine or ten hours later you give them another flake of hay, don't you?" I asked.

"That's right."

"Then maybe I should trade places with your horses, they eat better than I do, right?" He hung up the phone.

Eating made me feel better about the whole situation. I didn't blame the company for not wanting us to stop and eat. The more the crews ran straight through the better it was for the company, but it was still against the agreement between the brotherhoods and the company to be refused permission to eat. The company tried to tackle the problem by purchasing box lunches for the crews that were handed up at Mojave, if the crews ordered them ahead of time. This was fine for a while but I knew of one engineer who, when he arrived at Mojave on his way to Bakersfield, stopped the train after receiving his box lunch. The yardmaster wanted to know why he had stopped.

"I am eating my lunch," he replied.

"The idea is to keep you moving."

"I can't do that," the engineer responded on the radio. "You see, I have ulcers and can't run the engine and eat at the same time or they will act up." So many of us after that developed ulcers.

Back at the round-house, I planned my switching moves. There were many moves to make: uncoupling and coupling up air hoses, plus electric cables, and also handbrakes to release to tie down again. One move that I did was to get one unit out from a consist of five, leaving one set by itself until I switched out the one that was to go with me. All the units were supposed to be left with handbrakes secured on each one. I did not check the one I left by itself, and after it had been cut away from the rest, it started to roll towards the east end of the yard. In the darkness I could see small steplights. Oh my God! I thought. If that derail is lined, and most of the time it was, that unit will end up going to Lancaster. If any train is coming west, what a mess it will be.

I started to run in the dark, hoping not to stumble. Whichever way the engine ended up, it was slated for destruction if it couldn't be stopped. I felt the gravel and the ties beneath my feet and hoped every second that I would make it to the runaway unit. In my younger years I was in good shape, physically, so I used every ounce of strength available in my legs, at the same time blasting the bastard who had failed to secure the handbrake on the unit. My body was in deep sweat when finally my outstretched hand grabbed the grab iron of the diesel. I climbed on and forced myself to the cab. Luckily the door was not padlocked and the brake handle was left in the controls. The runaway stopped just before arriving at the derail, which happened to be properly lined. A photo finish, and no cameras around to catch the action! I ran the diesel back to its original position and after a minutes rest, and after securing the brakes and chaining the wheels, I left to continue my work.

I could hear him coming over the idling of the diesels. His roar was like that of a wild beast of the jungle, but my anger was bigger than all outdoors. I could feel the storm of the century approaching with its mighty roll of thunder and the quick snapping of lightning. I braced for the onslaught as Levi Franklin came in view of the round-house lights.

"What in the damnation are you doing?" He blasted me as

loud as he could.

"And what in the hell do you think I'm doing?" I roared back with the same intensity. I believe all Mojave must have heard the ensuing argument.

"I could fire you for this," Levi finally said. That hit me a little below the belt and maybe I should not have said any more. But too much had been said and we both were angry. Not with each other but with the company for allowing a situation like this to exist, so we had to have it out.

"Levi," I blasted, "whoever thought of this move should be fired! Look at it." I handed him the list of what had to be done.

"There isn't any switchman to pull the pins or to line the switches. They say it's the round-house responsibility, not the yardmasters. Also, the bastard that brought this bunch of units in and didn't tie the brakes on all of them should be fired, not me."

I told him about what I had just gone through, my face getting redder and redder as I got more and more heated about it.

"Do you know who came in on the units?" Levi asked, a little more subdued.

"No Levi, I don't," I replied with a little less anger. "If you want to help the situation, you can do it right here."

Levi and I took one hour and thirty-five minutes of hard work to get it all together. When we finished, we were wet with sweat.

"Thank you, Levi," I said.

"Don't mention it," he replied, back to his usual easy manner. "Let's sit down a minute and catch our breath. I want to show two hours on this work and then I'll personally see that this will not ever happen again. I will also find out who came in on the consist and didn't tie the brakes." I knew then the

208

sparks would fly again.

"Now get out of town," Levi said after we had rested. Then he walked away, forgetting his remarks about firing me or anything else. That was Levi's way. In all the years I knew him, he never fired anyone to my knowledge.

Back on the train, and waiting for the orders to leave, I figured the tonnage against the added power. Having much more than we needed it looked like we would fly up the mountain to Tehachapi, but with only two hours to work we could not begin to make Bakersfield.

Looking back towards the depot, I waited for the conductor to deliver our train orders from the operator stationed at the depot. Seeing his lantern appear I glanced at my watch. Fifteen minutes had lapsed since we were ready to continue, making our working time shorter. The conductor was a Los Angeles division person running off the miles that were owed to them because of the distance work by the San Joaquin crews between Los Angeles and Saugus belonging to Los Angeles division.

Upon arriving he handed me the orders.

"Why were you so long picking up the units? he said brusquely. "Usually it is only a short while to pick up some units but you were over three hours. The dispatcher is very upset because we won't make it in now. Also he wants to know why you went to eat without giving him notice."

"Mister," I began, slapping my hand on top of the control stand, "I'm going to repeat this just once more. You or none of your brakemen offered to help in picking up those units that were buried in three different consists. A three-hour job for one man—and I wasn't going to do all that work without eating, while the rest of you sat on your ass over here and slept. And besides, when I was eating I saw you and the rest of your henchmen sitting in the back dining room of the restaurant filling your guts while you thought I was doing all the work."

"But you have a contract and get paid for doing that work," the conductor insisted.

"Right you are, and also I have a contract to eat after being on duty a reasonable length of time. I think it says five hours and twenty-five minutes, and furthermore, if we don't all make the company as well as the men live up to the contract, the company will pull us off one by one. They already have started with the firemen—the brakemen are the next target and then who knows? Maybe you."

The conductor had had enough. He gently backed off the engine as I grinned to myself. I filled my pipe and reached down for my suitcase to play solitaire on the way up the hill, which helped me keep awake.

Arriving at Bakersfield at three-ten in the morning by carry-all, I debated whether or not to wake Mary to get a ride home, or to wait until six o'clock, when she arose to get ready for work. Then I could take her to breakfast. Looking at the clock in the crew dispatchers office, I saw that it would be a two hour and forty minute wait.

"Holy cow!" A loud voice came from the dispatcher.

"What's the matter with you?" I joking asked.

"There has been a major derailment out of Tehachapi with train #365," the dispatcher related as he listened on the telephone. I stood speechless, waiting for more news.

"Ralph Simmons and the head brakeman are both missing."

"By gosh," I said. "This was Ralph's last trip before going to San Francisco for an official job."

"Yes, that's right, sure hope he isn't hurt," the dispatcher remarked, just as a trainmaster came bustling excitedly through

210

the outer door.

"Did you hear about the derailment at Cable? he asked us.

"I thought it was just this side of Tehachapi," the dispatcher said.

"Yeah, between there and Cable," the trainmaster continued. "Four units left the rail on the second curve leaving Tehachapi and they were airborne across the Tehachapi Creek. And you know how deep a ravine that is? They all landed on the other bank. All the train is scattered along the right-of-way, but three cars are left on the rail, including the caboose. It's figured that the speed of the train was eighty miles per hour. The head brakeman was found dead, but they haven't found Ralph yet." The trainmaster left to carry the news to other offices.

I stayed at the crew dispatcher's office, waiting to find out about all the details about the wreck. Six o'clock came quickly. Ralph Simmons was finally found crushed to death, with his hand on the brake valve in emergency position.

Further investigations later showed that Ralph had played golf all day before going to work, and there was no alcohol or dope involved. It was assumed that both men fell asleep, but this was never substantiated. The only other doubt was whether the conductor, Warren Self, had put the train in emergency after finding the speed was too fast. What the outcome of any investigation revealed, I never knew.

The Move

Time elapsed and Mary and I enjoyed a happy relationship, in spite of the belief of others that we would be finished in less than a month. Engineer Hoot Mayo, a very good friend of mine, would stop by the office where Mary worked every week.

"Are you still married to Steffes?" he would ask. "I thought by now he would have flown the coop." Mary would smile and say, "things couldn't be better." Things were better for many years, until she passed away.

Mary and I talked many times about moving over to the desert, but I had rented the house out to a nice family and they were taking good care of the place. So thinking the situation over, we backed off for a while.

My second daughter, Charoline, had been dating a very nice boy and wanted to get married, and she did. The oldest girl was working and the youngest was about to finish school. I did not know that Margie had been sick with cancer until she passed away. The news was quite a shock to me. Things flashed though my mind, thinking back. Where did it all go wrong? There did not seem to be an answer. I guess the guilt lay with both of us, but I still felt remorse about it.

In 1965, for reasons of Mary's health, we decided to move to the desert. I still would work the pool job and drive to the desert every trip. We had all the time we needed to fix the house the way we wanted. When Mary sold her house in Bakersfield, she insisted upon using the money towards the desert home. When everything was complete, our home turned out to be a show place.

Rumors begin to circulate about the Palmdale cut-off to be built, running from Palmdale to Colton, a distance of seventy-eight miles. The track would start at Palmdale, run on the desert side of the San Gabriel Mountains to Cajon Pass, and then go down the mountains above the Santa Fe tracks into Colton and connect with the Southern Pacific track coming from Los Angeles. It would make it possible for all eastern trade from out of the Northwest to bypass the big city. I would be taking my pension in ten years and I never thought that I would see something like this happen before leaving the company. But I was to see a great many scientific advancements in my senior years.

The rumor came true. Early the next year, the Vinnell Corporation started excavating the right-of-way, putting in bridges and culverts. By February, the laying of the rail started and I bid on the work train that was to lay rail. I received the assignment. The second work train was the ballast-laying train and engineer Andy Smilehulla received the assignment on that one. My conductor was Harry Fielder, one good man for the job. Harry had bushy white hair, heavy sideburns, and blue eyes. He was a wiry man, who looked more like a sea captain than a conductor. Harry received the assignment with two of the best brakeman on the division, Herb Hunter and Eldon McLauren. Little Herb, as I always referred to him myself, always kept busy. He was short and stout and very precise and had a wife who was just as nice as he was. Eldon looked more like a businessman than a brakeman. He talked in a quiet refined manner, but when it came to the job of railroading, he was tops.

The new work law was in effect now so we were allowed twelve hours a day, even if we did not work that long. That was the company's incentive to get the job finished sooner. Also, no officials were allowed on any part of the cut-off, until we were finished with the job. We were to make our own rules of operation.

The job was finished two months ahead of schedule. With no accidents. Now if the Southern Pacific had taken our work as an example and removed all the unnecessary officials, like trainmasters, efficiency experts, and the like. If they had restored the honor system that we had had years before they would have gained the employees' respect. Discipline would have been taken care of by the senior employees, which would have been far more effective against the wrong doer, than discipline imposed by a company official. I witnessed the truth of this many times in my career. Overstaffing with officials was one more sign of the company's decline.

After my last run to Bakersfield out of Los Angeles, I would have to give up my regular room at Bakersfield. This was sad because I had had it for so many years; it was my home away from home. Since Mary and I had been married, I hardly went out on the streets of East Bakersfield, except to eat.

"Steffes must have a woman in his room—we never see him anymore when he is in town," some of my old friends remarked.

To hush that rumor up my landlady took a bunch of the doubters up to my room and showed them my hobby. I had been working on a model sailing ship and it was almost complete. When leaving for this last trip I gave it away.

After losing four days until the bulletins expired, I found when I arrived on the job that the work train had finished over two miles of track. The rail train consisted of many flat cars, measuring one quarter of a mile long. On these flat car contraptions were built to hold layers of quarter-mile long rails. Each car had a series of clamps to keep the rails stationary, but which allowed them to bend when taking making curves en route from where they were manufactured.

The morning I reported, Mary drove me to work. Later I found out that Harry Fielder had a carry-all assigned to him for picking up the crews and taking them to work, because the engine and caboose were to remain on the train wherever it tied up at night. The only time the train went to Palmdale was to change empty flats for loaded ones.

Each man on the job was issued a walkie-talkie to communicate on the radio with the engineer. Being on the rail train was very easy but the work was very precise. When shoving to spot the rail for the next pull, it had to be stopped on a dime. To accomplish this I shoved the train with air in the cars, in that way doing away with the roll in or out of the slack. When the cars in the train were spotted right, then the rails were pulled off by a special tractor from a car which had rollers and equipment to make the quarter-mile rail length slide easily.

The ties were laid out by a tie machine. This equipment was built by the Southern Pacific in Sacramento, California. It looked something like a forklift, and as it moved the ties would go through the machine and would be laid on the ground spaced exactly right. Trucks would deliver the ties in stacks four feet high and three or four feet wide along the right-of-way at given intervals. This machine worked fine when it was in good condition, but most of the time it was not, so the ties had to be laid out by the workmen. A gang of workmen would put tie plates on the ties for the rail to lay on and as the rail was pulled by the tractor, it was guided on the plates and then other men would spike the rail every fourth tie. When this operation was complete, it was our turn.

Harry and the crew would have me shove the rail train on this flimsy spiked rail for a quarter of a mile. At the end, the last car had to be spotted just right so that the operation could start all over. If I remember right, the complete operation took between forty-five minutes and one hour. Securing the rail at the rail joints was accomplished by clamps on each side of the two rails with a "dead man," a seven-inch piece of rail plug, between them. Then the rail was completely spiked by the automatic spiker, a machine which did the work of twenty men or more, and the rock ballast spread and tamped, automatically. Then the welder did his job. Two hydraulic twenty-one tons jacks worked in reverse as a stretcher clamped one on each rail. The welder took the "dead man" out and stretched (pulled) the rail together within a fraction of an inch, then welded the two ends of the rail together. This was done by putting ceramic on each side of the joints of the rail, making a mold, and then pouring molten metal into it. After it had cooled, a grinder came along, broke the ceramic mold off and dressed the weld down smoother.

As I sat on the engine waiting between moves, reading or playing cards, there was always the faint rat, tat, tat of the automatic spiking machine behind me, as it spiked down the rails. Sometimes the ballast train would come up behind me and then, and if I had time, I would visit with Andy.

One hot day in the early afternoon I was going back with a train of empties to exchange for a trainload of rails. The track did not have any ballast at this particular stretch of the road. I was traveling at a very slow speed, when the rails in front of me, without any warning, went into a double S curve. Before I could stop the train, the front trucks derailed, going on the ground with the wheels of the engine.

While we were waiting for a truck to being some ties to put under the engine wheels, I asked Willey, the foreman of the complete operation, why the rails had a tendency to do this in hot weather and why it did not happen when the ballast was holding the track in place.

"The track normally expands lengthwise but when it can't then it will expand up and down.," he explained to me. "The expansion is still there and it has to go in some direction."

After a time we rerailed the engine and I backed the train up a slight way. With steel bars and many strong backs the workmen were able to take the S curve out of the rail and put an extended bulge in the track so we could continue on our way.

That evening, when the steel rails cooled, the track straightened out by itself.

The Old War Horse

Jack Bones was a handsome, sharp blue-eyed man, with a slender, wiry build. His face was tanned by the desert sun and wind, and he was sort of a legend in and about the community of Little Rock. He grew up there with his brothers, and all of them, including Jack, owned vast beautiful acres of peach and pear orchards. Jack was quite a ladies' man, which was not a fault in his character—he was good-hearted, charitable and was good for the community.

It was a Sunday night when I took the car up to the gas station to fill it up. Jack Bones had just filled his as I pulled up.

"Hello, Charlie," he greeted me, "How in the hell are you? I saw you today out near 56th Street. What were all those guys doing around your engine? Was there anything wrong?"

With all the questions he asked, I forgot which was the first.

"No," I replied to the last question. "The heat turned the rail and my front trucks got derailed." I made out that it was like nothing.

"Hey," Jack continued, "How about taking Stella for a ride on the engine?" Stella was Jack's wife, a very pretty little woman with long wavy brown hair, big eyes, and a thin straight nose. I thought many times, how in the hell did Jack ever snag such a fine woman like her, but since he was a ladies' man that seemed to account for it. I paused for a moment's thought, knowing that taking a person on the engine was strictly against the rules. But the rules were different out there.

"Do you know where the first siding out of Palmdale is?" I asked.

"Yep, I know."

"OK, you bring Stella and I'll have Mary ready to go, and if you have one or two more who want to come have them there as well, if you like. I'll let them off at the crossing by Dewrea's place. Be sure you're there to pick them up. You do know where I'm talking about?"

"You bet—what time in the morning?" he inquired.

"No later than five after eight and wait there until I arrive."

"OK," he said, grinning, as he drove away.

I told Mary that she was going for a ride on the engine and that Stella would be there and maybe two more. Mary immediately phoned Stella to see what she was going to wear, just like all women do. The next morning was cold and brisk but the sun was out. I told Harry about the women going for a ride and he thought it was great, wishing his wife was going to be one of them, but she was down in Los Angeles for the day.

The train was sitting on the mainline at Palmdale number two, the first siding about two miles east of town. Bringing the loaded train from the house track where it was set out for us to use, we had pulled it out to Palmdale number two and left it overnight. Now the engine would have to back through the siding with the caboose, then come up the main to the other end of the train and shove it all to the end of the track for unloading and laying the rail. As I arrived at the train, Jack was there with the four women, all wide-eyed and laughing. This was a big event in their lifetimes. I helped them all on the engine, Eldon cut the engine off the train and Herb lined me down the pass track.

"Why are we going back, honey?" Mary asked, while the others hemmed and hawed about riding on the engine.

"We're running around our train to shove it out to the end of the track to start our rail laying," I explained to her. She

218

nodded her head in understanding.

"Here," I continued, "blow the whistle." She pulled the rope which the old 3900 diesel still had. Mary laughed when the others jumped and then laughed, so they all had to try. Women are little girls at heart; they still like dolls and in a crowd, when they let their hair down, they act like kids. This is fine, but they should not accuse us men of always being little boys until they look in the mirror and see themselves.

Herb Hunter and Eldon McLauren rode the lead car directing me with walkie-talkie radios as I shoved the train. And of course the speed was only fifteen miles per hour. Some mornings it was very chilly and little Herb would drop off as the train came close to the end of the track and catch the caboose or engine to get warm. He would always tell me that he wanted a cup of coffee or something, but I could see him shaking with cold. Harry Fielder would drive the carry-all to the destination and on his way flag any crossing against traffic en route. As we traveled along I let each woman sit in my seat to see how it felt to be an engineer. I have forgotten the names of the other two women—this was all a long time ago—but I think they were relatives of Stella Bones.

The ride and the excitement were over too soon. Dewrea's Ranch crossing came up and I stopped the train to let my passengers off. But no Jack Bones was around.

"What will we do?" Mary asked.

"I'll kill him when I catch him," Stella chirped in.

"Now Stella, he just got a little mixed up." I tried to smooth the situation over.

"His rear end is going to be mixed up when I get through with him," Stella said quietly.

About that time Harry drove up and saved the day, putting them all in the carry-all and taking them back to Little Rock, as we continued on to the job site. I never knew what happened to Jack, but I bet it was plenty.

One day, as the work was approaching the vicinity where a siding named Wash was to be located, Harry drove up in the carry-all and climbed on the engine.

"Morning," I greeted as he acknowledged me.

"Everything is bristling up there and everybody's in a state of confusion," he said, sitting down on the fireman's seat with a yawn.

"What's it all about Harry?" I inquired, a little puzzled.

"Well, word is out that D. J. Russell is flying here tomorrow in a helicopter to inspect the job and to see how the work is progressing."

"Isn't that too bad that the old war horse has to mar the day by showing up," I replied.

"I don't think that we're going to lay any rail today," Harry went on. "They got those greased monkeys stumbling all over themselves; trying to get things in order." Harry sleepily stretched out on the two seats with another yawn, then turned on his side and was snoring before I could say anything more. I went on playing solitary, hoping it would rain on the morrow, but that never happened.

As planned, the old bull of the woods came flying in on a 'copter. He went around telling everybody what a good job they were doing, of course, since the project was a month ahead of schedule. Saving money for his stockholders was not mentioned, but money was the prime object of this avaricious man's life. He must have hated engineers because he never came near the engine. But I figured the engine and the performance of the engineer were more important than his high-paying job which produced nothing. I realize that a certain amount of official personnel is required to run a business or a corporation but the Southern Pacific was getting top heavy, and sooner or later, the fiddler has to be paid. There were too many officials who were not producing anything to offset what they cost the company. One good official, of course, is worth more than a hundred bush men. A good official acts as a go-between for the employer and the employee. What he produces is then worth whatever he costs the company, because the employee will back him up and see that others do the same. Levi Franklin, Buck Brewer, Smokey Snider, Lee Master, Hastings and Gallington, to name only a few, and I am sure there were a lot more who belonged in this group. I was glad that Russell didn't come near me on that day. People like that made me queasy.

The work went on until reaching Highland, the top of Cajon pass some 4100 feet higher than Colton. We lost three working days on account of bad weather, one day of blowing wind and two days of being snowed out.

According to the agreement, my job would be turned over to the Los Angeles Division crews upon reaching Highland. In the timetable Highland was spelled as Hiland. This move left me with a bump, so I took several days off before bumping on the ballast job. The ballast train moved around very much, which I enjoyed for a change. When ballast was not being spread we did clean up work, such as picking up ties, left-over tie plates and so on. Spotting empty gondolas at the rockpit at Little Rock and pulling loads was the early morning job. This job was much harder work then the rail-laying job, but I was home and the job had the same conditions and entitlements that the other job had, except that I had to drive to Palmdale number two and back every day. The biggest drawback on this job was the dust that was created in unloading ballast, especially when the wind was blowing in my direction. The rock quarry was supposed to water the cars down but that was seldom accomplished.

The train crew on the ballast job was from Los Angeles Division. George, the conductor, was a tall dark-haired young fellow who talked with a slow Arkansas drawl, although whether he was actually from that state, I did not know. He also walked with a slight limp. George and I had something in common—we both liked woodworking. The two brakeman on the crew were Don Coats and Al Dew, both fine young men. Don was an easy going good-looking lad who took his job seriously. Al was something else, with black hair, and a dark complexion. He was a little shorter than the rest of the crew and had a short temper. Al and I became good friends later on in life.

While spreading ballast, sometimes one of the crew would relieve me and run the engine for a while. This always ended up in an argument between the other two, because of the friendly competition between all three. One little misinterpretation of the hand signals given from the other two on the ground would build into a mountain of friendly arguments between them. It reminded me of a bunch of kids, but this was one way of making the job pleasant.

All three trainmen lived down in the Colton area, or towards Indio, but they shared one auto to drive up through Palmdale. Then as the work progressed toward Hiland, one would drive the car along the railroad. They talked me into running the train back by myself from where the ballast cars were empty to Palmdale number two and tying the train down along with the engine. This was so they could go home from where they were on Saturday. The first time I tried this dangerous caper, it was a little scary. Every road crossing proved to be a nightmare, and then there was the thought of maybe

maybe derailing somewhere along the way. But fortunately nothing ever happened, and then it became almost an every night occurrence.

One day I had a good idea about using railroad ties for banking up my front yard. I figured it would take fifteen or sixteen to do the job. Going to work one Monday morning, I asked George, "what is done with the old ties they use under the gondola wheels to spread out the ballast with?"

"I guess they discard them. You need some?"

"Sure do, but I haven't anything to haul them with, even if I can get them."

"Well, we'll see what we can do about that," he said as he went off to talk to a foreman of the ballast gang. Not thinking of the ties anymore, we left for the rock pits at Little Rock. Digging out about thirty cars of ballast, was one day's work for us. The foreman and the train crew between them had perfected a unique system that increased production of car unloading immensely. We completed the job in record time so we were getting an early quit every day. Some days we would dig out fifty cars and store twenty at Wash to build up a backlog. In the operation, from what I could observe, the foreman in charge would open the doors on the bottom of the cars just enough to spread a light load of rock on the track. Then we would come back over the spread and stop at the beginning. The workmen would then take a tie and place it under the car against the wheels in the direction of travel. The oil in the creosoted tie would be enough to let the tie slip along the top of the rail, spreading the ballast as we moved along. And of course it was up to the supervisor to regulate the flow of ballast according to conditions.

The skill of these men and the potential of an early quit made a good combination. We were able to shave off the working hours and also receive the full twelve hours pay. Thirty cars unloaded was way above what was expected for that amount of time worked in a day. The system that the men had devised, and the results gained from it, should have been enough evidence of what the company could accomplish over the entire system. But instead it received a hard-nosed reception from many non-producing highly paid officials trying to make a name for themselves. True, the labor force needs officials, but to lead them, not push and badger them.

Arriving home that night after locking the engines up and securing the train, I felt tired as I filled out my time slip.

"Boy! three more weeks," I thought to myself, "then Mary and I will leave for a well deserved vacation." The most amazing coincidence however, was that the entire bunch of our crew was slated to have our vacation at that same time.

Several days went by and one night after work, upon driving into my long drive and coming to the front of the house, sat a nice neat stack of railroad ties, twenty in all.

"When did the ties get here?" I asked Mary.

"Oh, about noon. A yellow truck drove in and two men unloaded them." Mary seemed quite pleased.

"Didn't you give them a tip?"

"Should I have?" she asked.

"Well I'll find out who they were and give them five dollars apiece for their trouble. The ties are sure nice and now we can get the front fixed up the way you wanted it to be."

Work on the road continued. We had the ballast completed to Hiland and it looked good.

The Almost Fatal Accident

Downhill to Colton, thirty miles from Hiland, the grade was 2.2 percent. One day in the mid-morning, I tipped over

Hiland with the ballast train, having 6000 tons going downhill to Canyon. They wanted me to hold this train at a slow speed and spread ballast going downhill. I thought there was a chance it could be accomplished, if I did not have so much tonnage, and if the engine brakes would hold the train.

"Calling the conductor on the ballast train."

"Yeah, go ahead Charlie," he replied, as if he knew I would be calling on the radio.

"We have too much tonnage for me to hold the train downhill going that slow. Why don't we go to Canyon, set out half the cars and then spread ballast shoving up hill?" I suggested. After a little hesitation, George called back.

"Charlie, they want to try it this way for now."

"OK, we'll try. I'll do the best I can. Are you ready to spread?"

"We are ready to spread and the tie is placed under the car," George informed me.

Having twelve pounds of air reduction on the train line standing there, I knew that if I recharged the brakes, the engine alone could not hold the train from running out. So I reversed the engine and shoved against the train until the brake line was charged, then I used the feed valve to reduce the train line about four pounds of air. I put the engine in forward motion and let the engine brakes off. Nothing happened; the train held. Normally it should have started to roll, and then the speed could be governed by the engine brakes. Opening the throttle a notch, the train lurched forward and before I was able to check it with the engine brakes, the air went into emergency.

"I'm sorry George," I apologized over the radio. "I just couldn't hold it even with air in the train."

"I know," George came over the radio. We got a knuckle twenty-two cars back. We'll have a new one in it directly, then we'll take this train down to Canyon. Leave half of the gondolas there and shove the other half uphill and do it like you said. Maybe they will listen to the engineer sometime." I knew he was directing his remarks to foreman Willey, who also had a walkie-talkie. Willey was always in a hurry and cut corners, no matter what the cost.

"Charlie, the knuckle is in," George informed me. "Now back up about a half of a car to couple up."

"All right, they're coming back," I said, releasing the brakes and shoving against the cars.

Working till about noon that day, we finished all the ballast spreading with the cars we had hold of. I expected to return to Canyon but Willey directed us to leave for Hiland. As we arrived at the side track Hiland there was a dirt road leading off from Freeway at Cajon Pass, which connected to the railroad. There we saw a stationary black limousine. Several men stood by it waiting for us. In the side track, we had left a few empties and the caboose. We put the empties all together and went up the main line in order to come back to the side track to retrieve our train. I was puzzled about this move, but George climbed on the engine with one of the blue-suited officials. It was the first time any official had been on the engine since the beginning of this job.

"And who are you?" I asked. George introduced him to me but his name meant nothing to me. He was a slender man, about forty, and with an untanned face, indicating that he worked in an office. I was informed that he was the chief engineer in the engineering department, out of San Francisco.

"Have you traveled any fast speed on this rail yet?" he asked me. "Like forty or fifty miles per hour?"

"No, that's out of the question when there are so many people working around here," I cautioned him.

226

"We have all the people off the track and the right of way from here to Palmdale. What we want you to do when you get on the main line," he instructed me, "is to run forty-nine miles per hour all the way to Palmdale so we can test the track."

"What about the rail train? I know they're coming out with a load of rail." The rail train was working in the vicinity of a place called Devore, below Canyon.

"They are in the siding at Wash," George chipped in. "They have instructions to stay put until we've arrived."

"That is nice to let me know," I said, winking at George." And there isn't any written instruction on this move?"

"Yes, I have a wiregram about it," the general office man said, pulling it out of his pocket.

"Why in the hell didn't you show this to us at first, so we wouldn't be in the dark on everything that is taking place around here?" George scolded. Looking at George, I could tell he was getting a little upset, and this was unusual for him because he always hid his temper.

"Now once more," I repeated, stopping the train abruptly and hoping that Herb and Al were sitting down in the caboose. If they were not, they certainly were sitting down now. "You are certain everyone has been notified to be in the clear?"

"Yes, they are in the clear," he repeated, but he seemed perturbed.

"We've worked all these months without an accident and we don't want one now!" I cautioned. George shrugged his shoulders as if to indicate that he witnessed everything.

"OK, we'll give her a try. About where do you want to get off? I asked again.

"The limo will pick me up at 165th street, the first crossing below Wash," he informed me, as I started the engine and train rolling. Fifty miles per hour and riding smooth as glass. It was

227

fantastic how the curves were banked perfectly to accommodate such speed. When we were working at slow speed, I never realized the quality of engineering of grading and banking that went into the building of this project. I congratulated the man from the general office, although I still had an uneasy feeling. Years of experience teaches this kind of intuition to everyone who tries to do their job well. I sat back to enjoy the ride, kowing that I was the first to initiate the track at this speed.

It was just then that it happened. We were approaching the left-hand curve near Hi-volt, when George yelled stop! I saw the approaching motor car as I put the train into emergency. I knew the driver; his name was Bob White, a most likable person working on the project. Bob was young, always smiling or laughing, and worked with gusto on his job. His cute little wife and baby would make any man happy, and here he was coming towards us maybe to his death. Bob did all the welding or grinding and was on his way back to the rail head.

Bob's reflexes were quick, and he put the car into reverse as fast as could be done. Just as we were about to make contact, Bob jumped to the side, hitting the dirt and rolling in rock and dust. To my surprise. he regained his footing. The engine hit his car a good whack, and I thought it would splinter it into pieces. But this didn't happen; indeed, the car did not seem badly damaged. The locomotive stopped shortly after the impact, and to my relief, I saw Bob running alongside of my engine. I heard the grinding of metal in front of the diesel, then all of a sudden, the motor car, still on the rail, started back the way it had come, towards Palmdale. Bobby was running after it, and about ten yards in front of us, he caught and stopped it.

"Mister," I began after regaining my composure. "You just witnessed an almost fatal accident and it would have been your fault. You were so cocksure that everyone was off of this portion of the cut-off. Up till now we've been accident free and we've done a damn good job, without any official interference. But you people can't wait until work is finished and all the track people are out of the way. This is the ending of your testing as far as I am concerned."

Bobby was climbing up on the engine and I wondered what he was about to say. I looked at the poor fellow after I had finished dressing him down. He was shaking then. With Bob coming up to take another piece out of his posterior, he would not be able to sit down for a week.

"Which one of you is at fault?" Bob demanded, sternly.

"Charlie, you weren't supposed to be coming this way until four p.m." Bob said.

"I am responsible," the general office man said, taking the blame. I thought this was courageous of him. "I wasn't told of any time period and I am very sorry." That apology did not stop Bobby from dressing down his boss and I would not put in print what was said.

Taking an early quit that day, I told George that this was my last trip because I was going on a five-week vacation.

"You too?" And he began to laugh. "All three of us are going at the same time on a vacation. What a coincidence. Boy, they're going to have fun finishing up the job. There is only two weeks work left."

It was really a sad adieu between us because we had worked so closely together. It was the best job that I ever held working on the railroad, but it was over and good things seemed to end.

Working the Cut-off and the Later Years

Mary and I drove to Southern Illinois to visit Mary's aunt and on the return trip motored through the mountains in Arkansas to Eastern Oklahoma, to stay a few days with

Charoline. The narrow road followed the top of a ridge for several miles in Arkansas. As Mary and I traveled on this ridge, which was skirted with beautiful trees and brush, we came upon a turnout where stood a makeshift fruit and vegetable stand.

"Mary, let's stop and see what we might find here in the way of fruit," I said.

After parking the car we looked over the produce and noticed some large beautiful white potatoes, better than I have ever seen grown around Bakersfield.

"The potatoes are sure nice-looking," I remarked to the attendant. "Do you grow everything yourself?"

"Waul, most all things, I reckon sometimes we git other stuff some place else," he replied in his native drawl.

"Are these potatoes grown here? If they are they are better than anything around where we come from."

"I reckon we kin look at the bag to see if they come from around here," he said.

Looking at the burlap bag, Mary and I began to laugh. It read, grown in Bakersfield, California.

"You see dear, I told you all the number one grade produce is shipped out of the state and we have only inferior grade for ourselves," Mary said, still laughing. She should know, because before we were married, she worked during potato season as a bookkeeper in the shipping sheds. Looking further about, my eyes fell upon some short slabs of wood.

"Is that black walnut you have there?" I asked the attendant.

"Yep, that sure is," he replied, and he made the price so low that I could not resist buying as much as the station wagon would hold. Doing wood sculpturing as a hobby for much of my life, good walnut like this was at a premium, so our stop was far from a complete loss.

Five weeks went by fast and it was time to return home. Like the old saying goes, it is good to travel but it is sure good to come back home. I liked putting my feet down in my own flower bed. After making ourselves comfortable and unpacked the car, I phoned the agent at Palmdale.

"Palmdale. Can you hold a minute?" It was Ivan Upshaw's voice that answered the phone. I waited a few minutes until he came back on the line. "Yeah, this is Upshaw."

"Hello Ivan," I greeted him. "What you doing over here? You get tired of Bakersfield?"

"Well, this job came open, so I grabbed it. Charlie, they are so damn busy around here, the cut-off was finished yesterday and all the dignitaries, including the Governor, are going to be here tomorrow to drive the golden spike for the opening. Are you going to be here?"

"I don't think I'll be there, but thanks anyway. I know you're busy so I'll let you go, thanks." Then I hung up.

I found out later why it took five weeks to finish the job that we could have done in two weeks. The extra board crews that took our places ran into a lot of trouble. A trainmaster and a road foreman went out with them on the job. Keeping strictly to the book of rules, the brakemen had to do a useless job of flagging in both directions, leaving the conductor do all the work. At meal break the crew were taken to a restaurant in San Bernardino. They only managed to unload eight to ten gondolas of ballast a day to our thirty. And topping it all off, they had two derailments.

Dick Swartz our local chairman of the Brotherhood of Locomotive Engineers, did a very good job in negotiating a plan for working a split seniority territory with the Los Angeles Division. This left two of the job runs at Palmdale to Indio, the others worked out of Indio. I bid for one of the

231

Palmdale jobs and received it.

Shortly after I spoke to Ivan Upshaw the phone rang again. I let Mary answer it, believing it would be one of her many friends.

"It's for you, dear," she said, as I was about to leave and make my rounds of the yard. "It's Mr. Brewer, your boss." Wondering what he might want, I came back to the phone.

"Charlie, can Smoky Snider and I come over to see you? We're at Palmdale."

"Why certainly, you don't have to call and ask for that. What have I done now?" I inquired in a joking way.

"Nothing Charlie, we just want to ask some questions, if you don't mind."

"You know where I live. Mary will have the coffee on." As I hung up Mary was already hustling around trying to straighten things up in the house with a dust mop and a broom. I had no inkling of what they wanted to discuss with me, and turned on the television. But that did not quiet my nervousness about the two good officials coming to talk to me, so I went out on the patio and sat at the table by the water falls, sipping on a fresh cup of brewed coffee. A knock on the door announced their arrival. Mary escorted Smokey and Buck out to where I was sitting, then she disappeared, bringing back with her a tray with two cups of hot coffee for the gentlemen.

"Let's sit down," I gestured after shaking their hands.

"Tomorrow the first train is going to leave here for Indio, over the cut off, and it's too bad that you're not on it because you know the road," Brewer began. "One of us will have to ride with the engineer on that train, who is going to be an extra board man."

"Have you any idea who it will be?" I asked.

"Not yet. He's coming out of Los Angeles; he'll be called

tonight to dead head up here," Smoky Snider added.

"We don't know any more about this cut-off territory than the man that's coming up to work on it," Brewer admitted. "We figured you with the experience of working on the work train would know more about this than anyone else."

Boy! did I feel honored, having these distinguished gentlemen coming to my house and asking me how to handle a train, when I knew that they were both as good as could be found anywhere.

"It's all going to depend on how heavy a train you have from here to Hiland," I began. "If the tonnage is high, you'll be in run eight most all the way to Hiland. The speed will pick up in the swells but not much, not enough to shut the throttle down. But when you get close to Hiland, about a mile and half, I would make a running test with the air, that would bring the speed down from fifty to about thirty or thirty-five miles per hour, which I believe is going to be the speed through that territory. And also, if the air test is made there, when tipping over Hiland down to Colton, you will not have a soft train line, it will be fully charged.

"There are two ways of tipping over Hiland. First, gather up your slack in the train while going on the flat through Hiland, and after going into dynamic braking, you will be able to hold your train for some length until the train is partially on the descending grade. When the maximum dynamic will not hold the train back, use the air and then regulate the speed with the dynamic. Now, the way I would handle it over Hiland, I would have an initial reduction of air in the train line going through Hiland pulling on the train and regulating the speed with the throttle until the train was almost on the declining grade, then go into dynamic braking. And of course you must use your own judgment as to the tonnage, etc."

233

"That second way is a neat way of handling a train," Smokey spoke up. "But there are men that can't do that. They might try it, but they'd have the train torn in many pieces."

"That is very true," Brewer commented. "The first system is what we'll have to use in teaching these engineers that work over here."

"But," I cautioned, "remember this. If a train starts raging on you to where you can't control it in that first few minutes, you had better stop and start all over." They both agreed to that and after much more discussion they thanked both Mary and me and left.

The Coming of Pot

My first trip on the cut-off came a few days later. Fortunately I was called with a Los Angeles division train crew. The head brakeman could direct me on his part of the railroad from Colton to Indio because it had been a long time since I worked down that way and a great many things had changed.

Arriving at Slover, the siding just before the junction of the Southern Pacific main line running to the Eastern states through the Imperial Valley, we were stopped by a red signal, which was the starting of the Centralized Train Control known as C.T.C. The operator at Colton informed me on the radio that we would have a slight delay at Slover because Smoky Snider had not arrived yet to ride with me to Indio. But the helper engine was on the way to Slover and could be cut in the train there, and cut out at Beaumont, a distance of twenty-three miles.

I found out that Charlie Picket was the helper engineer, as he stopped by our engine on the side track to deliver our running orders, so we would not have to pick them up at Colton. Many years had passed since Charlie and I were kids firing steam locomotives around Indio and Colton. Charlie did not change much down through the ages. He was thin with a sandy-colored complexion, some gray hair mixed in with red, and with a few freckles on his smiling face. We grinned at each other and shook hands; then he took off up the siding to be cut in our train.

After some time a carry-all drove up on the maintenance road and let Smokey out.

"Sorry I'm late, but I was in Los Angeles when I got the call, and I got here as soon as possible," he apologized.

"We needed the rest any way, Smokey," I assured him.

Every engineer who was new on the district was to have a rider three times, but after the first time Smokey rode with me, that was it. It was a good thing the brakemen who were called to go with me were experienced on the territory—they helped me out as I needed it.

Indio in the summer was hotter than Hades, but from fall to spring it was heaven, except when the blasted wind blew. I stayed at the hotel where all the Los Angeles to Indio pool engineers resided, and the company paid the rent. The rooms were darkened for daytime sleeping and each room was air conditioned. Some difference from many years ago! It was then I realized how time had made me old.

Marijuana (pot) was becoming very popular at that time. Many people were also starting to use harder drugs. One close experience I had with pot happened in the side track at Wash on the cut-off, while I was waiting for a train coming out of Hiland. Being able to view the track ahead for a long distance, the head brakeman, Robert, and I, waited patiently for the expected train. Robert had worked with me many times and his alertness amazed me, along with his ability to interpret the rules of his work. But on this day, something was amiss. He

235

sat on his side of the cab, saying little and staring at nothing in particular until the approaching train showed in the distance. Then he left the cab of the engine, on his side of the engine, between the rails of the tracks. I took notice because he always left the cab of any locomotive on the opposite side to the adjoining rails and then walked across to the other side after satisfying himself it was safe to do so. On this day Robert did not cross over to the other side of the tracks to roll the other train by for inspecting his running gear. Instead he started to walk towards the approaching train. Reaching the five hundred foot board, which marked the distance to the fouling point of the main line. All trains were supposed to stop short of this point only if their train would fit in the side track and if not, when they were permitted by the board. Robert hesitated at that point.

Suddenly I jolted myself awake. A short while before, Jack Bones had arranged for a deputy sheriff to come up from Los Angeles to teach us people in the Search and Rescue Posse how to detect and smell anyone smoking pot. Now I recognized it. I could discern the lingering smell in and about the cab of the locomotive. I remembered that on the way from Palmdale, Robert would frequently leave the cab and go back through the units, checking them, and then telling me that one was giving us some trouble. I knew by experience that an engineer can usually tell if his units are all performing well or not, and these units were doing their work. The only nonfunctioning contrivance was Robert going back for a joint to smoke, and he was sure high on it.

To my amazement, as the approaching train came closer, Robert hurried towards the switch. For the love of Pete!, I thought to myself. He is going to throw the switch in front of that speeding train coming towards us!

Dropping off my engine, I ran as fast as my legs would carry me and just as he was putting his key into the lock, with the oncoming train only yards away, I pulled him back from the switch. The engineer on the approaching train had already put his train into emergency but there would have been a terrible head-on collision if I had not gotten there first. All this would have never happened if Robert had not been high on pot.

Foolish Things

Working out of Palmdale was probably the best paying job that I ever worked, but it was also the roughest piece of railroad working in the two combined districts. I enjoyed the job, although many times I was called to ride with other engineers who were not qualified, or who had not been over the territory. Sometimes it was fine, other times it turned out to be hard. But the pay was handsome.

One trip I remember quite well. A young engineer named Russell Bates, who fired for me in the steam engine days, came off the extra board from Los Angeles to work the one other assignment we had at Palmdale. Russell's curly hair, brown eyes and short stocky build made him look like his dad, an engineer whom I had the privilege of firing for in the early days. Bates had not been over the district so I was called to ride with him. Russell was an excellent engineer, so I thought, boy! this was going to be a piece of cake, this trip. We started out of Palmdale number two with Russ running the engine. I settled back in the fireman's seat, intent on having a little rest. With the head brakeman back in the second unit, I had the two seats to stretch out on. I did not have the thought of falling asleep—I was just observing how Russ was performing, and he was doing beautifully. The drone of the diesel motors was also beautiful, and it lulled me into dreamland. All of the sudden the end of a glorious lullaby came. The engines stopped and so did the train with a hissing blow at the brake valve. We were in emergency. I sat straight up, blinking my eyes and grabbing my pipe and lighter for a smoke.

"Where are we, Russell?" I asked.

"We just left Wash a few minutes ago. If we are not broke in-too, we could have a blown air hose."

"Or a broken trainline," I added.

"What is wrong up there?" The conductor came in on the radio. Russell told him what we thought it was, and about that time the brakeman came up from the second unit, looking for a wrench with an air hose in his hands. Finding what he needed he left in the dark, and it was exceptionally dark that night. I walked back through the units seeing that they were all right, then got on the opposite side of the ground that the brakeman had walked back on. I had no idea what prompted me to do this. Between fifteen or twenty cars back my flashlight started to act up, so I crossed over to the other side of the train. My flashlight quit entirely. Looking ahead towards the engine, I saw the light of the brakeman between me and the locomotive. It looked like he was ready to mount the steps to the engine, and to make things more complicated, Russell was releasing the air on the brakes and would be leaving soon. My first reaction was to run, but that would be useless. In the dark, the chances of staying on my feet would be nil. If I had gotten off the engine instead of going back through units, Russ would have known that I was not there. But as it was he thought that I was back in the units somewhere.

What in the hell was I to do? I did not dare to try climbing up on a ladder of a box car because most of them did not go all the way to the top, and to hang on to one for miles would mean certain death. One would not be able to maintain a grip for that length of time. Then other thoughts flashed into my mind. Maybe I could get to the highway some two miles across the desert from the tracks. But then, in this black of night, that would be ridiculous. And even if it could be accomplished, who would stop and pick up a hitchhiker at this time of night? And another thing. When the company found out about this, they would be sure to fire my ass. When it was discovered that I was missing on the head end somewhere down the track, maybe at Colton, then a search party would be sent out. Boy, I could not live down a dumb trick such as this. The train was picking up speed when an idea came to me—my lighter! It might work. I gave a slow stop sign with the lighter lit, hoping the rear brakeman was sitting on the right side of the caboose. I yelled stop as I gave the stop sign, and the rear brakeman was on the job. He related it all to the conductor who in turn told the head end to stop.

"What in the stupid hell are you doing out here, Charlie? Why aren't you up where you belong?" The conductor dressed me down much harder than I can write about, and of course I had no defense. He was right.

"Back up," he told Russell, "we got to pick up a jackass." And I sure felt like one, but luckily I did not get left in the desert.

9. Mary's Adventure

Mary wanted to do something for herself. Being married to a railroad engineer is not an easy life for a woman. It's a bit like being a doctor's wife. They never know what to expect or how to plan a home life.

"What did you have in mind?" I asked.

"Well, we have a lot of space in the garage downstairs," she said, and hesitated, looking at me with her searching, beautiful green eyes. I knew something was stirring around in her pretty head. The house was built on three levels—the large four-car garage below, with three bedrooms and a bath above. Then there was a kitchen and family room with a master bedroom and bath leading off from an entry hall which opened into a sunken living room. All this was half between the garage and the bedrooms, with a short set of stairs down from the family room to the garage or up to the bedrooms.

"Go on," I said trying to be stern but not succeeding.

"We could take the garage door off and make windows with a regular door in its place and then go through the block wall and put in a sliding glass door for an entry door on the front end." She stopped for a moment to see what effect her words were having.

"Yes, go on," I said, slowly.

240

"Then with the room we have in the back with the big tall trees as a windbreak we could have a growing nursery, and very quickly downstairs a flower and gift shop with a nice counter to wait on customers. And out in front we could put up a sign by the side of the road with the name 'Hurstmont Nursery.' We have plenty of parking space back here also."

Mary was out of breath by this time and was looking at me out of the corner of her eye, as she always did when she wanted something. I looked at her, up and down, then looked away, thinking about this concoction she cooked up. Mary had had a second job at a nursery at Bakersfield for a long time and she was very good at it. I could see the possibilities for it working at our house.

"It will be a lot of work and I still will have to work at my job," I said, finally.

"Oh sure," she said. "I think it will work fine and give us a little more income, although maybe not much."

"OK, let's do it," I agreed.

Between trips I worked with Mary on the nursery project. While I was on trips, Mary planned of her inventory and calculated how much money we had to cover it with. As usual, there was never enough money, so we borrowed some. It took some time to set the nursery in motion because of the remodeling involved. Having a harsh winter that year made things go more slowly.

The Blizzard

It was raining hard one early afternoon, and by nightfall it had started to snow. The cold seemed to bite as I left for work, even though my clothes were heavy enough to withstand considerable cold weather. I was called to ride with a young Los Angeles division engineer. he was supposed to have had an official ride with him out of Indio. But for some reason the official was called back to Colton, so that made me number one boy for the job. But when I arrived at Palmdale, my call was canceled.

"Who is going to ride with the Los Angeles engineer?" I asked Jay Glass, the crew dispatcher on duty at that time.

"I don't know Charles, I just do as I'm told. The dispatcher said to hold you on duty for the next train because there is no other engineer in town. I believe there'll be someone at Hiland to ride with Ron down the hill."

Ron was the young engineer I was supposed to ride with. I found out that he had just been promoted as an engineer and now he had to go out on the most wicked pieces of railroad in the country in a snow storm.

I phoned up Mary while I waited for my train to arrive. She told me there was almost nine inches of snow on the ground and it was getting awful cold with a wind starting up. Two hours later my train went by the depot on its way to Palmdale number two siding. With much difficulty the carry-all drove us out to the train, and the snow was really blowing hard by then.

The engineer I relieved informed me that the radio did not work and there were no power packs to trade out on the rest of the units. Fred, my head brakeman, knew something about radios and he tinkered with the power pack as we started to leave the side track. But he discovered that a condenser or something like that was burned out and nothing could be done with it. Checking the orders on the way out of the siding, we found we had the right of way over everything to Hiland, and we would take siding there to meet two trains.

Figuring that the train was out of the siding, I started to work the engine to increase the speed. The snow caked on the windshield so heavily that it was difficult for the wipers to work. Visibility turned to almost zero. It was as if a white sheet had been thrown over the cab of the engine, as the storm approached near blizzard conditions. Never in my life have I ever experienced a storm like that. As the speed picked up a little, visibility became even worse. As the front of the engine plowed into snow over a foot deep it threw snow everywhere, much of it landing on the already snow-laden windshield.

"Do you think we should continue, Fred?" I asked.

"I don't know, but if we don't, we can't go back. We'll just be marooned out here."

"I think you're right. We'll keep going as far as we can. The train ahead of us should be almost to Colton by now. He's well over two hours beyond us," I said, making a wild guess. I eased the throttle down a notch, trying to keep the snow from kicking up in front of us, but to no avail. Looking out of the side window for a glimpse at the landscape, I caught a glance at the top of the mileboard approaching Wash.

"Wash is one mile ahead, Fred," I yelled, closing the window to keep out the vicious storm. Fred nodded his head; his eyes showed signs of fright, and maybe mine did too.

It showed up against the white snow—a weird-looking thing loomed up in front of us, and it looked like it was going to swallow us. And it did, but it spit us out just as fast. It was the overpass of highway #18 we traveled under, and the roaring muffled sound made Fred and I wince slightly, because we were very tense. In a blowing snow storm everything looked odd and took on unnatural shapes.

The grade increased somewhat after leaving the overpass, but the snow was getting deeper. I was puzzled because the snow on each side of the track was a foot or more higher than where we were traveling on the track. I figured if the snow was level across the track, we would be stalled and snowbound, but as it was we could keep moving. Plowing on in the curtain of white, we came to another object much bigger than the last one. It happened to be highway #15 from San Bernardino to Barstow. The speed of the train accelerated to forty miles per hour going under the overpass. Before arriving at Hiland, there was a stretch of many curves. The grade ascended a short way then leveled off.

That certain feeling was gnawing at me. It was as if I could smell disaster ahead. As if to compound the feeling, a fog had set in with wisps of snow flying in it. In the snow country this was called a "white out," making visibility zero. Figuring that Hiland was about a mile and a half further ahead, and we had to head in there for opposing trains, I slowed the train to twenty-five miles per hour. Then there was a hole in the sheet of white, just like somebody had torn a piece out of it. Across a ravine and around a right-hand curve, less than thirty car lengths away, stood a caboose. Someone was standing on the rear platform giving a slow stop sign with a fusee (a colored flare). Immediately I put the train in emergency, which immediately killed all the units of my engine. Fred made an exit through the window, and I ran to the back steps along the walkway. Jumping off and wallowing in deep snow, I hoped to escape the impending crash and derailment of box cars. To my surprise, the train stopped, making a nice gentle coupling into the caboose, just as I pissed in my pants. I was shaken, but beyond being angry. Plowing through the snow, getting completely wet from my waist down, I climbed on the caboose, confronting the conductor and the rear brakeman.

"You two nincompoops sit here on your ass and didn't give me any flag protection. You bastards never dropped one fusee or put out any torpedoes and you know that I didn't have a radio. What in the hell is wrong with you? Don't you know the rules?" The more I talked, the more angry I became, and if it weren't for Fred we would have come to blows. Fred finally persuaded me to leave the caboose. I learned later that the conductor and that same brakeman bid off the job.

The communication between the dispatcher and the operator at Hiland about how severe the storm was should have been enough to shut down all operations. The train ahead of us started to move, disappearing into the white mist, illuminated by our headlight. The awful silence was very weird because I had not started my units up, and the air was leaking off in the trainline. So, cold and wet, I shook myself and started to get things going again. After getting everything back to normal I went through the procedure of calling in the flag and waiting a few minutes, figuring if he was out, he would have time to come in. Then I moved the train forward very slowly, searching for the siding switch at Hiland and at the same time watching out for the train moving head. When we arrived at the switch, Fred had a very hard time getting the switch lined for us to enter into the siding on account of the freezing weather. But when the task was finally completed, I started to move into the siding, and after an hour of pushing and shoving the snow we made it into the siding and down to the train order office.

I found out that the engineer on the train ahead of me had a brakeman who was also making his first trip over the territory, and both of them were lost. So taking extreme measures, they had felt their way along until reaching Hiland, which accounted for the long time it had taken them to arrive there. The engine he was running had a snow-spreader in the front of the lead unit, and that explained why the snow was lying as shallow as it was on the top of the rail.

The poor young engineer who was supposed to pick up an

instructor at Hiland did not materialize, because the Cojon Pass had been closed to all traffic much earlier, and no one could drive up to help him. Of all the wrong things for a dispatcher to do, ordering an engineer down the mountain by himself in a terrible snow storm such as this was about the worst. I could not help but think of that bewildered young engineer attempting to take that train down a 2.2 percent grade by himself. Then I remembered that youth has no conception of fear. The young go blindly into the bowels of hell because they have not yet learned the meaning of fear or the lesson of safety. I thought back to my young years of learning—no one escapes that time of life.

The young competent faithful gladiator went down in the jaws of destruction. Getting his train a short distance out of Hiland he then pulled a draw-bar out of a box car, derailing two cars. There was nothing for us to do but sit and wait. The hours of service overtook us at Hiland and it was eighteen hours later before we were able to leave by automobile. Boy, was I hungry.

For three days after arriving back home from Hiland it rained and snowed. Not being called the second day, I called Ivan, the chief crew dispatcher.

"Is the railroad shut down?" I asked.

"You haven't heard about all wash-out on the cut-off?" he started in. "Why, there's more than twenty different places washed out from here to Colton. They figured it would be a week before things open up."

"That figures, from what I was in the other night, I can see there would be many wash-outs. But anyway, let me know when things clear up, please?"

"Sure will, Charlie, and have a good day." With that Ivan hung up.

246

In the time off I built a hot house which housed a long growing table. But I was stumped for some type of watering system for it until Mary came to my rescue and showed me how to construct a fogger system. She did it by putting a long pipe above the table with fogger sprinklers, as were used on vegetables in the stores, spaced evenly along the pipe and a time clock in which to operate the watering.

"Darn but you're smart," I complimented her. Women have much more brains and know-how than men give them credit for. The trouble with men in the time I am writing about was that they had dominated women and their world for too long. There are a great many things a woman can accomplish better than a man, and men should realize the woman's potential. For instance, I would rather have the care of a woman nurse than a man. To have a woman's hand on my aching head is much better than a man's, and there are many, many more jobs suitable for women than are suitable for men. God made men and women to be partners, not to be always sparring with each other to see who is better than the other because neither one is any better than the other. Man should not invade a woman's world, nor should women invade a man's world. There are jobs in a man's world that I think a woman should not undertake, like in law enforcement (except in clerical jobs), or in fire prevention, or any hard, dangerous manual work such as railroading. I know there are women who think they are men in a man's world, and we will always have that revolutionary element in our society. Now for myself, I think a woman is the most precious, beautiful, intelligent creature that ever inhabited this earth, and she was made for man to cherish and to hold in reverence because she is the center of his being here on earth. What more is there than having the love of a good woman?

I fixed the sprinklers like Mary suggested and it worked fine. Looking about for something to put in the soil on the table for growing, I found half a pound of Oregon pine seeds, so I used the bagful for the table. Just as the last seed was planted, the phone rang. For nine days there had been peace and quiet but now I was called for work. The railroad was on the move again!

The operator at Palmdale handed me the train orders and they contained several pages of slow orders, one eighteen miles long from Hiland to Dike of fifteen miles per hour. On viewing the condition of the track, I understood why. Other than that the complete trip was routine.

Living nine miles from the depot in the desert at Little Rock, I had a slight wait for Mary to drive over and pick me up to take me home—that is, if she wanted the car while I was on a trip, and most of the time she did.

"We have company," she said after giving me a warm greeting.

"Yeah, who?" I asked, getting into the station wagon.

"Jack something or the other, he's an engineer working on the Los Angeles extra board. He says he's on the San Joaquin Division."

"Oh that will be nice to see Jack. He's a good engineer and he has fired for me out of Los Angeles a lot of times," I told her. I am using the name Jack because I don't want to cast any shadow on his character.

"And how is Jack?"

"Well, he is not very well. He is sound asleep at home—I hope that is all right?"

"Oh yes, Jack is honest and trustworthy but he has a problem," I told Mary.

"Oh! what kind of problem?" Mary became alarmed.

"Nothing for you to worry about," I laughed. "Women is his problem. He has been married several times and he can't seem to find the right woman or the right woman find him."

"I see," Mary said, "that accounts for what he told me. Some girl kicked him out and he thought he was going insane, so he wanted to get away for a while." I began to laugh.

"So he picked your shoulder for sympathy?"

"Now, don't you say that," she scolded. "If a man needs help, we'll give it to him." And that was that.

When we arrived at home, there lay Jack on the divan, sound asleep, with his mouth wide open, playing a tune from bass to low alto, then repeating it. "Pretty good rhythm," I remarked to Mary.

"I don't think we ought to disturb him," she replied.

"And why not? There are three bedrooms upstairs with beds and he doesn't need to snore and snort down here where I can hear him in the next room. And besides, maybe I might want a little, you know how horny I am." She had no defense against that.

"OK, wake him. I'll go up and pull the covers down for him," Mary said.

Getting sleeping Jack upstairs was not easy, but finally I goosed him and he jumped to the top of the stairs. Whether he undressed for bed or not, I did not wait to see, because the smell of the dinner Mary was cooking was too much for me. Finishing off a big steak and other goodies, Mary and I went down to inspect the nursery. The fluorescent lights lit up the hothouse like day.

"Holy mackerel! Look Mary, the whole table is green and only four or five days," I said to her, and she nodded her head, smiling. It was then that I took hold of the nursery idea. I thought of all the multitudes of things we could grow and propagate. Boy, was I excited, but Mary took hold of my hand and led me upstairs to the house and to our bedroom.

Jack was still asleep when Mary and I were cooking breakfast. It was a wonder the smell of coffee brewing and lean bacon sizzling, and hot biscuits coming out of the oven, as well as the sound of eggs crackling in the frying pan, didn't wake him.

"Look what is coming down the stairs," Mary said, and there came Jack.

"Good morning," he grinned. "What smells so good?"

"Mary's cooking. What else?"

One thing Jack wasn't, and that was lazy. After eating, we went out into the nursery and he worked hard all day long helping us. He was very enthusiastic about Mary's adventure, especially the hot table.

"What are you going to do with all those trees, Mary?" he inquired.

"We'll leave them grow a little higher, then call the Forest Department and see if they might want them." As it turned out they did, and later came with large boxes filled with peat moss and transplanted them, intending to take them far back into the mountains for reforesting.

Jack had left to return to work in Los Angeles, but promised to return soon, which he did many times to help in the nursery. Mary reminded him to bring his laundry so she could wash it for him. I gave her a bad look, but women are women.

Just after Jack left I was called to make a patch (to relieve a crew whose hours of service were up) at Hiland. Not losing much time at Hiland, changing crews, we were on our way to Palmdale. The trip seemed too easy until we came by the Little Rock gravel pits, where I hit something on the track. It was a very large iron woodburning kitchen stove, worth its weight in gold as an antique. It rumbled and tumbled under the units. Not knowing if all the units were on the rail, I put the train into emergency.

"Calling the operator at Palmdale," I said over the radio.

"This is the operator, go ahead, Charlie."

"I'm out here by the rock pit. I hit something on the rail, it looked like an old iron cooking stove. After I make an inspection I'll let you know if everything is all right."

"OK, I have a train going into the siding at #2 Palmdale. When you're ready to travel, come down to the depot here and change crews. Over and out."

Climbing off the lead unit, I found the big part of the stove in front of the engine. The brakeman and I removed it. Going back on one side of the engine, we found that all the wheels were on the rail. The brakeman went further back, inspecting the train for a short distance. I crossed over to the opposite side of the units to walk to the front of the engine, when I saw a sheriff's car coming towards me on the service road. The deputy sheriff took my statement about what happened and then left. When everything was back in order and the flag returned we continued on our way.

Arriving home about noon, Mary took me to lunch at Palmdale, in a little place so neat and nice called the Tea Room. I do not know if it still exists today, but at that time it was great. I was telling Mary about the stove incident.

"And I've been looking for one of those stoves for a long time and you had to wreck one, oh, Chucker," she said in playful disgust. Well the day had not turned out too bad after all. Going out with Mary was a pleasure.

The next morning, awakened late by the smell of coffee and the sound of someone fluttering around in the kitchen, I slipped out of bed, took a shower and then put on my robe and went to the kitchen.

"Well, look what we have here, Mr. Celebrity!" Mary smiled as she poured me some coffee.

"What did you call me?" I asked, puzzled.

"Mr. Celebrity. Your name is in the paper."

"What paper? We don't get any paper but that little twice weekly local paper," I said, a bit mixed up, as I took a sip of coffee.

"Well, it's on the train thing of yesterday. Let me read it to you. It says, brave engineer . . . "

"Why in the hell do they call the engineer brave?" I cut in. "We're just ordinary people, and just as scared as anyone else."

"Now don't interrupt me and listen. It says 'brave engineer saves train from derailing. Our own citizen of Little Rock, Mr. C. F. Steffes, a locomotive engineer, was driving a train towards Palmdale' . . . "

"Damn it," I cut in again. "I don't drive a train, it drives itself. I run a train."

"Will you stop butting in and listen? 'Some vandals placed a large iron stove on the rail near the rock pits trying to derail the train that engineer Steffes was commanding, but it failed to derail the freight train going at a high speed due to the quick action of Mr. Steffes.'"

"I wasn't commanding nothing. I just ran the train."

"Oh poof on your perfection." Mary said, and walked away.

The Opening of the Nursery

Mary opened the nursery the next week and it proved a success. But I would have to keep working, as she predicted. Her plan was to hire help when the time came and it came fast.

252

Mary hired a young man named Robert (I do not recall his last name). He was hardy and tall, with a dark complexion and coal-black eyes. He knew nursery work at its best and wasn't afraid to work, but he also liked the alcohol once in a while. But Mary thought he was worth a try and he turned out to be one of our best employees.

During the week of our opening, Jack came up for a visit, spending most of his time in the hot house putting in cuttings on the growing table or helping Robert pot plants. I relieved Mary so she could go to town on a shopping spree. I was sitting on a stool behind the counter, noting how nice everything had turned out to be, when two good-looking women drove up and walked into the shop, intent on buying some potted flowers. One of the women was a blonde with a fair complexion and a Marilyn Monroe figure. The other woman, attractive and dark-haired, was a neighbor of ours and later Mary had her come in to help in the house.

"And what does your husband work at?" I asked the blonde, just as Jack walked in the door.

"I'm single now," she said, not seeing Jack.

"You're not married?" Jack said with his eyes lighting up like a Las Vegas electric sign. The blonde returned the look. It was like two shock waves coming together. I could feel the tremendous impulse of the two just standing there watching. I was looking at the dark-headed girl and shaking my head, when Mary came in the shop, and I was thankful because I had to contribute to the amber stream.

After the two left, Mary had Robert close the nursery because it was five o'clock.

"Where is lover boy Jack?" I asked Mary, when she came up the stairs from the garden shop.

"He is outside talking to Mary Lou. I think they're going

out to dinner. I believe he wants to borrow our car to take her out. Is it all right?"

"I guess so. I'm laying off so we won't need it tonight. What do you think?" I said, knowing her answer would be yes, and I was right.

Jack came bustling into the house like a schoolboy, with little cherubs and their bows and arrows flying all about him.

"I have a date with the most wonderful, beautiful woman. I think I'm in love," he exclaimed.

"Hell Jack, you're just horny. You fall in and out of love like the change of weather. Take our car and go see how it is. There is even a pad in the back of the station wagon you can use," I said, as he went upstairs to clean up. Boy, did I get a dressing down from Mary for that last remark.

The next morning Jack drove in. His clothes were ruffled, with his shirt tail out in back. His eyes were red as stop signs and he was in need of a shave. But he was as happy as a jaybird.

"Well how. . . ." Mary was standing beside me and gave me a bump with her hip, so that I knew not to finish my sentence.

"Jack go upstairs and get some sleep and don't pay any attention to this old goat," Mary told him.

The Sugar Beets and the Ninety Day Wonders

Three weeks later the Southern Pacific started to haul sugar beets out of Imperial Valley north to somewhere in San Joaquin Valley. The old beet cars were gondolas with three-foot wood extensions at the top of them and for years they were used like that. But greed ensured that they would be used for carrying heavier loads. So another extension rack was applied on top of the existing one, making the tonnage way out of line for the braking power of the original gondola. But it satisfied the company. I happened to be the lucky one getting the first

254

trainload of beets out of Indio with a through helper.

We sat in the Indio yard for long periods of time trying to charge the hundred and ten car train line up to ninety pounds of air with a tonnage of over eleven thousand tons. We finally pumped the train up to where I could have an air test for setting the brakes and also include the checking of the leakage on the train line. As I went through this procedure, the brakeman riding with me walked back to check for hand brakes. With the brake handle on lap position the leakage was over fifteen pounds per minute, which was way over the limit. I told the car men that we couldn't leave with this amount of leakage, and we were delayed another hour and a half, making a three-hour delay in all.

When the train was cleared to leave town my head brakeman climbed on the engine.

"You know Charlie," he said to me, "I walked back after you had set the air on the train and for thirty cars, every third or fourth car, the brakes were inoperative." We were on the move by then and there was not much that could be done about it after that. When we reached Beaumont, the top of the grade, I stopped the train and told the brakeman that according to the rules we needed forty-five retainers, which he gladly turned up for me one each car.

While waiting for the retainers, the Los Angeles dispatcher called on the radio, wanting to know the reason for the delay.

"We are turning up retainers according to the rules," I told him.

"That is the first time that I heard of an engineer stopping for retainers since the coming of the diesels," he laughed.

"Maybe so," I replied. "But this is the first time I have ever been so far over the tonnage per operative brake that by the rules I had to have retainers. And furthermore, one fourth of these brakes are inoperative." There was complete silence on the airways after I told him that.

At Colton the retainers were returned to their original position, and with five hours to work, we started up the Cajon Pass towards Palmdale making the fast speed of nine miles per hour. We were struggling up the mountain and about to reach the siding at Canyon, when on a long curve the brakeman spotted a car with smoking wheels, sixty cars back.

"I think we have either a hand brake set or one sticking," he said, and I agreed with him. "But if we stop," I said, "our chances of starting and holding together are about sixty percent against us. Do you think if you dropped off and rolled 'em back to the car at this speed you'd be able to knock off a brake or bleed the car off on the go?"

"Sure," he grinned, "but I can't run that fast to return back up here."

"Oh no," I said, "you roll on back and catch the caboose. I'll take care of your things when we arrive in Palmdale."

Upon leaving Canyon and receiving a 'high ball' over the radio from the caboose, I knew things were all right. It seemed strange being by myself but that had become the policy of the company. Before, it had always been two in the cab of a locomotive, but to operate without a fireman, the company had to form a new and different policy.

Finally reaching Hiland with enough time to make Palmdale on the hours of service law, we received an order to meet a train at Wash. He would be in the siding for us, without delaying our train. Letting the helper shove our train to get up our speed, I went into dynamic braking because we were on a downhill pull. I did not want to use the air along with the dynamic but with the tremendous weight behind me it looked like it might be necessary. Running over two torpedoes was the indication that a lighted fusee could be a mile ahead. Or then again they could have been put down by another train in flagging protection going in either direction, but in either case the safe course had to be taken. If it was a test and an engineer failed to stop short of a fusee in none block territory, he was subject to dismissal.

With twenty-five pounds of air and the brake system and the dynamic brake on maximum, I called the helper to revert to dynamic braking also. The air was at the equalizing point, which meant there was no braking power left, but still the train scarcely slowed down. Passing under the Barstow underpass, the train slowed down slightly, but only a quarter of a mile further down the track I saw a slither of red flickering from a fusee. Knowing that it was impossible to stop, I angrily put the train in emergency. But it was useless. We went many cars beyond the fusee before stopping, and I didn't really caring anymore, thinking that any damn fool who would pull a test on a train like this being on short time wasn't much of an official. I sat there with a hostile feeling in my soul for officials, especially for ninety-day wonders that came out of Berkeley or Stanford at that time.

Here they came, two blue suitors, neither of whom had I seen before. They climbed up on the engine with a cocky, sarcastic attitude.

"Where is the head brakeman?" was their first demand.

"In the caboose," I replied.

"The caboose, the caboose?" One of them looked around the cab in a shocked manner.

"Yeah, the rear end of the train, the back end, you know," I said with heavy sarcasm. I must have been their first pigeon because they never asked why or what for.

"Why didn't you stop behind the red fusee, like you were

supposed to?" one of the men, who had a hooked nose and expressionless face, asked me.

"Because I couldn't stop." The heat was rising within me.

"The book says that you will stop short of a . . . "

"Mister," I cut him short. "I used everything within my power to stop this train." I stood up and pushed his finger away from my face. Thinking that I would be fired anyway, I figured that a little more self-justification would not hurt. So I went on.

"You're not talking to someone that just hired out here this morning. I know the rules better than both of you. Now the both of you are disrupting my work and adding to my stress. If the two of you would kindly get your ass off of my engine and let me do my work, I'll be obliged. And furthermore, save your breath for the investigation."

"We have a right to be on this engine," the scrummy-faced thin one said, his narrow thin nose twitching.

"Yes," I said, "but so long as you don't interfere or hinder my work, which you two bird dogs are doing right now. So get your butts off of my engine and let me go about my work."

If looks could kill, I would have been drawn and quartered and hung out to dry, but they did remove themselves from the engine. I knew if they had taken the initiative they could have relieved me on the spot, and taken over the operation. I was gambling on their inexperience. Also, a good, experienced official would have had a much different approach then these college grads.

We were all relieved at siding Wash. The carry-all with a rested crew was waiting for us there and so was the train we were to meet. Everyone was buzzing and wanting to know about the test that I failed. Parts of it had been picked up on the radio. All that I would tell them was, I figured that I was due for a long vacation, and with my job insurance, plus the railroad unemployment insurance and the one hundred percent club insurance that I carried I would be getting more money than I was making on the job.

Having dinner with Mary after arriving at Palmdale, I related what had happened out on the cut-off. Her faraway look indicated that she was deep in thought.

"If you are fired," she said, "we could let Bob go and you could spend your time in the nursery. We might be eating beans but I think we can make it."

Beans, hell!" I exploded and then told her about the insurance and all. That relieved her monetary worries and we ate.

After arriving home that night it was still early, so I called Bakersfield to talk to Dick Swartz, our local chairman of the Brotherhood of Locomotive Engineers.

"Hello." He had a quick way of saying hello on the phone.

"Dick, this is Charlie Steffes at Little Rock."

"Yeah, I know what you want. It's already out about you getting by a fusee. I don't want to hear about it over the phone. I'll be over your place the day after tomorrow." He hung up. He was one hell of a great man. He wasn't just a man—he was our leader and we looked to him for help when it was needed.

The next morning was a busy day for the telephone. Ivan Upshaw was the first to call, letting me know that a carrier was on his way out, bringing papers for me to sign about the pending investigation. I thanked Ivan and went downstairs into the garden shop, where Mary was talking to two well-dressed gentlemen. Thinking that maybe they were state officials or the likes and not wanting to interfere, I went out to the greenhouse where Robert was potting some plants. After being there only a short while, when the phone range again. Mary answered it.

259

"It's for you, Chucker, better take it upstairs because I believe it's long distance." So upstairs again I went.

"This is the general office of the Southern Pacific Transportation Department calling for Mr. Steffes."

"I am Mr. Steffes," I said rather gruffly, thinking it was about the fusee incident.

"Will you hold a minute, please?" a pleasant voice said on the other end of the line. The gentleman I finally talked to was an acquaintance of mine, one of the old guard who was still at the general office.

"Charlie, I have a letter from engineer Jack - - - - - , stating that he wishes to join our official staff. Again I would like your opinion of him and his marital status." This was not the first time that I had been called from San Francisco to discuss whether an employee should or not be given an official job. Many of the older engineers and conductors were consulted in this way, although the practice was fast disappearing as the new regime took over.

"He might make a good man for you, and as for his marital situation, he is not married right now but plans to be very soon."

"OK, Charlie, thanks a lot," he said, and then hung up. As I was hanging up the phone, up drove the carrier with my summons for a formal investigation the following Monday at the depot in Palmdale.

Because Dick Swartz was coming the next day, I called Ivan and marked off the board.

"Charlie," Ivan said, "Bill Riesen is here to fill Kenny Osborn's vacancy and he said he would like to come over to see you, if he may."

"Tell him anytime he wants to," I said and hung up, to turn my attention to some pipe work that needed doing on the nursery grounds. Then Mary wanted to talk to me upstairs.

"Do you know who those two men were, that were here this morning?" she asked.

"Probably from the IRS or Palmdale Chamber of Commerce."

"No, they are developers and they are building a very large mobile home park, with mobile homes already on the sites, for Lockheed Corporation, who are going to expand the operation at Palmdale. They need more housing for their employees to live in because of the housing shortage here at Palmdale. Now they want us to put a bid on landscaping, the whole bit, including all the grounds and club house." Mary was quite excited.

"Mary, that's too much for us, and besides we're going on a vacation." So the idea was shelved for the time being.

The Great Investigation

I didn't know at that moment but the pending investigation would be the largest one of its kind at that time.

Dick and June Swartz arrived at ten in the morning the next day. They looked about the nursery and were amazed at what had been accomplished. Leaving Mary to entertain June, Dick and I retired to the living room to discus the details of the upcoming event. After relating to him every detail of the entire trip, which Dick wrote down on a large pad, he asked many questions. When he was finished, he cupped his hands behind his head, like he always did.

"You have, beyond a doubt, one of the biggest investigations coming up that I've ever witnessed. We are going to have them all subpoenaed to be there."

"Who will that be?" I asked Dick.

"Well to start with. your helper crew and train crew, if they are not already summoned to be there. The car men at Indio, the Interstate Commerce Commission, the Federal Transportation Department, and any other that I might think of," Dick said, taking a sip of ice tea. "And if we can't get them all together by next Monday, we will have it postponed until they can all be there, but I think they will make it."

"It's going to be like a regular court trial, isn't it?" I said.

"Of the highest degree, Charlie. No one has yet beat the case of getting by a fusee but I think we have a good chance. Now June and I must go."

Many customers came and left after the Swartz's had gone, and then Bill Riesen came, looking the same as he always did, with his lean face, thinning light hair, and slim, wiry build. Looking about, he was amazed. "Great, super," he kept repeating. "What does it take to get a piece of this action?"

"Money, money!" I jokingly laughed, not meaning it.

"How much? really how much?"

"We are doing fine, Bill, what we need is someone to come in and help run the place so Mary can have a little rest." The phone was again ringing off the hook until Mary answered it.

"Oh, just a moment please, " Mary said over the phone and then turned towards me. "Honey, Mr. Harvey wants to know about the Lockheed contract?"

"Tell him to bring the plans over and I'll take a look at them, but I'm not promising that we'll do it." Then I turned to Bill and explained. "That guy has a hundred thousand dollar job for us to do but I don't know if we should do it." Amazement and excitement seemed to overtake Bill; maybe I should not have mentioned the contract to him.

"Why don't you let me help, I can do a lot. I have a little money and I'm looking for investment."

"Like I have said Bill, we need someone to work with us in

the nursery."

"Name your price and I'll work with you too."

"How can you work with us when you live in Los Angeles? That is too far away," I pointed out.

"I'm going to bid this job in and I stand to get it. If I do, will you let me in?" I looked at Mary and she lifted her shoulder slightly. It was her way of saying, what the hell!

"I'll think it over Bill," I promised. With that he was satisfied and left for Palmdale.

It had been a long day with much activity, so we decided to have dinner at Lancaster, twenty miles away.

"I don't want this business to get out of hand," Mary remarked as we were driving into town.

"Sometimes that can't be helped, Mary, but maybe if Bill would help run the place?" I broke off, thinking.

"What are you thinking of?" Mary asked.

"How did you know I was thinking?"

"I can tell. I know a lot about you even when you don't say anything, Chucker."

"We could form a closed corporation, cut up the shares and Bill would only be allowed so many shares," I said.

"What do you mean?" Mary wanted to know.

"Well for instance, we have an inventory of $20,000 and so much in pending business of, say $25,000 at a net worth of $13,000. That makes us worth $33,000. Now if we have shares worth $100 a share, that gives us three hundred and thirty shares. If we allot one hundred shares to be sold, Bill can buy any part of that. The only thing that's bad, is that he can sell his stock to anyone else, which we can't stop. But if he does buy in he must help us take care of the business and in working for the enterprise, he can receive payment in shares for his labor."

263

"Sounds good to me," Mary commented." I didn't know you were a financier."

"I'm not. A lawyer will have to draw it up."

The next day Mr. Harvey arrived with his plans. "Do you think that you'll be able to handle this big job? It's going to take a lot of man power," he said.

"We'll let you know after we look at the plans," I informed him, as he was leaving. I told him it would take ten days or more before we would have a quote for him.

In the interim, Bill received the job and was moving to Little Rock. We revealed our plans to him but told him that he would have to wait until the lawyer drew up the papers.

The big day, which fell on a Monday, was rolling around fast. The day of the ax. Driving into Palmdale that morning I found a great crowd of people gathered at the depot, including the two head hunters. I glared at them as I went into the depot, wondering if they knew how much they were costing the company. With such a large crowd the investigation had to be moved into a big room next to the storage shed at the depot. Buck Brewer was holding the investigation and like any court, there were many formalities to go through before getting down to real business.

The two clowns were put on the stand first. The one without any expression on his face did the talking and ended with the remark, "As an official of the company, he told us to get our ass off of the engine."

"And you did," Dick Swartz remarked. "Isn't that strange. As an official you could have relieved Mr. Steffes on the spot but you didn't. So that left him in charge of his engine and the working conditions, and he decided that both of you were making it impossible for him to go about his duties. So he was in his rights to remove both of you."

A silence followed, letting the men and women secretaries who were recording in shorthand catch up on the proceedings for each individual group of the government agencies and the railroads.

After that session Buck Brewer started at the beginning of the trip, taking it step by step, drawing from each witness their account of their involvement in what happened. Finally it was my turn.

"Charlie, when you told your brakeman to drop off at Canyon to roll the train by, to take care of the smoking car, wouldn't it have been better to have stopped and let the brakeman return to the engine before going on?" Buck asked me.

"It was my judgment not to do so, because of the chance of breaking the train in too by starting. We were only doing nine miles per hour and also the equipment was old and not trustworthy." That remark started a low hum of talk in the audience.

"I see, and what was your speed when you came across the torpedoes?"

"I was doing about forty-five miles," I replied.

"Why did you let the speed get so high when you knew that the brakes were not working properly?" I was almost stumped on this question and had to think for a moment. The entire room waited for my answer in silence as the old big railroad clock ticked away on the wall, as if it was counting the time to my execution.

"Just what speed would be right in this condition? I was let out of Indio yards with the assumption that my brakes were in perfect working condition. And another reason, we were on short time for making Palmdale under the twelve hour law. And one more thing," I continued, "never in my life would I

265

believe a couple of grown men, that are supposed to have intelligence, would be so stupid as to pull a dumb trick like this without first finding out the condition of the train and how much time they had left to work."

"I object!" one of them exclaimed. "We are not stupid. We're both graduates from Stanford." Buck looked at them weakly and winked at Dick, thinking no one noticed. But I happened to see it and it gave me a warm feeling inside, realizing that I had an ally on our side.

It was lunch break already. Time seemed to leap forward that day. I went to lunch with Dick Swartz and the rest of the train crew.

"Things look good so far," Dick said." But where did the company pick up such neophyte dummies as those two?" No one knew the answer but someone remarked, "That is the new regime the company is hiring, the downfall of Rome." After thinking about his remark, I concluded he was right.

Dick was in his element. He loved a good fight and being in the position he was on that day, he was going to give it all he had. "Maybe you won't get fired, Charlie," he assured me.

"Oh, but I have my vacation all planned, I don't want to be disappointed," I said as they laughed, not knowing how true it was.

The investigation reconvened at one o'clock, but Buck Brewer was not conducting it that afternoon. Some man out of the general office was holding it instead. He did not look like a railroad person. He was rather stout in build, tall, slightly balding, and he wore pinch on nose glasses.

It was Dick's time for interrogation of any witness. He asked the head brakeman what he found when he walked the train at Indio.

"One out of every three or four cars had inoperative

brakes."

"I object!" the new commander shouted, who I shall call Mr. Q, not remembering his name. "How did you know the brakes were not working? Maybe they were slow in reacting."

"That I can't tell you, but some were completely cut out for some reason," the brakeman replied.

"Mr. Q, don't you think an engineer needs the brakes when he applies the brakes, not when they decide to work sometime in the future?" Dick asked. Mr. Q's face was turning crimson. Then the man from the Federal Transportation Department spoke up.

"As each of you know, everything you say is being taken down. Now we have tagged each car so they can't be used again and we will assemble the train and find out just how it was."

"Mr. Steffes, are you sure you can operate a locomotive with a train over the piece of territory involved," Mr. Q asked me. "You know certain engineers can only operate switch engines and others are more adapted to mainline work." I was about to take Mr. Q apart piece by piece, but Dick knew that was what he wanted me to do. So Dick sat me down.

"I believe I have the floor, Mr. Q," he said, "and I want to talk to those two gentlemen that pulled the test." Dick turned to the two.

"Have you both been working long for the Southern Pacific?" he asked.

"No. I started a week before and he started four days before."

"And this was the first time either of you worked on the railroad?" They both agreed that was true. "You say that you both have a degree?"

"Yes," one of them said. "A Ph.D. in sociology." Dick took

267

in a deep breath and I sensed something was coming.

"Not to make little of your education, but does the Southern Pacific pay you both the wages that your education calls for?" There was complete silence.

"And education is the finest thing that can be had, if used right," Dick continued. "But you both were hired by the company and came up here, pulled a very technical test, and neither of you knew what a caboose was nor on which end of the train it was located." The room went into an uproar. Mr. Q's face was ashen, with a look of contempt—not against his colleagues but against us, the "human element."

"Gentlemen," Mr. Q called out after regaining a little composure. "Let's get on with the investigation."

By the time Dick had finished with his part of the questioning it was getting late. Mr. Q then took over and I knew he was either going to try to ridicule me or was going to resume the investigation on the next day. Either way was too much for me. I stood up, with everyone looking at me in amazement, and Mr. Q's mouth hung open. The heat of battle sprung high inside of me.

"Gentlemen, and you, Mr. Q," I said loudly and with a clear voice. "For thirty-three years I have run a locomotive with a train up and down the tracks anywhere on my division and I'll wager that is a whole lot longer than you have been here, Mr. Q. My work has been in the interests of the company and my record is very clean.

"Mr. Q, you probably were hired by the company and taught to hate your fellow man especially if he is not quite as educated as you are. And many of us in this room here have not your degree of education, but down through the years I have gotten more education than you'll ever have. I know you are out to have me fired. Well fire me right now because I have had it with you and your two green horn jumping jackasses that still have their diapers on. Good night, sir." I walked out of the room. The investigation was closed.

10. The Last Years

Mary wanted to hear everything about the investigation, and when I had finished the story, she looked out far into the desert.

"They will probably fry you for this."

"Yes I know," I answered quietly. But I was battle-scarred, and weary, and did not care much who won the war. I wanted to report and make one more trip before getting the news of my dismissal, so I could get my things out of the locker in Indio. But my turn happened to be out of town and I would have to wait until it returned.

"What now my dear lady?" I asked, turning to Mary.

"Well," she began. Mary used "well" many times to start her sentences, since she was from the Midwest. "Jack wants to be married at our house!"

"When and to whom?" I sneezed for no real reason.

"Next Saturday and to Mary Lou, silly."

"Who's going to do all the work?" I inquired.

"Oh, there won't be much work. They're going to be married in the patio and Mary Lou and I are going to arrange it." I sneezed again and looked at Mary blurry-eyed. All at once I felt lousy. Mary put her hand on my forehead.

"You have a fever, you are coming down with something.

Come on off to bed you go," she commanded. I did not put up much of a resistance. Nothing seemed of much importance to me for the next week because I had a bad case of the flu.

Poor Mary had to take care of everything that week. She signed the contract with Mr. Harvey, prepared for Jack and Mary Lou's wedding and took care of the incorporation papers from the lawyer. She did all this while I fought the bugs in bed.

The wedding night came but I did not feel like getting up to see it. After some persuasion from Mary, I climbed out of bed but I had to hold up the walls because they seemed like they wanted to fall over. Mary set me in a chair and wrapped me up in a blanket out on the patio under the wisteria vine, so as not to be noticed. The patio never looked so beautiful. At the end of the ceremony, I was ready to retire. It took two more days before there was any glimpse of hope for me to rejoin the human race.

Bill Reisen invested five thousand dollars in the corporation as it was, and said he would work in helping run the business until he arrived at eight thousand dollars. But his wife said no! They were going to Europe first. They did go to Europe and when they returned all was forgotten about the working part.

Not hearing anything from the railroad about the outcome of the investigation, I decided to report for work and drove over to the dispatcher's office, just to look things over. After I arrived there and was standing in the registering room, looking over some bulletins, Ivan said he had something for me.

"I know," I replied.

"It's not as bad as you think, Charlie. They're only assessing you eighty demerits—you're not being fired."

"Hell, there goes my extended vacation," I growled.

"Charlie," Ivan came back at me. "You are the only man that didn't get fired for going by a fusee—you established a record."

"I guess," I said reluctantly, and left for home. Mary was very pleased that I had not been dismissed, and maybe she was right.

"I really hate to burden you so soon after being sick but we must start the Harvey job in ten days. What are we going to do for manpower or money?"

"We can get the money at the bank on the strength of the contract but the manpower, that is a problem. But we'll go to the bank first," I suggested.

We were driving back to the nursery after having a successful trip to the bank, in which we had obtained the cash necessary to see us through the contract, when I looked at the orchards starting to bloom out.

"That 's it!" I cried out, "that's it, Joe."

"Who in the hell is Joe?" Mary asked, perplexed.

"You know Jack Bones's Joe, the Mexican fellow that contracts blue card labor out of Mexico."

"Oh! that's it," Mary exclaimed, jumping out of her doldrums. The old fire was rekindled and we were ready to go. We drove up the lane to the nursery and found Robert very busy with customers. Mary hurried to help him, and before we had got some groceries out of the station wagon, Jack the newlywed drove up. It was the first time we had seen him since the wedding.

"I got the appointment," he announced, stepping out of his car.

"I know," I remarked loosely, on my way up the walk to the front door, carrying the bag of food.

"I go to Bakersfield tomorrow, then to classes for sometime."

"So they are going to brainwash you too?" I replied with a little disgust. "But don't be like those bastards that pulled a test on me, and I know you won't." Jack departed in a hurry, not bothering to say hello to Mary.

Running Two Jobs

Thirty days in which I sandwiched the work on the railroad with that on the job site made me look like a scarecrow with hollowed eyes. But it was going good. Mary had hired a young fellow named Ron, and he was perfect for running the job. Bill Reisen traveled the country and when he was off, most of the time I had to ride with his replacement out of Los Angeles because most of the young engineers were not qualified for the cut-off.

And to my biggest surprise, I received a letter from Dick Swartz, stating that the eighty demerits had been removed from my personnel record, and also that I would be paid for all the time spent at the investigation. The FTD had completed their test and found the company was in complete default.

Before the Harvey job was completed, other small jobs came to us. Jack Bones warned me that we were going too fast and told both Mary and I to slow down, but I didn't know how to. One day while I was asleep (having worked all night), a gentleman came into the nursery carrying a set of plans. Mary awakened me from a deep sleep.

"I don't know what to do. I need your help, please forgive me?" She apologized. I rubbed my eyes, which felt like crackling sparks of electric with a sting with each spark. I was still half-asleep.

"What is it the house burning down or what?" I mumbled.

"No, there is a man downstairs and he has a. . ." Before

Mary could finish she started to cough. In my stupor, still not being fully awake, I jumped out of bed, grabbed my thirty-eight special handgun and ran for the garden shop in my undershorts. Bob was waiting on three women and a man was sitting in one of the lounge chairs holding a set of plans.

The women burst out laughing and Bob let out a big hee-haw. The man was trying to suppress his laughter, as Mary rushed after me down the stairs, dragging my pants.

"You don't need a gun, we're going to buy something," one of the women laughed.

"Here, dear, you forgot these." Mary said, handing me my trousers. Finally it dawned on me what was taking place, I grabbed my pants and ran back upstairs, leaving Mary to explain.

After a while I returned downstairs to meet the gentleman with the plans.

"I'm Mr. Quigbly and I own a landscaping business out of Los Angeles. I bid on a job with HUD at Acton and it looks like a money job. It is further than what I thought from where I live, and I see you have manpower and I haven't. I would like to sell you the contract."

"Well," I said. "I'm not really interested in any more work but you leave me a set of plans and we will look them over. It will take about a week." With that he left.

"You're on duty at 8:30 a.m.," Ivan called the next morning.

"Getting out kind of quick, ain't I?"

"Yeah, we ran a whole lot last night, and by the way, your friend Jack has been assigned to work out of Palmdale," Ivan said. Boy, was I surprised and stunned.

"You don't say," was all I could say. Going into the door to the crew dispatcher's office I came face to face with Jack, who was all decked out in a Jim Clinton blue suit.

274

"Well good morning, Mr. Road Foreman!" I said politely. He glared at me and walked away with only a grunt. Oh gad, I thought, how the company has brainwashed this guy. Dismissing the incident, I went about my business.

Working on the plans at Indio, it looked very much like I could make money on them, but I would let my lawyer check them over first. Then I went to sleep with the idea of moving the nursery up to the highway at Little Rock so we could have privacy at the house. I knew Mary was getting tired of it so close to our living quarters.

Going back home, the trip was routine, so when I arrived, I stopped at my lawyer's office with the plans. I told him to look them over and give me his opinion about buying the contract. Leaving the office I stopped at the Harvey job site, which was about finished. Joe was standing watching his men working.

"Joe," I said. "Looks like another week on this job, but can you hold onto three of your best men?"

"I can keep as many as you want until their green card expires," he told me.

"I might move the nursery up to the highway, so I'll need them for a little while, just three of them," I said.

Back at home I sank into my comfortable chair and kicked off my heavy shoes. I looked at Mary, who looked tired and drawn. All this was getting to her. I could see she was going downhill fast, so the move of the nursery was urgent.

"Mary, there is a piece of ground next to Woody's market and we can rent it cheap. So what do you think about moving the nursery up there?"

"Why?"

"Because you are tired and going downhill and we sure as hell don't have any privacy here," I told her. After much discussion, we both agreed it would be for the best. We designed a nice plan of a fenced-in place and ordered the material. We would start to move as soon as the Harvey job was completed. Just about that time the buzzer rang from downstairs. Mary went to see who it was.

A short period expired, while I checked the drawings on the new nursery, before Mary returned with two people.

"Dear, this man and his wife are interesting in buying our business."

"Are you really interested in buying this nursery?" I asked.

"Yes," the man answered. "We live in Los Angeles and we're wanting to move and we thought buying a little business like this would be good for us."

"This isn't such a little business any more," I said, and explained our operation, and also told him we were moving the nursery up to the highway. He thought it would be better for him.

"What price would you want for the business?" he asked

"We are a corporation and have a little stock hanging out, but with the outlying stock and our large inventory I would say at a ballpark figure, one hundred thousand dollars."

"That's reasonable enough, but that will have to include the corporate stock, or no deal. How long would it take?"

"Give me a week," I said, very excited as they left.

Immediately I gave Bill a call. Receiving no answer, I called the crew dispatcher, leaving word for Bill Reisen to call me when he arrived home from his trip.

The Quigbly Contract

With everything buzzing concerning the move and the contracts, I took off of work for a week, to give Mary some relief. The next afternoon I went to see my lawyer.

276

"I haven't any idea about the nursery end of the thing but I certainly would not offer Quigbly any more than five hundred dollars for this contract," he advised.

Reisen showed up two days later at the nursery

"What's taking place up at the corner?" he inquired.

"We're moving the nursery up to the highway, getting it out of my home."

"Well, I wasn't told about it."

"Maybe if you would come around more often and do some work, you might know what's taking place," I reprimanded him. "One more thing, which is what I called to talk to you about. Someone wants to buy the place out of Los Angeles, lock, stock and barrel. . .,"

"I don't want to sell, not my stock," he cut in, before I could finish.

"Now just a minute, let me finish," I continued. "He will pay one hundred fifty dollars per share and I'll give you another fifty. That makes you double your money inside of a year." But the answer was still no.

"Well, I'm going to sell him my shares, in that way he'll have charge of the nursery, I added, thinking to bluff him a little.

"You can't do that because I have first choice. I'll see my lawyer in the morning." With that he pranced out the door. The situation left me in a bad mood.

The next morning Mr. Quigbly was at the door wanting his answer. I was not really ready for him but I made my mind up that I was going to stand up and tell him what my lawyer recommended.

"What do you want for the contact?" I asked.

"I'm asking three for it," he said softly.

"Three what, Mr. Quigbly?"

"Three thousand," he said, testing the ground. I folded the plans up and handed them to him. "Mr. Quigbly, I'll give you five hundred and that's it." Knowing that it was useless, he took the money and left.

My week passed and I returned to work, after first taking Mary to a doctor. The diagnosis was pneumonia, and she had to be hospitalized immediately. I let Bob and Ron take care of the business, and after I knew Mary was out of danger, I made five trips to Indio and back. On leaving for my fifth trip, I stopped by the hospital and was informed by the doctor that Mary was to be released the following day. It was too late for me to lay off, so I left a note for Jack to pick up Mary at the hospital and see that she was taken home and that I should be home that evening.

The trip was routine down and back from Indio, and when I was tying up at Palmdale, I asked the afternoon crew dispatcher, Jay Glass, if he knew whether Mary made it home all right.

"Yeah," he said. "I took her home and she was feeling fine. The Indian lady, Dawn Littlesky, was there to take care of her." I felt the adrenalin creeping through my body like the ocean waves pounding the seashore.

"You took her home! What in the hell happened to Jack?" I demanded.

"Jack said he couldn't take her home. He said he was an official, not a taxi driver." I turned white and then crimson red, and then I began to shake.

"Have you his home phone number?" My voice quivered as I asked.

"Take it easy driving home," Jay said, handing me his home phone number.

"Don't worry, I will, and thank you so very much for taking

care of my wife."

Driving home, I formulated what Mr. Road Foreman would hear when I finally reached him on the phone. My blood was at a high boil when turning down 77th Street to our home. The house was dark except for the downstairs bedroom. With the key in my hand I ran to the front entry door, unlocking it and rushing into the bedroom. There she sat in bed with her usual sweet smile. Boy! Mary was a sight for sore eyes, and after hugging and kissing her, my blood started to percolate.

"Now wait," Mary said, sensing my anguish. "Take it easy or you might have a heart attack."

"I'll more than have a heart attack if I don't get this off of my mind," I told her and went into the kitchen for a drink of water. Looking at the clock I saw it was only seven-thirty; Jack should be home by now.

"Hello," Mary Lou answered.

"Mary Lou, I would like to talk to Jack."

"Just a moment please," she said. After a short wait, Jack finally answered the phone and I think he knew what was in store for him.

"Go ahead, this is Road Foreman Ja. . ." I would not let him finish his sentence.

"Jack, I don't know what kind of a road foreman you are and I don't give a damn. But as a friend, you're pretty low down on my list. Of all the things Mary has done for you, nursed you when you could hardly hold your head up, washed your clothes and fed you many times, then planned your wedding and footed most of the expenses. What in the hell is wrong with you? Did the company brainwash you that much or are you debased with power? If you had played this trick on anyone else, they would take a gun and shoot you. Now you blundering jack-ass . . . " I was getting wound up when Mary walked into the kitchen, shaking her finger at me. But I kept going. "You stay out of my way. If I come in the crew dispatcher's office, you leave—don't cross my path again, understand?"

"I don't have to listen to this kind of talk," he bellowed.

"You better, because I mean business," I said, as he slammed the receiver down. I grinned at Mary. All the heat and frustration had left my body. I felt good.

"Why, Jack will have you fired," Mary warned.

"No he won't, he knows I'm right. I should have told San Francisco the truth about things and it would have been better for him. He is so zealous about this job that he has forgotten where the center of the earth is. The policy of the company in the new generation has fallen into the wrong hands and it is like in the old days of Nazi Germany. They have a way of brainwashing every would-be official, although there are still some of the old guard left within the company. But when they are gone, it will be like the termites eating the pillars that hold up the building, it will fall."

"How do you know these things, Chucker?" Mary asked, puzzled.

"It's not just me knowing this but every veteran employee working out there can see what is happening. The morale is broken between the company and all of the workers, and no company can succeed without it."

HUD, the Beginning of the End

"Breakfast is served," came the musical voice through the rooms of the house, after I had finished my shower. I scooted for the kitchen just as the phone rang.

"Yes, yes, thank you, I will tell him, thank you, good day," Mary said, as she turned to me.

"That was HUD—the job is ready to start." And that we did. But the project was jinxed from start to finish. I learned a very dear lesson. Never get caught up in a government contract. It is never what it seems to be. Red tape is a mild expression for what we went through.

For three weeks, after every trip on the road, there were problems waiting for me at home. Bob and Ron were doing a fine job, but there were always changes or irregularities that would come up, and mostly these meant more costs for us.

One morning, after a good night's sleep at Indio, I was called to run a train back to Palmdale. Mine was the second train to be called. As was the usual procedure, I had a much lighter train in tonnage then the train ahead of me. For some reason, the Southern Pacific liked to run trains in that manner. When both of us reached the cut-off out of Colton, radio contact between his caboose and my engine was perfect, so I could keep the required ten minutes behind him. At that time we were in the nonblock territory for seventy-eight miles. When we approached Palmdale the operator informed both of our trains that the first train would continue on to Palmdale proper to exchange crews, and the second train would exchange crews at Palmdale #2.

Traveling through Little Rock, I ran over two torpedoes. I knew the train ahead of me had cleared the circuit beyond me because of radio contact. He hadn't stopped en route. So the only conclusion was that Jack was in the neighborhood. We passed the yard limit board and also a distant signal in green position, because we were entering automatic block signal territory. Slowing my train down to twenty miles per hour, and before reaching the home signal, I came upon a lighted fusee, which I continued on by. This was according to the rules of having my train under control to stop short of a train, engine,

281

car, switch, or any misplaced object. Everything was in order, so going down and stopping between switches at #2, we changed crews.

I was making out my time slip when Jack came in like a tornado.

"I got you now! I'll see that you'll get fired for sure this time," he bellowed out sarcastically.

"For what?" I calmly asked.

"For what? For failing the test I pulled on you," he replied bitterly.

"What test?" I needled him.

"That fusee test at mile post 418." He stammered and started to shake a little. It was then I felt very sorry for Jack. He had been a good friend and a fine fellow in the past, and to have become infected with the company disease was devastating for him. The test that he thought he pulled on me, I had responded to perfectly. And in his rage he didn't know? Besides, in pulling tests of that sort, two personnel are required. Jack was trying so hard to be a good official, he was overlooking some of the rules.

"You better look up the rules and quit threatening me. Now get the hell out of here and leave me alone to finish my work," I demanded.

"Jack, you're wanted on the phone," Jay called from the office. Jack turned and left, and I believe he was relieved.

Driving home deep in thought, I came to the conclusion that one of us had to leave. Jack's vengeance was very real; he needed some kind of help. There was nothing Jack could not do concerning the running and maintenance of the units, or to keep the trains running, but as for human nature, Jack lacked a great deal. Personally I liked Jack, he was a great fellow, but the job mesmerized him. He was like Dr. Jekyll and Mr. Hyde, and it was the company's fault. They tried to mold the officials so that they would be feared by the employees. It might have worked in medieval times but it was not working now.

In my possessions, hidden away, was a telephone number to San Francisco that I was to use in case I needed it. But it had never been used and I hesitated to do so. But one of us was going to have to leave and it wasn't going to be me.

More problems confronted me on the HUD job and I was going well into the red, moneywise. I had to work harder to pay the two employees I had. A week later, making a routine trip to Indio and back, I was checking over some bulletins in the dispatcher's office. Everything seemed subdued and quiet, but when I turned to leave I almost bumped into Jack, who was coming out of his office carrying a suitcase. Jack did not have the old swashbuckling attitude he used to have.

"I want to thank you for costing me my job." He half-smiled as he spoke to me.

"I am really sorry but just maybe some day you will thank me and understand why I did it, and hopefully you will make your friends come first, not your job." What happened to Jack after that I never heard.

"What a shame, where do you think he'll end up?" Ivan Upshaw asked. I couldn't answer that. Driving home I thought about Jack and all of his women. about his ambitions, and his ever-present need to do something.

Mary was upset when I arrived home to face the problems of the HUD job, and she had a right to be.

"What is it they want this time?" I asked, becoming irate, not with Mary but with the HUD people.

"They called and said that the twenty-five big wooden container trees are unacceptable, that they were the wrong kind, although we purchased what the plans called for."

"Mary, this job is breaking us. Do you have the telephone number of HUD?"

"Yes, and I'll even dial them for you," she said, and she did.

"Hello, I want to talk to someone who is handling the Acton job please," I said over the phone. Finally a man answered.

"I'm Mr. Steffes, we're doing the Acton job and I understand you won't accept the trees we're planting because you say they are the wrong kind?"

"Yes, that's right," he stated.

"According to the plans they are exactly the ones we are planting."

"I know that but they're wrong and we don't want them."

"My dear fellow," I burst out, "I've had enough of you people, not wanting this and not wanting that. We are doing this strictly to the plans and contract now these trees will be planted. If you insist not, it will be a breach of contract and you'll have to pay us for the complete job." There was complete silence for ten seconds.

"All right, Mr. Steffes, the trees stay," came the eventual response.

"And one more thing," I added. "Stay away from the job site until my men have finished the job which will be at the end of the week. Then inspect it and then I will expect my pay."

"It will be as you wish, Mr. Steffes, good day."

Mary looked at me with beaming eyes and parted her red lips in a smile of approval. "I sure don't want you mad at me because you have a positive way of telling people off," she commented.

There is an old saying, the proof of the pudding is in the eating. And the pudding turned out sour, I found out after going to my bookkeeper when the HUD job was completed. $18,000 sour. All the profit from the Harvey job out of the nursery business had gone into this job.

The hardest thing was to face Mary and tell her the bad news. All she ever wanted was a small place that she and I could take care of by ourselves. Jack Bones was right.

Mary had tears in her eyes, big tears, when I related the bad news to her. And I never felt lower in my life than I did then.

"What are we going to do?" she asked.

"I don't know," I said, sinking into a soft chair.

"If only Riesen had not been so unreasonable, we would have all come out in fine shape," Mary said between sobs.

"Yes," I agreed, "he is the contributing cause of our being in this condition."

"Well there is only one thing left to do," Mary said, regaining her composure, which she could quickly do in a crisis — it always amazed me.

"And what is that?" I asked, a little puzzled.

"Bankrupt the corporation." The shock of hearing what she just said was like a mule kicking me or rather biting me in the ass. I could hardly face this thing.

"That takes in Riesen also." I finally could talk.

"Everything connected to the nursery. We will lose it all," Mary said.

"Not our house too?" I cried out in dismay.

"No, not our personal property, just what's in the corporation," Mary explained. I remembered that Mary had been a legal secretary in the past and knew about these things.

Three days later a bankruptcy was filed against the corporation of the nursery and the doors were closed.

The very next day Riesen came like a bolt of lightning down from Juniper Hills community where he lived

"Where in the hell is my money?" he demanded.

"The same place where our money is, gone!"

"But I want my money. I lost a lot of it," he insisted.

"Bill, I lost ten times the money you did plus all of Mary's and my time, you lost hardly nothing, and it is your fault."

"My fault?" He drew back, looking amazed. "Why my fault?" he asked indignantly.

"If you can collect your memory together. A while back you could have sold your shares and doubled your money. Then I could have sold the nursery, but no, you wouldn't hear of it. You cost Mary and me many thousands of dollars. Now get your ass out of here before I throw it out and don't ever come back." I opened the door and shoved him out.

Many stories were spread by him on the railroad but I don't know if anyone was interested. I was never asked for my side of the conflict and it didn't matter to me much anyway.

Quake

February, 1972. Day was breaking as I sat on the edge of our bed after a long night's sleep. Mary was still sleeping peacefully as I rubbed my hand over the top of my partially bald head (which had been that way since the age of twenty-seven). I was starting to stand up to go on my usual path to the bathroom to ring out my sock, when I was thrown back on the bed. There was a terrific sound around me, like grinding boulders under my feet. Finally regaining my foothold by holding onto the window sill, I looked down the lane to the house, and it was the first time that I ever saw electric poles doing the hula dance, or the ground moving like waves of the ocean. Mary, awake by now, was trying to stand up, getting out of the way of the bed that was doing the Saint Vitus dance. The house acted like a ship on the high seas. I held on to Mary as we watched nature in her angry display as it rearranged the earth. We had ringside seats, and what a sight it was!

286

When it was over, we inspected the house for damage. I found only a few dishes lying broken on the floor, but no cracks in the entire structure.

"You stood well!" I whispered to my house.

"I wonder where the center of the quake was?" Mary said.

"I don't know. Try turning on the TV or radio," I suggested. We found out that the center had been at Newhall, fifty miles away. Later we discovered that all traffic and rail lines were out from Los Angeles to Palmdale. That meant all rail traffic would be going over the cut-off.

"Mary," I said, "I'm going to lay off, and let's get out of here for a while."

"I'm ready, let's go," she replied, and we did—to Arizona.

For ten days we had a ball together, then we returned.

"Just think," Mary remarked. "Four more years you'll be sixty and then you can retire—then we'll be able to do this all the time."

"Yes, it seemed like yesterday I started out, today I'm working, and tomorrow I take my pension. My uncle once told me, 'boy you only pass this way once, get everything out of it you can because there is no way back,' and how right he was," I reminisced to Mary as she was getting out of the car. As she opened the door of the house the phone rang.

"Dick Swartz wants you on the phone," she called to me as I was taking things out of the station wagon.

"Yeah, Dick, what goes?" I asked.

"Hell, I been trying to get you for days, don't you ever stay home?"

"We took off to Arizona for a while. What goes?"

"First I'm sending you some papers to sign so I can close out your investigation, and you did know that they removed all of your demerits?"

287

"Oh yeah, I was told."

"Also," Dick continued, "did you hear about the new computerized classification yard going in at Colton?"

"No," I replied, "tell me about it."

"At first they were going to build it at Palmdale but then they selected Colton. It has a price tag of thirty-five to forty million dollars and it's going to handle seven thousand cars a day, so they say. Now they're closing Palmdale down, when it's finished. I'm meeting tomorrow with the people out of Frisco in the superintendent's office to discuss the matter."

"Oh, my gosh, where does that leave us over here?" I asked.

"Well, I'm afraid you'll have to pack and leave, but the company will buy your places and also pay for all of your moving. But this is costing me money, long distance. When I find more out I'll send you a memo in the mail, so goodbye for now."

Mary had been taking a shower while Dick and I were talking. It would be bad to break the news to her because I knew the move over here from Bakersfield had been a hard chore in her life.

She came into the living room smelling like a bouquet of delicate flowers, wearing a pink fluffy robe with her dark wavy hair flowing around her shoulders. Oh boy! She was alluring.

"Well," she said slowly and teasingly, "are you going to take a shower and are we going to bed?" I knew what was coming.

"But first aren't you interested in what Dick Swartz had to say?" I asked.

"Later, dear, later," she smiled back and it was much later. It was the next morning, because I was tranquilized to sleep.

The most appetizing breakfast was waiting me on the table

the next morning after I had been kissed awake. The smell of fresh perked coffee and sizzling bacon should have awakened me, but I had had a hard night sawing up a cord of wood—at least that was Mary's comment on my snoring. Finishing the last bite of the gourmet breakfast, I took Mary's hand and told her of the conversation with Dick.

"Oh! no," she cried. "I thought we were set once and for all."

"Yes, and I thought so too."

"You mean to say that we have to do all that packing and rent a truck or use that old pickup and rent a trailer?"

"Not this time. The company will pay to have it all moved. They will pack it and unpack it," I assured her.

"But I like my house here." she said, with tears swelling in her eyes.

"Well, we could keep the house and I could drive over the mountain every trip like I did before," I offered.

"No way you'll do that. It's becoming too dangerous driving on that mountain. We'll go back to Bakersfield," she said in a determined manner. And so that was it.

Eleven months passed before the move was upon us. The company gave us a fair market price for our home, moved us, and gave us an extra thousand dollars for the inconvenience.

We had found a nice place in Bakersfield near the Valley Plaza, close to where, many years ago, a young couple were parked out in the country one night, not knowing it was a farmer's front yard.

Being the oldest engineer at Palmdale in seniority, I was last to leave in the changeover of the pool freight runs that now would be Bakersfield to Colton and back. Mary stayed at our new home in Bakersfield while I slept on the floor of our empty house at Little Rock. But that would only be for one week.

The week ended quickly and I had to bid a final goodbye to my house. I guess there is no fool like an old fool. Tears flowed freely down my face. With upstretched arms, I went into the living room, calling out in a sobbing voice.

"You are the love of the other side of my life. We stood together in many battles and weathered great storms. When I was down, you brought me comfort. When I was hurt in spirit, you put your arms around me and when I was troubled, you told me, you are a man and must stand tall by yourself. But most of all," I continued, with my voice strengthening with the adoration and love I had for my house, "I leave part of me with you just as an artist or a sculptor leaves part of himself with his work. Somehow those that come after me will know this and understand. Treat them well."

I walked into the family room and kitchen that once rang with laughter and joy and had the aroma of good food spread out for everyone. Now it was stilled and empty. I left the house, not being able to stand anymore. A stage in my life was ended. It will remain in my memory until that too, is obliterated.

The home in Bakersfield was less important to me. But with Mary's help, I remodeled and landscaped it. When finished, it turned out nice. While doing all this work, I had bid on the Bakersfield to Colton pool freight job, which gave me much time at home to accomplish the project.

Because many engineers never worked beyond Palmdale, the officials were busy riding with them as instructors over the cut-off. After being called several times as an instructor, I finally refused. I only had a short few years to work, and I just wanted to coast out.

One cool evening Mary and I were sitting on our patio, discussing our different views on things and I said to her.

"Mary, you and I have come a long way together and we have a long way to go," I said to her. "You wouldn't believe how advanced the railroad has progressed. When I was waiting for the limo to take me to San Bernardino to my lodging the, travel Lodge, a first class motel, I had a chance to visit the building that housed all the computers and the yard master's tower. it was too much for me to understand but it was all there and I was like a young lad going to his first baseball game. I just did not fit in the picture anymore. They ought to turn us old horses out to pasture or shoot us, for what good we are."

"I know dear," Mary said. "But it was your footsteps of yesterday that made the ladder they're climbing on today. Remember if it weren't for Washington, Jefferson, Adams and all those fine men back then, we wouldn't have this fine great country we have today." Her intelligence and wisdom always amazed me, and she was always right. Each generation's footsteps are ladders for future generations, and my era was fast coming to a close. There was no room for me in the new regime, and I felt like a mother chicken sitting and keeping her chicks warm and watching them grow, hoping no one would exploit them as they developed.

The company had let many fireman go, and as a result found themselves short of personnel to promote to engineers. So they hired a number of them back. One trip I remember clearly when I had one of these fireman, a man named Don Starr. He was a very handsome young man, with meticulously groomed dark brown wavy hair, dark eyes and muscular build. Anywhere his travels took him, women would stumble all over each other to walk by him. But even with his women trouble, Don was a damn good engineer. He could run a train like a pro. If Don thought I wasn't watching or was napping a little, he would get a little speed up with the train. But he didn't fool me with my years of experience. Even with my eyes closed, I knew what he was up to, and after a few attempts, which were followed by my censure, he would settle down to the rules. But we all did the same, when we were young.

The trainmaster informed us at Colton about the great many whores, or call girls as they were known in that time, walking the streets of San Bernardino and to be on our alert for them. Of course at my age, they would have to be on the alert for me! But to be truthful, there was so much cheating among the respectable ladies that the whores didn't have much chance.

There was a large swimming pool situated in the middle of the horseshoe-shaped two story motel and the young lions that I worked with used the second floor for a diving platform into the pool. Don Starr had to be one of them and to sure all the females were watching, adding to his ego. His room and mine were on the top floor, four doors apart. After so much diving, the excitement died down. That was too much for Don, so to liven things up he slipped out of his bathing suit. The women went wild and some even started to climb the stairs to the second story. This was done when the practice of "streaking" was very common among students in college.

Not being able to withstand it any more, and fearing that the police would arrive any minute, I got to Don just in time, before the hoard of women reached him, and dispatched him to his room.

"What the hell are you trying to do out there? Have all of us in trouble?" I fired questions at him, but he just looked at me. "Now either dress or get your ass in bed and go to sleep." He never had anyone talk to him like I just did.

"I'll get some sleep," he answered meekly. Later, when I knew Don better, I realized there was not a nicer fellow. His only flaw was being too damn good-looking; the women would not leave him alone. He had a beautifully-shaped wife, who was just as beautiful inside.

The Remotes

As we traveled by the nudist camp at Devore, pulling our train up the long hill out of Colton on our way back to Bakersfield, every eye was strained in that direction. Sometimes the display was beautiful, when the female population was out and about, but we turned away in disgust when the males showed up, and today was one of those days.

"Did you see the remote slaves units at Bakersfield before we left?" Don asked me.

"I saw four controlling units sitting on the track over by the shops but I never climbed on them," I replied, lighting up my pipe.

"Well I did, and it is just like these units only it has another console sitting on top of this one, hooked up to a radio-sending device so that whatever is done or controlled up here is picked up by the slave unit and duplicated. And of course the slave unit can operate as many regular units behind as will be required for helper service," Don explained.

"What a great expense the company will incur just to cut one helper crew out of a train," I remarked. "Just think of the thousands of dollars it's going to take in getting these units and then the expense of maintaining them alone will cost more than they'll save by cutting out the manpower."

"Lee Master said everyone must attend classes on these remotes, and that includes trainmen," Don said. Lee Master was the new road foreman of engines at Bakersfield since Brewer left.

"I see they're putting antennas and wiring the tunnels for

293

transmission," the head brakeman commented.

"Yeah," I said, blowing smoke rings. "When the Santa Fe ran their   radio-controlled helper units out of Bakersfield, that's where they had trouble, losing transmission in the tunnels."

The hours of service was creeping up on us as we went flying through Mojave.

"We should be able to make it in if we're not jockeyed around too much," I told Don, who was half asleep by then because he had run the engine to Lancaster and now it was my turn at the helm. Upon arriving at Tehachapi we had an hour and thirty-five minutes left to work, which was just enough time to make the yard at Bakersfield. Filling my pipe with fresh tobacco and lighting it up, I watched the blue smoke curl upwards. I wished that we were tied up and that I was eating a steak and some potatoes. The sandwich of long ago did not keep the hunger pains down there were gnawing inside of me now.

At Woodford we went through the siding for a S.P. train, losing five minutes, but we still could make it by exceeding the speed a mile or so. The traffic on the hill was very heavy, and then I realized, when the dispatcher put us in the siding at Bealville for two trains, that he had no intention of our making it in. I called the dispatcher and reminded him of our short time to work.

"Keep moving," was all the response I received.

The twelve hour law was up on double track at Magunden, and also we were stopped on a red signal because a train ahead of ours was waiting to get into Bakersfield yard. I called on the radio to our caboose.

"Do we clear that crossing back there?" I asked.

"No we don't," came the reply.

"Cut it short because I have one to cut up here," I instructed.

"Don't cut any crossing out there, we're going to get you in here soon," someone at the yard radioed us.

"Our time to work is up and we will cut the crossing," I repeated.

"We will take care of your violation of the twelve hour law, just stay intact and do what you are told."

My age stopped me from flaring up like I did when I was young, but I was getting close to the boiling point at this time. At least the person instructing me could have said, "please."

"And who is telling me to break the law?" I demanded.

"This, Mr. Steffes, is Joe E. Neal, assistant superintendent."

"Engineer Steffes, come in please." Another voice came on the radio, along with many others, urging a good fight.

"Go ahead, this is Steffes."

"This is Dick Swartz. I'm leaving the yard for Fresno and the violation of the law will be taken care of when I return. In the meantime do as the man tells you."

"Yeah, OK, Dick." I acknowledged. "Mr. Neal, come in please." Joe did not like me and I didn't care for him. So we were like a couple of bulldogs when it came to talking to each other, and the entire division knew it.

"This is Neal, Mr. Steffes."

"Mr. Neal, I shall bring the train into town but first, whether I will cut these crossings or not will be up to the conductor. But either way, I will have the head brakeman tie down the necessary brakes on this train and then we shall cross the street to Banducci's Restaurant and then we shall eat. I've gone long enough without eating."

It was like a touchdown at a college football game, the hurrahs and the hoopla that came over the airways from every direction in support of me.

Don Starr, the head brakeman, and I, had a full meal. When we were almost finished the rear brakeman and the conductor arrived.

"Do you know there are trains stopped behind us and backed all the way to Mojave?" the conductor laughed.

"I suspected there would be but no one cares, so why should I?"

It was late when our train came to a rest in Bakersfield yard. On arriving home it was close to midnight, but Mary was waiting up for me. After cleaning up I told her about the incident.

"I bet they'll be glad when you take your pension," she laughed.

"You are so right. There's not many old fish in the pond and when they get us all fished out, they will manage things the way they want, without restrictions. I'm afraid that will be the final blow to the goose that laid the golden eggs," I warned.

Qualifying for the radio remote helper engines didn't take long. But I didn't catch any for a long time.

The first remote helper in my train came out of Colton and it was the first one I had operated by myself. We were without a fireman, and the head brakeman, whom I will call Elmer, and I, struggled up towards Hiland with all the tonnage every unit was rated for. The weather was fine with the sun shining brightly. But as we left siding Canyon, a very swift wind started to blow. Sometimes such a heavy wind will slow a train down one mile per hour or even more. In our case we slowed down almost a mile per hour.

Struggling within two miles of station Hiland, the slave remote unit stopped, showing a red light on my console, and the train dragged to a standstill.

"Anyone back there in the caboose know anything about a slave unit?" I called on the radio.

"No, neither one of us do, we are both out of Los Angeles and never been on one, I'm sorry," the conductor informed me.

"Well, there are two things we can do," I said. "We can cut the train and double into Hiland or I can walk back and try to find the trouble and start the units. Either one will take some time. Which one would you prefer?"

"Maybe you better walk back," he suggested.

"All right, I'll secure the engines and Elmer will tie the brakes on the head end cars while you do your things back there," I said.

Sixty-five cars seemed like a five-mile walk by the time I reached the helper engine with the slave unit. When I arrived, the units were all quiet, the motors had stopped running. What a queer and ghostly feeling I experienced, climbing up on the engines. The only sound was the sweeping wind, whispering, as if to say, "you don't belong here." Starting all the units and making sure that the radio controlled slave unit was on the right wave length frequency as my controlling leading unit, I started on the long walk back, another sixty-five cars.

Finally we were on our way again and everything worked fine. Leaving Tehachapi with the dynamic brakes working, the train handled easily. If it gained too much speed, six pounds of air set and release would control it for a long distance. But when going around siding Cliff, I felt a surge in the train followed by a slowing down. I thought that maybe the dynamic brake on the slave unit was acting up and slipping, and I dismissed the incident.

Leaving tunnel #5 the approach signal was yellow over green, an indication that we were going into the siding at

Bealville. Under a rule put out by the engineering department, this train was restricted to fifteen miles per hour in entering a siding downhill for so many hundred feet. Then the speed could be increased to twenty miles.

I was harboring a thought that all was not well because of the way the train was performing. Going against he rules, I used the engine brakes in conjunction with the dynamic brake to maintain my speed. An engineer does everything possible to keep his train going regardless of rules—if he can do it in a safe manner. Every engineer, when arriving at a difficult bit of train handling and in an unyielding condition, could stop and call for the help of someone in a higher capacity, but the instructor, or whoever it was, wouldn't be able to do any different themselves, so what the hell!

Bealville siding is over two miles in length with a double crossover (at that time) in the middle, making an upper and a lower siding. Heading towards Bakersfield, an advance signal close to the ground, five hundred feet from the main crossover signal, was installed to indicate the proceeding signal by displaying either yellow or green, whichever the case might be. This operation only effected the siding, not the mainline.

Entering the siding with my train, I tried to keep the speed low because most signals on the Tehachapi Mountains cannot be seen very far away, on account of the terrain, which was full of curves and obstructing mountains. To complicate matters a Santa Fe train stood waiting for me on the mainline. Coming down and receiving a yellow advance signal and not yet being able to see the next home signal, which was only five hundred feet ahead, I begin to sweat a bit. Using the train air, the air gauge would not indicate any reduction.

With a feeling of helplessness, realizing that the slave units were malfunctioning, pumping the air back into the trainline as fast as I was reducing it for setting the air on the brakes. In the meantime the Santa Fe started to leave next to me. Seeing a red signal before me, I put the train in emergency, going by the red signal and stopping within twenty feet of a caboose in the lower siding waiting for a S.P. train coming out of Caliente siding. I put my engine in reverse motion so as to hold the train from running away, while Elmer started to secure hand brakes on the box cars.

I noticed the air gauge was trying to rise and then the pointer hand would fall, an indication that the slave helper was trying to pump the train line up. On the lead engine controls was a switch to isolate and shut the engines down on the helper. I used it immediately, stopping all operations of the slave units. I became angry, thinking of how easily Elmer and I could have been hurt or killed, as well as anyone on the caboose. I called the dispatcher on the radio and let him know our condition, and why we went by the red CTC signal. Later, after things cleared up, the dispatcher radioed me for us to continue down the siding, and then we left Bealville for Bakersfield.

"What is your story?" the master mechanic growled at me when I arrived at the round house. I looked at all of the officials that were greeting me. I related my complete trip to them.

"You have the complete story and I don't give a damn if you believe or not," I said to them. "And you can tell the company to shove them up their ass because they will never pan out. Good day gentlemen!"

The Helper Job

Time was up for me handling the heavy trains over the mountain, so I put a bid on a helper job and that let me take one more trip to Colton before the assignments were up.

I said goodbye to all my friends at Colton and made the rounds of all the habitats, such as the little cafes off the beaten path, and the stores such as the pipe and tobacco shop. It sure was a sad adieu, but that is the way it is.

My final return trip came at 8:10 that night. I received orders to run as regular train 519 and meet extra 4844 east at Dike. Siding Dike was only thirteen miles from Colton, and being a superior train we would hold the main line. We arrived at the mile post of Dike much earlier than expected because of light tonnage and much power. The operator at Dike came over the radio, calling the conductor and me, to inform us that we had train orders to advance our train by Dike. This was a new rule implemented by the company to keep trains moving over the cut-off. Upon receiving orders at Dike, advancing our train to Canyon for the extra 4844, we were to take siding.

At Canyon in the siding we waited in the dark of the night, not hearing anything of extra 4844 over the radio until he made his running air test coming into Hiland. After he had left Hiland, we heard the conductor on his train asking why he had stopped. I was not able to recognize the engineer by his voice, but he related to the caboose that he had only two dynamic brakes working and that he was having the brakeman put up retainers. Soon after that the engineer called the flag in by radio. Most flagman had walkie-talkie radios. It was then I recognized who the engineer was on the extra. It was Jack Crumply, and a short time later Jack came on the air telling the caboose that he just ran over two torpedoes.

The terrain from Hiland down to Dike was 2.2 percent down grade with endless curves twisting around the mountains. The track ahead of us in the daylight leaving Canyon could be followed for some distance, winding through the numerous huge rocks. But when pitch darkness set in, everything was a blank, until a fusee lit up the landscape not far up the tracks from us. It was shimmering on the giant rocks and mountain sides, casting weird shadows, like dancing, shapeless forms. The fusee was placed in a position that would make it very hard for an engineer to stop a train when coming upon it, because the curve it was on was short blind and reversed. Knowing Jack was having a hard time with his train, I thought it was as my duty to inform him of the impending danger.

"Engineer on 519 calling extra 4844, come in please."

"Go ahead, this is 4844," came the quick response.

"We are in the siding at Canyon but there is a fusee burning about a half of a mile from us. It's on a curve and will be hard for you to see and to stop short of. If I were coming down the hill with a train like yours being hard to handle, I would stop short and send a flag out because there might be some rocks on the rail or other obstruction. Over and out."

"Thank you, Charlie," Jack said, "I'll do that."

Another unidentified voice came over the airwaves.

"Steffes, we would appreciate if you would mind your own business and stop putting your nose in places it doesn't belong."

That made me angry, very angry.

"Just one minute mister, whoever you are," I said. "That is my business and if you don't think it is, make yourself familiar with the book of rules. When I hired out with the Southern Pacific, one of the first rules stated that employees should protect company property and report any unsafe condition, which you people are creating." And I added, which maybe I should not have done, "go do your bird dogging somewhere else in a safer manner."

The fusee was extinguished and everything remained quiet but a lot of thinking was being done. Jack rolled by me with his cab light on, grinning like a cow eating oats. We pulled out of Canyon on the watch out for the head hunters, but I believe they gave it up for a lost cause.

Six more weeks to work until my retirement—hardly believable! Looking back over my life, there were things that I could have changed but not concerning my job. The learning and romance of the railroad was far beyond any expectation a man could conceive or imagine. I came as a young boy and worked up through the golden years of railroading. The transition and expansion in that decade was beyond anything that I experienced, and it would never return. The railroads will continue to progress, but it will not be like those years of 1938 to 1976. The growth during the war years was tremendous, along with the exciting era of the great steam locomotives, which soon gave way to the first diesels. Before this golden age, railroads were busy buying and acquiring right of ways, laying track, buying rolling stock and improving the steam power to carry heavier loads. When hiring out as a young man and choosing to become a fireman, I did not believe that someday I would go to work in good street clothes and be talking over a gadget called a radio to other trains and to the dispatcher one hundred miles away. It was inconceivable. Radios were hardly known in my young life—we were just coming out of the windup victrola days.

Other developments would have seemed incredible to me in those long gone days, such as computer read-outs telling the location of loaded or empty cars, and every unit of locomotive power. It's like in a grocery store, when the clerk drags an item over the scanner and it picks the UPC code and reads out the price and prints it. Similarly, there are now codes on all rolling equipment, and scanners at given locations along the route that will pick up this code as the train speeds by. The readouts relays the information to a central office and there it is determined what is in the loads, or records if it is empty. In my early times it was nothing for the company to lose a car or even a string of cars. If they contained perishables of any kind, they would rot, and the company was liable. Today that does not happen because of the readouts. Along the track at given intervals there is what's called a hot box snifter, for detecting hot bearings, and also drag detectors. When any of this equipment is activated, further down the track, the engineer is alerted by a series of readout signals.

What was the most important thing of all? The fact that I was associated with men and women on the San Joaquin Division—a close-knit bunch of people, making up a large family who cared and shared the happiness and sorrows of each other. But we are a vanishing race today. From my research, I find that this brotherhood of closeness and caring is fast disappearing. I am hoping that someone will pick up the banner and try to put things back together. I do not blame the rank-and-file for this erosion but I do blame the previous generation of officials who badgered, aggravated, annoyed, and exploited the employees. A good official leads his people— he does not push them. For what reason no one knows, but the once proud and prosperous Southern Pacific has become a poverty-stricken railroad, so it is said.

The money that is made for a corporation is made by those who earn it, not by those who oversee the earnings. When a company or a corporation realizes that the most precious assets they have are their employees and a good relationship with them, it builds a sound, good, lasting business. The Southern Pacific on its rise was perhaps the best railroad to work for and it made money where some other roads did not. But on reaching its peak, greed and power took over on the part of those who ran the business. And the employment of over-educated people, immature in the ways of railroading, added to it's decline. It is my hope, and that of many others, that the company will eventually get back to the kind of industrial relations that existed early in my time.

My Last Trip

Six weeks rolled around and was to make my last trip on the helper to Summit switch and return, on January 1, 1976. Mary had typed out my resignation for me.

"Shall I come down to the yard and greet you when you bring your engine to the relieving track?" she asked.

"No honey," I said. "I just want to get off the job and come home as always, with no fuss but never to return." I was choking back the tears and emotions.

Since it was my last trip, I ran the engine both ways, and on my return with a light engine, I got the urge to speed down the mountain or to run a red signal, but years of stringent obedience to the rules and regulations stopped me from doing so.

As I arrived at the yard in Bakersfield the herder put me down the #1 yard track. After getting to the yardmaster's tower and sitting there for thirty minutes, I finally called on the radio.

"Are we going to stay here long yardmaster?" I asked.

"Yeah, Charlie we have a lot of switching to do, you'll be there a little while."

"No I won't Charlie." His name was Charlie also. "The fireman might but not me. I am quitting for good. You can take this engine to the house yourself or let the fireman make an engineer's day in pay. I'm walking in, over and out for good."

The cheering section over the airwaves, from Fresno to Tehachapi and Bakersfield, was great. They all wished me a

happy retirement. Arriving at the washroom, no one was there, nor at the crew dispatcher's office, where Ivan Upshaw and others had already wished me happy retirement. That was the policy of the company; the officials never thought much of their employees.

GLOSSARY

Atomizer................ On the Fireman's side of cab a valve to brake up oil and spread it out in the fire-box on a steam locomotive. Note: Western U.S. used oil instead of coal for energy on railroads.

Automatic Brake Valve................... Used by the Engineer to operate the train (box cars and etc.) brakes and it will apply the engine brakes. The valve has many features such as first service, lap position, service, emergency. On newer valves it has a maintaining feature, which takes care of the leakage in a train line.

Ballast................. A gravel bed for ties and steel rails to lay on.

Block Signal............ Can be a signal either of bullet type lite or arm signal. Early in the century arm signals were used by all railroads. They were signal mast with arms, red, green or yellow. During and after W.W.II most railroads changed to bullet lite type signals.

Block Signal Limit............ Is actuated by a train with-in its territory making its most restrictive indication shown on the signal and will also indicate broken rails and such.

Blower.................. To create draft through the fire box in conjunction with the atomizer.

Console.................. A stand on the operating unit that holds all the controls for running the train.

Dead-Head............. An employee or employees to ride from one point to another on passenger train or bus or any other type of transportation to balance crews or to job destination.

Demoter................ A fireman who has taken and passed the test to become an Engineer and is not yet on the Engineer roster or has been on the roster and on account of the decrease in business, has been cut off the list and taken his job as a fireman and then is called to make a trip as an Engineer in an emergency.

Drawbar............... A long heavy piece of iron protruding out from each end of the car onto which is fastened a knuckle, used for coupling to another car.

Feed Valve........... A valve mounted below the automatic brake valve to adjust the amount of air carried in the train-line. 90 lbs for freight and 110 lbs. for passenger trains.

Flat Spots....... Flat spots on drivers (wheel rims) caused by improper handling of engine brakes or in an emergency condition, making the engine slide on rails.

Fusee................. Looks like a stick of dynamite when ignited it lights up with a red color used by railroads and highways in certain conditions.

High-Ball............ A hand signal or by radio to the Engineer that everyone is aboard and the train can travel maximum speed.

Independent Brake Valve.................. A valve used by the Engineer to operate the Engine only.

Jam................... Slang for independent brake valve.

Loco Freight........ A train that spots or picks up cars at different locations, usually daily.

Long Oiler.......... An oil can with a long spout used for hard to reach oil cups on steam locomotives.

Malley............... One of the largest and most powerful steam locomotives made with the cab in front. Used primarily in mountainous country where many tunnels are prevalent.

Mile Post............ A 12" wide board, painted white, planted in the ground with the mileage printed on it to or from San Francisco; at intervals of one mile, so that the Engineer can check the speed of his train with his watch or see how many miles it is to the next station. (This was a Southern Pacific System)

Rail Dead Man.................... A piece of rail about six to eight inches long that is clamped between adjoining ends of rail. When laying 1/4 mile ribbon rail, the dead man piece of rail is removed and the rail stretched together with hydraulic clamps, and the two rails welded.

Retainers............. A regulating valve on each car in the train with a handle for use by trainman on descending grades.Incorporated with the valve is a weight to restrict the flow of air from the brake cylinder on the car to the atmosphere, there by helping the Engineer recharge his train-line with air pressure.

Reverse Lever....... A lever mounted on a third circle of notched metal, making it possible for the Engineer to keep the lever at a pre-set position. Sometimes referred to as a quadrant.

Running Air Test.............. This test is completed by the Engineer when the train is in motion, he would apply 6 lbs to the air brakes and when the train slowed a little, he would release the brakes there upon getting a "high-ball" from the conductor, completing the test.

Slave Unit....... Diesel helper units operated by a slave unit, that is controlled by radio from the Engineer at the head of the train.

Spur.................. A track of any length coming off the main line or side track for purpose of storing railroad cars.

Tons Per-operative Brake................ The weight of the train divided by the amount of cars in the train, gives the tons per-operative determines the speed and conditions of which the train can operate.

Torpedo............. A small amount of explosive powder, wrapped in water proof material, with light metal straps for fastening to the rail so when a locomotive runs over it, a loud bang erupts; warning the Engineer of danger.

Train-Line.......... Pipe and hose couplings extending to rear end of the train used for charging the air brake reservoir for each car.

Train Order
Station & Signal.... A station or place where train orders can be received if the order signal is red.

Units.................. One diesel unit represents one single locomotive. When coupled together, they can be controlled by one Engineer.